ArcGIS 9

Using ArcGIS® Geostatistical Analyst

DATA CREDITS

Carpathian Mountains data supplied by USDA Forest Service, Riverside, California, and is used here with permission.

Radioceasium data supplied by International Sakharov Environmental University, Minsk, Belarus, and is used here with permission. Copyright © 1996.

Air quality data for California supplied by California Environmental Protection Agency, Air Resource Board, and is used here with permission. Copyright © 1997.

Radioceasium contamination in forest berries data supplied by the Institute of Radiation Safety "BELRAD", Minsk, Belarus, and is used here with permission. Copyright © 1996.

CONTRIBUTING WRITERS
Kevin Johnston, Jay M. Ver Hoef, Konstantin Krivoruchko, and Neil Lucas

DATA DISCLAIMER

U. S. GOVERNMENT RESTRICTED/LIMITED RIGHTS

Contents

1 Welcome to ArcGIS Geostatistical Analyst   1

Exploratory spatial data analysis   2
Semivariogram modeling   3
Surface prediction and error modeling   4
Threshold mapping   5
Model validation and diagnostics   6
Surface prediction using cokriging   7
Tips on learning Geostatistical Analyst   8

2 Quick-start tutorial   11

Introduction to the tutorial   12
Exercise 1: Creating a surface using default parameters   14
Exercise 2: Exploring your data   19
Exercise 3: Mapping ozone concentration   26
Exercise 4: Comparing models   38
Exercise 5: Mapping the probability of ozone exceeding a critical threshold   39
Exercise 6: Producing the final map   42

3 The principles of geostatistical analysis   49

Understanding deterministic methods   50
Understanding geostatistical methods   53
Working through a problem   54
Basic principles behind geostatistical methods   59
Modeling a semivariogram   61
Kriging   74
A guide to the Geostatistical Analyst extension   78

4 Exploratory Spatial Data Analysis   81

What is Exploratory Spatial Data Analysis?   82
Exploratory Spatial Data Analysis   83
Exploratory Spatial Data Analysis tools   84
Examining the distribution of the data   95

specify

Nutrients , USGS.
DEQ —

Examining the distribution of your data   98
Looking for global and local outliers   99
Identifying global and local outliers   101
Looking for global trends   103
Looking for global trends   105
Examining spatial autocorrelation and directional variation   106
Examining spatial structure and directional variation   108
Understanding covariation among multiple datasets   109
Understanding spatial covariation among multiple datasets   111

5 Deterministic methods for spatial interpolation   113
How Inverse Distance Weighted interpolation works   114
Creating a map using IDW   118
How global polynomial interpolation works   120
Creating a map using global polynomial interpolation   122
How local polynomial interpolation works   123
Creating a map using local polynomial interpolation   125
How radial basis functions work   126
Creating a map using RBFs   129

6 Creating a surface with geostatistical techniques   131
What are geostatistical interpolation techniques?   132
Understanding the different kriging models   133
Understanding output surface types   135
Creating a kriging map using defaults   136
Understanding transformations and trends   137
Understanding ordinary kriging   138
Creating a map using ordinary kriging   139
Understanding simple kriging   143
Creating a map using simple kriging   144
Understanding universal kriging   150

Creating a map using universal kriging   151
Understanding thresholds   153
Understanding indicator kriging   154
Creating a map using indicator kriging   155
Understanding probability kriging   156
Creating a map using probability kriging   157
Understanding disjunctive kriging   159
Creating a map using disjunctive kriging   160
Understanding cokriging   165
Creating a map using cokriging   166

7   Using analytical tools when generating surfaces   167

Investigating spatial structure: variography   168
Modeling semivariograms and covariance functions   175
Determining the neighborhood search size   181
Determining the neighborhood search size   185
Performing cross-validation and validation   189
Performing cross-validation to assess parameter selections   193
Assessing decision protocol using validation   195
Comparing one model with another   197
Comparing one model with another   199
Modeling distributions and determining transformations   200
Using transformations (log, Box–Cox, and arcsine)   204
Using the normal score transformation   205
Checking for the bivariate normal distribution   206
Checking for bivariate distribution   209
Implementing declustering to adjust for preferential sampling   211
Declustering to adjust for preferential sampling   214
Removing trends from the data   216
Removing global and local trends from the data: detrending   218

8 Displaying and managing geostatistical layers 219

What is a geostatistical layer? 220
Adding layers 222
Working with layers in a map 223
Managing layers 224
Viewing geostatistical layers in ArcCatalog 225
Representing a geostatistical layer 227
Changing the symbology of a geostatistical layer 229
Data classification 230
Classifying data 233
Setting the scales at which a geostatistical layer will be displayed 235
Predicting values for locations outside the area of interest 236
Saving and exporting geostatistical layers 237

9 Additional geostatistical analysis tools 239

Changing the parameters of a geostatistical layer: method properties 240
Predicting values for specified locations 241
Performing validation on a geostatistical layer created from a subset 243

Appendix A 247

Appendix B 275

Glossary 279

References 285

Index 287

Welcome to ArcGIS Geostatistical Analyst

1

IN THIS CHAPTER

- **Exploratory spatial data analysis**

- **Semivariogram modeling**

- **Surface prediction and error modeling**

- **Threshold mapping**

- **Model validation and diagnostics**

- **Surface prediction using cokriging**

- **Tips on learning Geostatistical Analyst**

Welcome to the ESRI® ArcGIS® Geostatistical Analyst extension for advanced surface modeling using deterministic and geostatistical methods. Geostatistical Analyst extends ArcMap™ by adding an advanced toolbar containing tools for exploratory spatial data analysis and a geostatistical wizard to lead you through the process of creating a statistically valid surface. New surfaces generated with Geostatistical Analyst can subsequently be used in geographic information system (GIS) models and in visualization using ArcGIS extensions such as ArcGIS Spatial Analyst and ArcGIS 3D Analyst™.

Geostatistical Analyst is revolutionary because it bridges the gap between geostatistics and GIS. For some time, geostatistical tools have been available, but never integrated tightly within GIS modeling environments. Integration is important because, for the first time, GIS professionals can begin to quantify the quality of their surface models by measuring the statistical error of predicted surfaces.

Surface fitting using Geostatistical Analyst involves three key steps (demonstrated on the following pages):

- Exploratory spatial data analysis

- Structural analysis (calculation and modeling of the surface properties of nearby locations)

- Surface prediction and assessment of results

The software contains a series of easy-to-use tools and wizards that guide you through each of these steps. It also includes a number of unique tools for statistical spatial data analysis.

Exploratory spatial data analysis

Using measured sample points from a study area, Geostatistical Analyst can create accurate predictions for other unmeasured locations within the same area. Exploratory spatial data analysis tools included with Geostatistical Analyst are used to assess the statistical properties of data such as spatial data variability, spatial data dependence, and global trends.

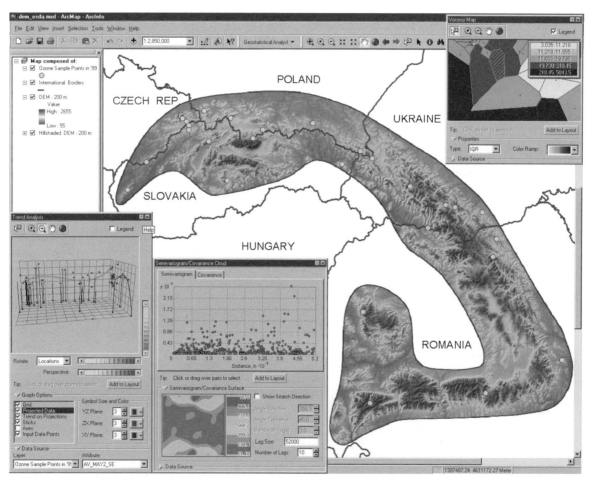

A number of exploratory spatial data analysis tools are used to investigate the properties of ozone measurements taken at monitoring stations in the Carpathian Mountains.

Semivariogram modeling

Geostatistical analysis of data occurs in two phases: 1) modeling the semivariogram or covariance to analyze surface properties, and 2) kriging. A number of kriging methods are available for surface creation in Geostatistical Analyst, including ordinary, simple, universal, indicator, probability, and disjunctive kriging.

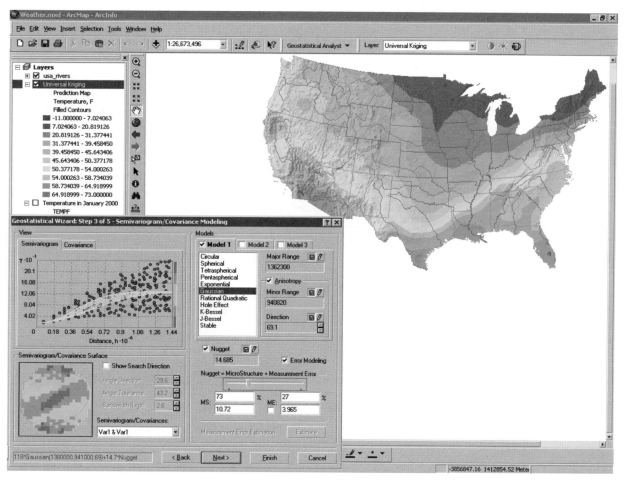

The two phases of geostatistical analysis of data are illustrated above. First, the semivariogram/covariance wizard was used to fit a model to winter temperature data for the USA. This model was then used to create the temperature distribution map.

Surface prediction and error modeling

Various types of map layers can be produced using Geostatistical Analyst, including prediction maps, quantile maps, probability maps, and prediction standard error maps.

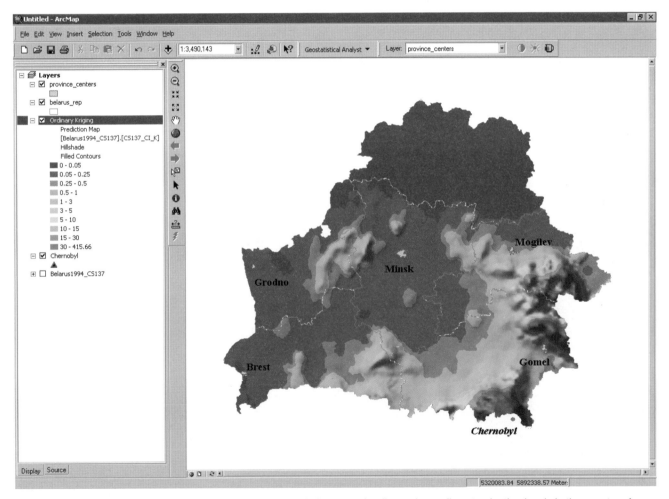

Here, Geostatistical Analyst has been used to produce a prediction map of radioceasium soil contamination levels in the country of Belarus after the Chernobyl nuclear power plant accident.

Threshold mapping

Probability maps can be generated to predict where values exceed a critical threshold.

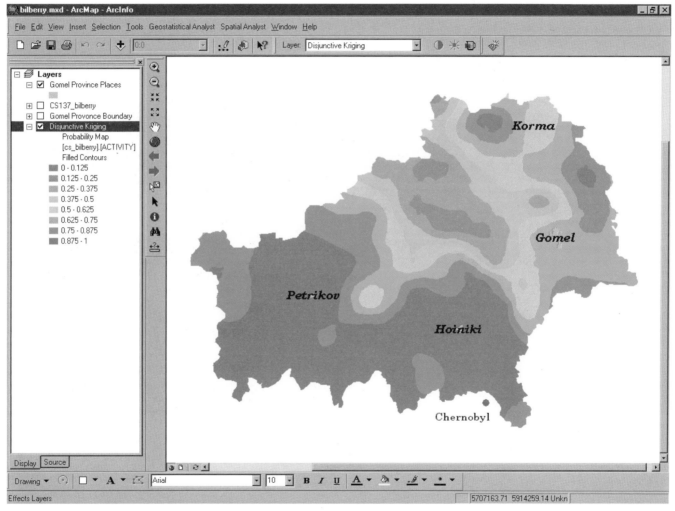

Locations shown in dark orange and red indicate a probability greater than 62.5% that radioceasium contamination exceeds the upper permissible level (critical threshold) in forest berries.

Model validation and diagnostics

Input data can be split into two subsets. The first subset of the available data can be used to develop a model for prediction. The predicted values are then compared with the known values at the remaining locations using the Validation tool.

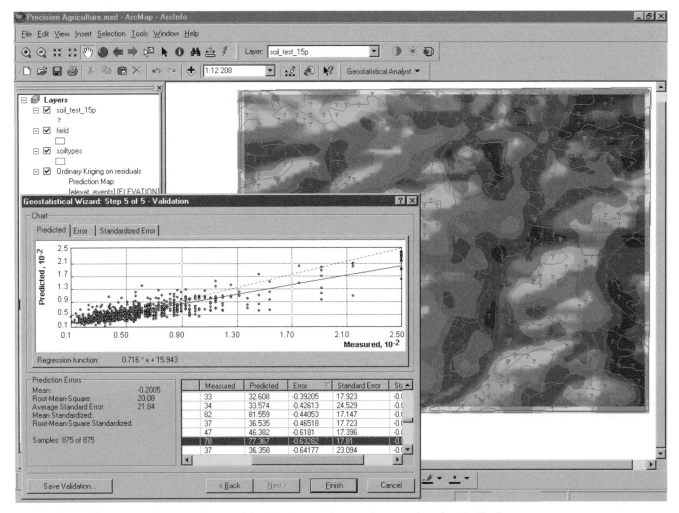

The validation wizard is used to assess a model developed to predict organic matter for a farm in Illinois.

Surface prediction using cokriging

Cokriging, an advanced surface modeling method included in Geostatistical Analyst, can be used to improve surface prediction of a primary variable by taking into account secondary variables, provided that the primary and secondary variables are spatially correlated.

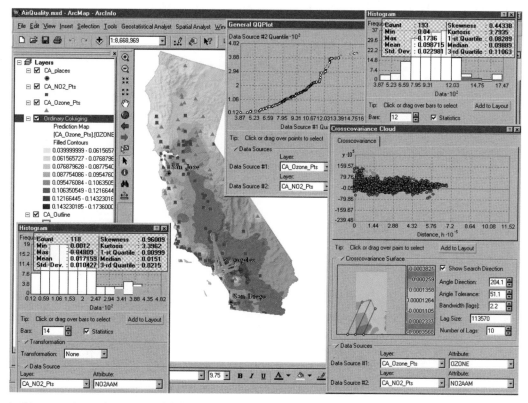

In this example, exploratory spatial data analysis tools are used to explore spatial correlation between ozone (primary variable) and nitrogen dioxide (secondary variable) in California. Because the variables are spatially correlated, cokriging can use the nitrogen dioxide data to improve predictions when mapping ozone.

Additionally, Geostatistical Analyst contains a number of unique tools to improve prediction, including tools for data transformation; data detrending using local polynomial interpolation; identification of the shift parameter in a cross-covariance model; error modeling to define the proportion of error resulting from microscale variations and measurement errors; examination of data for bivariate distribution; optimal searching neighborhood selection; and quantile map production.

Tips on learning Geostatistical Analyst

If you are new to the concept of geostatistics, remember that you don't have to know everything about Geostatistical Analyst to get immediate results. Begin learning Geostatistical Analyst by reading Chapter 2, 'Quick-start tutorial'. This chapter introduces you to some of the tasks you can accomplish using Geostatistical Analyst and provides an excellent starting point as you begin to think about how to tackle your own spatial problems. Geostatistical Analyst comes with the data used in the tutorial, so you can follow along step by step at your computer.

If you prefer to jump right in and experiment on your own, use Chapter 5, 'Deterministic methods for spatial interpolation', and Chapter 6, 'Creating a surface with geostatistical techniques', as a guide to learn the concepts and the steps to perform a certain task.

Finding answers to questions

Like most people, your goal is to complete your tasks while investing a minimum amount of time and effort on learning how to use software. You want intuitive, easy-to-use software that gives you immediate results without having to read pages of documentation. However, when you do have a question, you want the answer quickly so you can complete your task. That's what this book is all about—getting the answers you need, when you need them.

This book describes geostatistical analysis tasks—from basic to advanced—that you'll perform with Geostatistical Analyst. Although you can read this book from start to finish, you'll likely use it more as a reference. When you want to know how to do a particular task, such as identifying global outliers, just look it up in the table of contents or the index. What you'll find is a concise, step-by-step description of how to complete the task. Some chapters also include detailed information that you can

read if you want to learn more about the concepts behind the tasks. You may also refer to the glossary in this book if you come across any unfamiliar geostatistical terms or need to refresh your memory.

About this book

This book is designed to help you perform geostatistical analyses by giving you conceptual information and teaching you how to perform tasks to solve your geostatistical problems. Topics covered in Chapter 2 assume you are familiar with the fundamentals of a Geographic Information System (GIS) and have a basic knowledge of ArcGIS. If you are new to GIS or ArcMap, you are encouraged to take some time to read *Getting Started with ArcGIS* and *Using ArcMap*, which you received in your ArcGIS package. It is not necessary to do so to continue with this book; simply use the books as references.

Chapter 3 takes you through the basic principles of geostatistics, helping you understand the different interpolation methods and how they work conceptually. Chapter 4 covers Exploratory Spatial Data Analysis (ESDA), which allows you to understand your data better. Chapter 5 explains the deterministic interpolation methods. Chapter 6 discusses the various geostatistical methods, and Chapter 7 discusses the wide variety of tools that you use when performing interpolation. Chapter 8 describes the various display and management tools that are applicable to geostatistical layers. Chapter 9 covers a series of other geostatistical–analysis concepts and tasks. Appendix A provides detailed mathematical formulas for the various functions and methods used in Geostatistical Analyst. Finally, a glossary gives definitions to various geostatistical terms used in this book.

Getting help on your computer

In addition to this book, use the ArcMap online Help system to learn how to use Geostatistical Analyst and ArcMap. To learn how to use Help, see the book *Using ArcMap*.

Contacting ESRI

If you need to contact ESRI for technical support, see the product registration and support card you received with ArcGIS Geostatistical Analyst, or refer to 'Contacting Technical Support' in the 'Getting more help' section of the ArcGIS Desktop Help system. You can also visit ESRI on the Web at *www.esri.com* and *support.esri.com* for more information on Geostatistical Analyst and ArcGIS.

ESRI education solutions

ESRI provides educational opportunities related to geographic information science, GIS applications, and technology. You can choose among instructor-led courses, Web-based courses, and self-study workbooks to find education solutions that fit your learning style. For more information, go to *www.esri.com/ education*.

Quick-start tutorial

2

IN THIS CHAPTER

- Exercise 1: Creating a surface using default parameters

- Exercise 2: Exploring your data

- Exercise 3: Mapping ozone concentration

- Exercise 4: Comparing models

- Exercise 5: Mapping the probability of ozone exceeding a critical threshold

- Exercise 6: Producing the final map

With Geostatistical Analyst, you can easily create a continuous surface, or map, from measured sample points stored in a point-feature layer, raster layer, or by using polygon centroids. The sample points may be measurements such as elevation, depth to the water table, or levels of pollution, as is the case in this tutorial. When used in conjunction with ArcMap, Geostatistical Analyst provides a comprehensive set of tools for creating surfaces that can be used to visualize, analyze, and understand spatial phenomena.

Tutorial scenario

The U.S. Environmental Protection Agency is responsible for monitoring atmospheric ozone concentration in California. Ozone concentration is mea-

sured at monitoring stations throughout the state. The locations of the stations are shown here. The concentration levels of ozone are known for all of the stations, but we are also interested in knowing the level for every location in California. However, due to cost and practicality, monitoring stations cannot be everywhere. Geostatistical Analyst provides tools that make the best predictions possible by examining the relationships between all of the sample points and producing a continuous surface of ozone concentration, standard errors (uncertainty) of predictions, and probabilities that critical values are exceeded.

Introduction to the tutorial

The data you'll need for this tutorial is included on the Geostatistical Analyst installation disk. The datasets were provided courtesy of the California Air Resources Board.

The datasets are:

Dataset	Description
ca_outline	Outline map of California
ca_ozone_pts	Ozone point samples (ppm)
ca_cities	Location of major California cities
ca_hillshade	A hillshade map of California

The ozone dataset (ca_ozone_pts) represents the 1996 maximum eight-hour average concentration of ozone in parts per million (ppm). (The measurements were taken daily and grouped into eight-hour blocks.) The original data has been modified for the purposes of the tutorial and should not be taken to be accurate data.

From the ozone point samples (measurements), you will produce two continuous surfaces (maps), predicting the values of ozone concentration for every location in the State of California based on the sample points that you have. The first map that you create will simply use all default options to show you how easy it is to create a surface from your sample points. The second map that you produce will allow you to incorporate more of the spatial relationships that are discovered among the points. When creating this second map, you will use the ESDA tools to examine your data. You will also be introduced to some of the geostatistical options that you can use to create a surface such as removing trends and modeling spatial autocorrelation. By

using the ESDA tools and working with the geostatistical parameters, you will be able to create a more accurate surface.

Many times it is not the actual values of some caustic health risk that is of concern, but rather if it is above some toxic level. If this is the case, immediate action must be taken. The third surface you create will assess the probability that a critical ozone threshold value has been exceeded.

For this tutorial, the critical threshold will be if the maximum average of ozone goes above 0.12 ppm in any eight-hour period during the year; then the location should be closely monitored. You will use Geostatistical Analyst to predict the probability of values complying with this standard.

This tutorial is divided into individual tasks that are designed to let you explore the capabilities of Geostatistical Analyst at your own pace. To get additional help, explore the ArcMap online Help system or see *Using ArcMap*.

- Exercise 1 takes you through accessing Geostatistical Analyst and through the process of creating a surface of ozone concentration to show you how easy it is to create a surface using the default parameters.

- Exercise 2 guides you through the process of exploring your data before you create the surface in order to spot outliers in the data and to recognize trends.

- Exercise 3 creates the second surface that considers more of the spatial relationships discovered in Exercise 2 and improves on the surface you created in Exercise 1. This exercise also introduces you to some of the basic concepts of geostatistics.

- Exercise 4 shows you how to compare the results of the two surfaces that you created in Exercises 1 and 3 in order to decide which provides the better predictions of the unknown values.

- Exercise 5 takes you through the process of mapping the probability that ozone exceeds a critical threshold, thus creating the third surface.

- Exercise 6 shows you how to present the surfaces you created in Exercises 3 and 5 for final display, using ArcMap functionality.

You will need a few hours of focused time to complete the tutorial. However, you can also perform the exercises one at a time if you wish, saving your results after each exercise.

Exercise 1: Creating a surface using default parameters

Before you begin you must first start ArcMap and enable Geostatistical Analyst.

Starting ArcMap and enable Geostatistical Analyst

Click the Start button on the Windows taskbar, point to Programs, point to ArcGIS, and click ArcMap. In ArcMap, click Tools, click Extensions, and check Geostatistical Analyst. Click Close.

Adding the Geostatistical Analyst toolbar to ArcMap

Click View, point to Toolbars, and click Geostatistical Analyst.

Adding data layers to ArcMap

Once the data has been added, you can use ArcMap to display the data and, if necessary, to change the properties of each layer (symbology, and so on).

1. Click the Add Data button on the Standard toolbar.

2. Navigate to the folder where you installed the tutorial data (the default installation path is C:\ArcGIS\ArcTutor\Geostatistics), hold down the Ctrl key, then click and highlight the ca_ozone_pts and ca_outline datasets.

3. Click Add.

4. Click the ca_outline layer legend in the table of contents to open the Symbol Selector dialog box.

5. Click the Fill Color dropdown arrow and click No Color.

6. Click OK on the Symbol Selector dialog box.

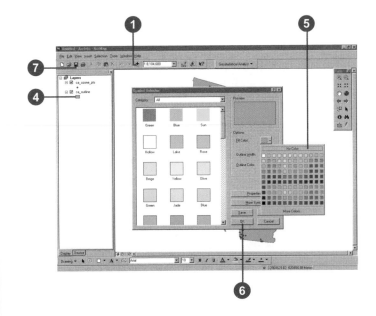

The ca_outline layer is now displayed transparently with just the outline visible. This allows you to see the layers that you will create in this tutorial underneath this layer.

Saving your map

It is recommended that you save your map after each exercise.

7. Click the Save button on the Standard toolbar.

   You will need to provide a name for the map because this is the first time you have saved it (we suggest Ozone Prediction Map.mxd). To save in the future, click Save.

Creating a surface using the defaults

Next you will create (interpolate) a surface of ozone concentration using the default settings of the Geostatistical Analyst. You will use the ozone point dataset (ca_ozone_pts) as the input dataset and interpolate the ozone values at the locations where values are not known using ordinary kriging. You will click Next in many of the dialog boxes, thus accepting the defaults. Do not worry about the details of the dialog boxes in this exercise. Each dialog box will be revisited in later exercises. The intent of this exercise is to create a surface using the default options.

1. Click the Geostatistical Analyst toolbar, then click Geostatistical Wizard.

2. Click the Input Data dropdown arrow and click ca_ozone_pts.

3. Click the Attribute dropdown arrow and click the OZONE attribute.

4. Click Kriging in the Methods dialog box.

5. Click Next.

   By default, Ordinary Kriging and Prediction Map will be selected in the Geostatistical Method Selection dialog box.

Note that having selected the method to map the ozone surface, you could click Finish here to create a surface using the default parameters. However, steps 6 to 10 will expose you to many of the different dialog boxes.

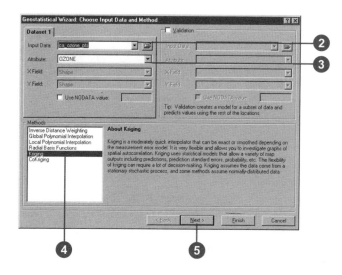

6. Click Next on the Geostatistical Method Selection dialog box.

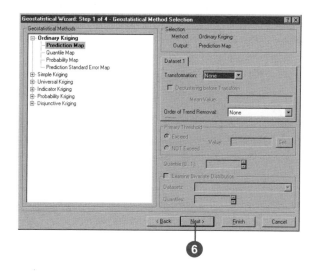

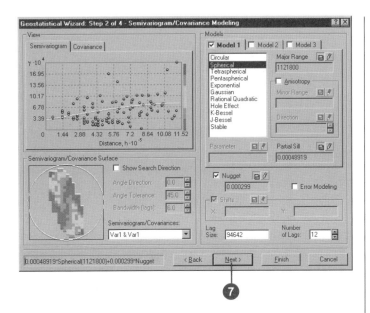

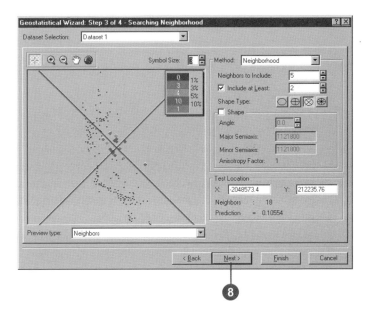

7

8

The Semivariogram/Covariance Modeling dialog box allows you to examine spatial relationships between measured points. You assume things that are close are more alike. The semivariogram allows you to explore this assumption. The process of fitting a semivariogram model while capturing the spatial relationships is known as variography.

7. Click Next.

The crosshairs show a location that has no measured value. To predict a value at the crosshairs you can use the values at the measured locations. You know that the values of the closer measured locations are more like the value of the unmeasured location that you are trying to predict. The red points in the above image are going to be weighted (or influence the unknown value) more than the green points since they are closer to the location you are predicting. Using the surrounding points, with the model fitted in the Semivariogram Modeling dialog box, you can predict a more accurate value for the unmeasured location.

8. Click Next.

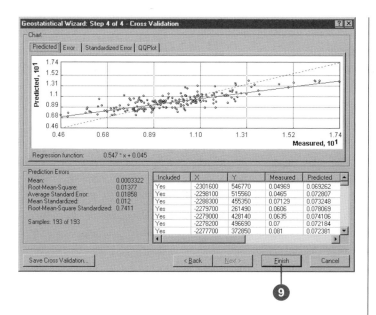

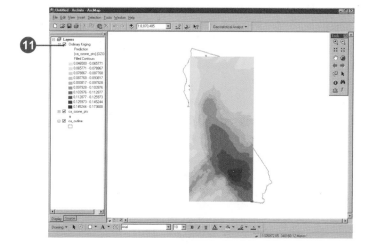

The Cross Validation dialog box gives you some idea of "how well" the model predicts the values at the unknown locations. You will learn how to use the graph and understand the statistics in Exercise 4.

9. Click Finish.

The Output Layer Information dialog box summarizes information on the method (and its associated parameters) that will be used to create the output surface.

10. Click OK.

The predicted ozone map will appear as the top layer in the table of contents.

11. Click the layer in the table of contents to highlight it, then click again, and change the layer name to "Default".

This name change will help you distinguish this layer from the one you will create in Exercise 4.

12. Click save on the ArcMap Standard toolbar.

Notice that the interpolation continues into the ocean. You will learn in Exercise 6 how to restrict the prediction surface to stay within California.

Surface-fitting methodology

You have now created a map of ozone concentration and completed Exercise 1 of the tutorial. While it is a simple task to create a map (surface) using the Geostatistical Analyst, it is important to follow a structured process as shown below:

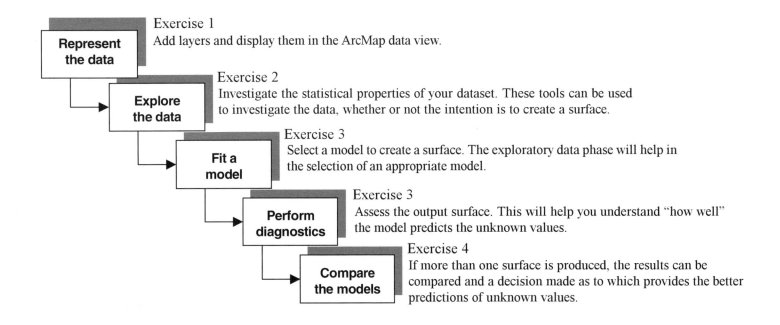

Represent the data

Exercise 1
Add layers and display them in the ArcMap data view.

Explore the data

Exercise 2
Investigate the statistical properties of your dataset. These tools can be used to investigate the data, whether or not the intention is to create a surface.

Fit a model

Exercise 3
Select a model to create a surface. The exploratory data phase will help in the selection of an appropriate model.

Perform diagnostics

Exercise 3
Assess the output surface. This will help you understand "how well" the model predicts the unknown values.

Compare the models

Exercise 4
If more than one surface is produced, the results can be compared and a decision made as to which provides the better predictions of unknown values.

You will follow this structured process in the following exercises of the tutorial. In addition, in Exercise 5, you will create a surface of those locations that exceed a specified threshold and, in Exercise 6, you will create a final presentation layout of the results of the analysis performed in the tutorial.

Note that you have already performed the first step of this process, representing the data, in Exercise 1. In Exercise 2, you will explore the data.

Exercise 2: Exploring your data

In this exercise you will explore your data. As the structured process on the previous page suggests, to make better decisions when creating a surface you should first explore your dataset to gain a better understanding of it. When exploring your data you should look for obvious errors in the input sample data that may drastically affect the output prediction surface, examine how the data is distributed, look for global trends, etc.

The Geostatistical Analyst provides many data-exploration tools.

In this tutorial you will explore your data in three ways:

- Examine the distribution of your data.

- Identify the trends in your data, if any.

- Understand the spatial autocorrelation and directional influences.

If you closed the map after Exercise 1, click the File menu and click Open. In the dialog box, click the Look in box dropdown arrow and navigate to the folder where you saved the map document (Ozone Prediction Map.mxd). Click Open.

Examining the distribution of your data

Histogram

The interpolation methods that are used to generate a surface give the best results if the data is normally distributed (a bell-shaped curve). If your data is skewed (lopsided) you may choose to transform the data to make it normal. Thus, it is important to understand the distribution of your data before creating a surface. The Histogram tool

plots frequency histograms for the attributes in the dataset, enabling you to examine the univariate (one-variable) distribution of the dataset for each attribute. Next, you will explore the distribution of ozone for the ca_ozone_pts layer.

1. Click ca_ozone_pts, move it to the top of the table of contents, then place ca_outline underneath ca_ozone_pts.

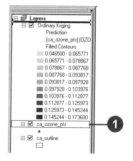

2. Click the Geostatistical Analyst toolbar, point to Explore Data, and click Histogram.

You may wish to resize the Histogram dialog box so you can also see the map, as the following diagram shows.

3. Click the Layer dropdown arrow and click ca_ozone_pts.

4. Click the Attribute dropdown arrow and click OZONE.

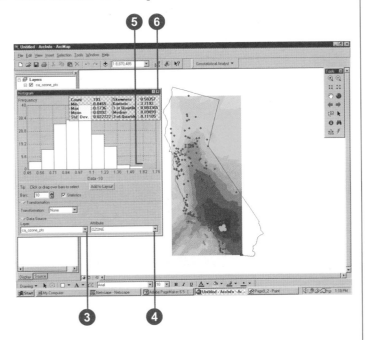

The distribution of the ozone attribute is depicted by a histogram with the range of values separated into 10 classes. The relative proportion (density) of data within each class is represented by the height of each bar.

Generally, the important features of the distribution are its central value, its spread, and its symmetry. As a quick check, if the mean and the median are approximately the same value, you have one piece of evidence that the data may be normally distributed.

The histogram shown above indicates that the data is unimodal (one hump) and fairly symmetric. It appears to be close to a normal distribution. The right tail of the distribution indicates the presence of a relatively small number of sample points with large ozone concentration values.

5. Click the histogram bar with ozone values ranging from 0.162 to 0.175 ppm.

   The sample points within this range are highlighted on the map. Note that these sample points are located within the Los Angeles region.

6. Click to close the dialog box.

Normal QQPlot

The QQPlot is where you compare the distribution of the data to a standard normal distribution, providing yet another measure of the normality of the data. The closer the points are to creating a straight line, the closer the distribution is to being normally distributed.

1. Click the Geostatistical Analyst toolbar, point to Explore Data, and click Normal QQPlot.

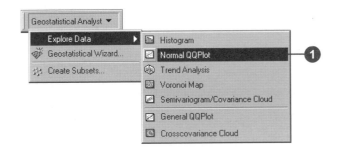

2. Click the Layer dropdown arrow and click ca_ozone_pts.

3. Click the Attribute dropdown arrow and click OZONE.

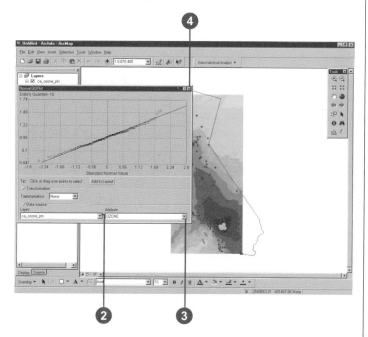

A General QQPlot is a graph on which the quantiles from two distributions are plotted versus each other. For two identical distributions, the QQPlot will be a straight line. Therefore, it is possible to check the normality of the ozone data by plotting the quantiles of that data versus the quantiles of a standard normal distribution. From the Normal QQPlot above you can see that the plot is very close to a straight line. The main departure from this line occurs at high values of ozone concentration (which were highlighted in the histogram plot so they are highlighted here also).

If the data did not exhibit a normal distribution in either the Histogram or the Normal QQPlot, it may be necessary to transform the data to make it comform to a normal distribution before using certain kriging interpolation techniques.

4. Click to exit the dialog box.

Identifying global trends in your data

If a trend exists in your data, it is the nonrandom (deterministic) component of a surface that can be represented by some mathematical formula. For instance, a gently sloping hillside can be represented by a plane. A valley would be represented by a more complex formula (a second-order polynomial) that creates a "U" shape. This formula may produce the representation of the surface you desire. However, many times the formula is too smooth to accurately depict the surface because no hillside is a perfect plane nor is a valley a perfect "U" shape. If the trend surface does not adequately portray your surface for your particular need, you may want to remove it and continue with your analysis, modeling the residuals, which is what remains after the trend is removed. When modeling the residuals, you will be analyzing the short-range variation in the surface. This is the part that isn't captured by the perfect plane or the perfect "U".

The Trend Analysis tool enables you to identify the presence/absence of trends in the input dataset.

1. Click the Geostatistical Analyst toolbar, point to Explore Data, and click Trend Analysis.

2. Click the Layer dropdown arrow and click ca_ozone_pts.

East–West trend line   North–South trend line

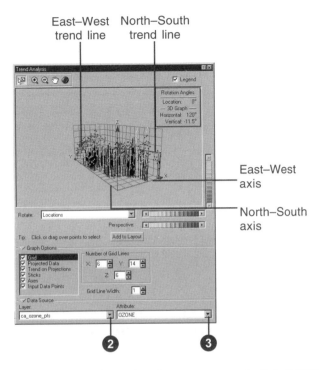

East–West axis

North–South axis

② ③

3. Click the Attribute dropdown arrow and click OZONE.

Each vertical stick in the trend analysis plot represents the location and value (height) of each data point. The points are projected onto the perpendicular planes, an east–west and a north–south plane. A best-fit line (a polynomial) is drawn through the projected points, which model trends in specific directions. If the line were flat, this would indicate that there would be no trend. However, if you look at the light green line in the image above, you can see it starts out with low values and increases as it moves east until it levels out. This demonstrates that the data seems to exhibit a strong trend in the east–west direction and a weaker one in the north–south direction.

4. Click the Rotate Projection scroll bar and scroll left until the rotation angle is 30°.

This rotation enables you to see the shape of the east–west trend more clearly. You can see that the projection actually exhibits an upside-down "U" shape. Because the trend is "U" shaped, a second-order polynomial is a good choice to use for the global trend. Even though the trend is being exhibited on the east–west projection plane, because we rotated the points 30°, the actual trend is northeast to southwest. The trend seen is possibly caused by the fact that the pollution is low at the coast, but moving inland there are large human populations that taper off again at the mountains. You will remove these trends in Exercise 4.

5. Click to exit the dialog box.

"U" shape trend

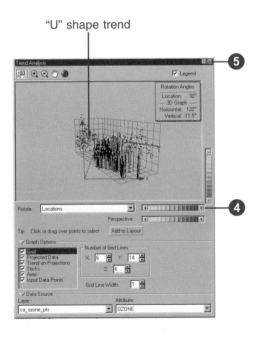

⑤

④

Understanding spatial autocorrelation and directional influences

1. Click the Geostatistical Analyst toolbar, point to Explore Data, and click Semivariogram/Covariance Cloud.

2. Click the Layer dropdown arrow and click ca_ozone_pts.

3. Click the Attribute dropdown arrow and click OZONE.

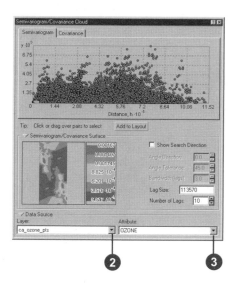

The Semivariogram/Covariance Cloud allows you to examine the spatial autocorrelation between the measured sample points. In spatial autocorrelation, it is assumed that things that are close to one another are more alike. The Semivariogram/Covariance Cloud lets you examine this relationship. To do so, a semivariogram value, which is the difference squared between the values of each pair of locations, is plotted on the y-axis relative to the distance separating each pair on the x-axis.

Each red dot in the Semivariogram/Covariance Cloud represents a pair of locations. Since closer locations should be more alike, in the semivariogram the close locations (far left on the x-axis) should have small semivariogram values (low on the y-axis). As the distance between the pairs of locations increases (move right on the x-axis), the semivariogram values should also increase (move up on the y-axis). However, a certain distance is reached where the cloud flattens out, indicating that the relationship between the pairs of locations beyond this distance is no longer correlated.

Looking at the semivariogram, if it appears that some data locations that are close together (near zero on the x-axis) have a higher semivariogram value (high on the y-axis) than you would expect, you should investigate these pairs of locations to see if there is the possibility that the data is inaccurate.

4. Click and drag the Selection pointer over these points to highlight them. (Use the following diagram as a guide. It is not important to highlight the exact points the diagram displays.)

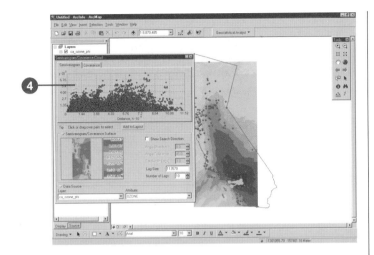

The pairs of sample locations that are selected in the semivariogram are highlighted on the map, and lines link the locations, indicating the pairing.

There are many reasons why the data values differ more among sample locations between the Los Angeles area and other areas. One possibility is that there are more cars in the Los Angeles area than in other areas, which will invariably produce more pollution, contributing to a higher ozone buildup in the Los Angeles area.

Besides global trends that were discussed in the previous section, there may also be directional influences affecting the data. The reasons for these directional influences may not be known, but they can be statistically quantified. These directional influences will affect the accuracy of the surface you create in the next exercise. However, once you know if one exists, the Geostatistical Analyst provides tools to account for it in the surface-creation process. To explore for a directional influence in the semivariogram cloud, you use the Search Direction tools.

5. Check Show Search Direction.

6. Click and move the directional pointer to any angle.

The direction the pointer is facing determines which pairs of data locations are plotted on the semivariogram. For example, if the pointer is facing an east–west direction, only the pairs of data locations that are east or west of one another will be plotted on the semivariogram. This enables you to eliminate pairs you are not interested in and to explore the directional influences on the data.

7. Click and drag the Selection tool along the values with the highest semivariogram values to highlight them on the plot and in the map. (Use the following diagram as a guide. It is not important to highlight the exact points in the diagram or to use the same search direction.)

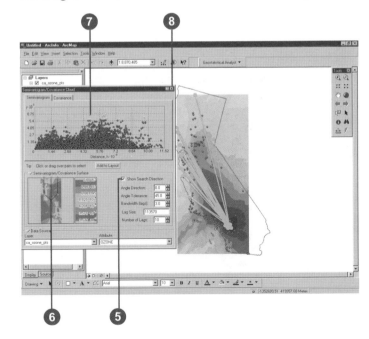

    USING ArcGIS GEOSTATISTICAL ANALYST

You will notice that the majority of the linked locations (representing pairs of points on the map), regardless of distance, correspond to one of the sample points from the Los Angeles region. Taking more pairs of points, at any distance, into consideration, shows that it is not just pairs of points from the Los Angeles region out to the coast that have high semivariogram values. Many of the pairs of data locations from the Los Angeles region to other inland areas also have high semivariogram values. This is because the values of ozone in the Los Angeles area are so much higher than anywhere else in California.

8. Click to exit the dialog box.

9. Click Selection and click Clear Selected Features to clear the highlighted points on the map.

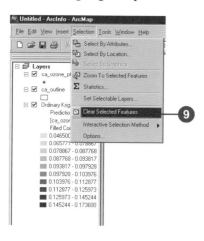

In this exercise we learned:

1. The ozone data is close to a normal distribution. They are unimodal and fairly symmetrical around the mean/median line as seen in the histogram.

2. The Normal QQPlot reaffirmed that the data is normally distributed since the points in the plot created a fairly straight line, and transformation is not necessary.

3. Using the Trend Analysis tool you saw that the data exhibited a trend and, once refined, identified that the trend would be best fit by a second-order polynomial in the southeast to northwest direction (330 degrees).

4. From the Semiovariogram/Covariance Cloud we found that the high values of ozone concentration in Los Angeles create high semivariance values with locations nearby as well as far away.

5. The semivariogram surface indicates there is a spatial autocorrelation in the data.

Knowing that there are no outlier (or erroneous) sample points in the dataset and that the distribution is close to normal, you can proceed with confidence to the surface interpolation. Also, you will be able to create a more accurate surface because you know that there is a trend in the data that you can adjust for in the interpolation.

Exercise 3: Mapping ozone concentration

In Exercise 1, you used the default parameters to map ozone concentration. However, you did not take into account the statistical properties of the sample data. For example, from exploring the data in Exercise 2, it appeared that the data exhibited a trend. This can be incorporated into the interpolation process.

In this exercise you will:

- Improve on the map of ozone concentration created in Exercise 1.

- Be introduced to some basic geostatistical concepts.

Again you will use the ordinary kriging interpolation method and will incorporate the trend in your model to create better predictions.

1. Click the Geostatistical Analyst toolbar and click Geostatistical Wizard.

2. Click the Input Data dropdown and click ca_ozone_pts.

3. Click the Attribute dropdown arrow and click the OZONE attribute.

4. Click Kriging in the Methods box.

5. Click Next.

    By default, Ordinary Kriging and Prediction are selected.

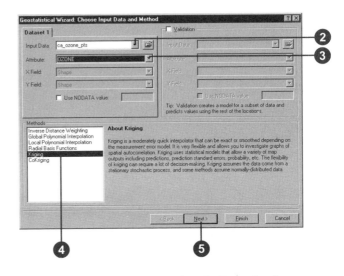

From the exploration of your data in Exercise 2, you discovered that there was a global trend in your data. After refinement with the Trend Analysis tool, you discovered that a second-order polynomial seemed reasonable and the trend was from the southeast to the northwest. This trend can be represented by a mathematical formula and removed from the data. Once the trend is removed, the statistical analysis will be performed on the residuals or the short-range variation component of the surface. The trend will automatically be added back before the final surface is created so that the predictions will produce meaningful results. By removing the trend, the analysis that is to follow will not be influenced by the trend, and once it is added back a more accurate surface will be produced.

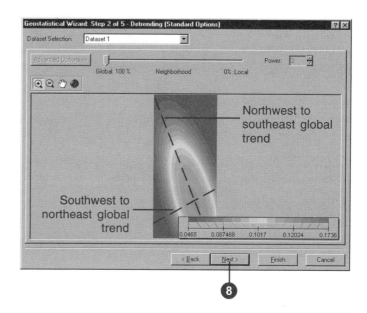

6. On the Geostatistical Method Selection dialog box, click the Order of Trend Removal dropdown arrow and click Second.

A second-order polynomial will be fitted because a U-shaped curve was detected in the southwest to northeast direction in the Trend Analysis dialog box in Exercise 2.

7. Click Next on the Geostatistical Method Selection dialog box.

By default, the Geostatistical Analyst maps the global trend in the dataset. The surface indicates the most rapid change in the southwest to northeast direction and a more gradual change in the northwest–southeast direction (causing the ellipse shape).

Trends should only be removed if there is justification for doing so. The southwest to northeast trend in air quality can be attributed to an ozone buildup between the mountains and the coast. The elevation and the prevailing wind direction are contributing factors to the relatively low values in the mountains and at the coast. The high concentration of humans also leads to high levels of pollution between the mountains and coast. The northwest to southeast trend varies much more slowly due to the higher populations around Los Angeles and extending to lesser numbers in San Francisco. Hence we can justifiably remove these trends.

8. Click Next on the Detrending dialog box.

Semivariogram/Covariance modeling

In the Semivariogram/Covariance Cloud in Exercise 2, you explored the overall spatial autocorrelation of the measured points. To do so, you examined the semivariogram, which showed the difference-squared of the values between each pair of points at different distances. The goal of Semivariance/Covariance modeling is to determine the best fit for a model that will pass through the points in the semivariogram (the yellow line in the diagram).

The semivariogram is a function that relates semivariance (or dissimilarity) of data points to the distance that separates them. Its graphical representation can be used to provide a picture of the spatial correlation of data points with their neighbors.

The Semivariogram/Covariance Modeling dialog box allows you to model the spatial relationship in the dataset. By default, optimal parameters for a spherical semivariogram model are calculated. The Geostatistical Analyst first determines a good lag size for grouping semivariogram values. The lag size is the size of a distance class into which pairs of locations are grouped in order to reduce the large number of possible combinations. This is called binning. As a result of the binning, notice that there are fewer points in this semivariogram than the one in Exercise 2. A good lag distance can also help reveal spatial correlations. The dialog box displays the semivariogram values as a surface and as a scatterplot related to distance. Then it fits a spherical semivariogram model (best fit for all directions) and its associated parameter values, which are typically called the nugget, range, and partial sill.

Try to fit the semivariogram at small lags (distances). It is possible to use different bin sizes and refit the default spherical model by changing the lag size and number of lags.

9. Type a new Lag Size value of 12000.

10. Click in the input box and type 10 for the Number of Lags.

Reducing the lag size means that you are effectively zooming in to model the details of the local variation between neighboring sample points. You will notice that with a smaller lag size, the fitted semivariogram (the yellow line) rises sharply and then levels off. The range is the distance where it levels off. This flattening out of the semivariogram indicates that there is little autocorrelation beyond the range.

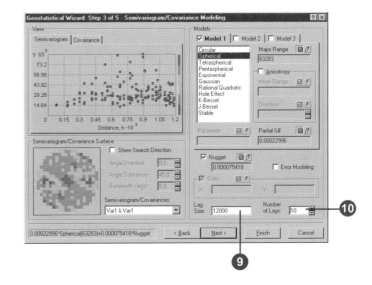

By removing the trend, the semivariogram will model the spatial autocorrelation among data points without having to consider the trend in the data. The trend will be automatically added back to the calculations before the final surface is produced.

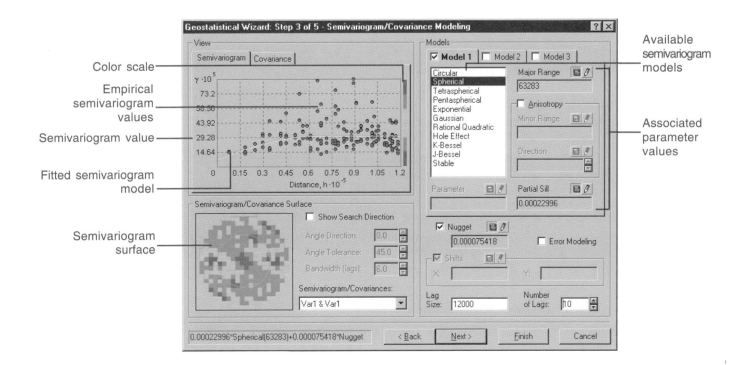

The following labels appear on the figure:

- Color scale
- Empirical semivariogram values
- Semivariogram value
- Fitted semivariogram model
- Semivariogram surface
- Available semivariogram models
- Associated parameter values

Geostatistical Wizard: Step 3 of 5 - Semivariogram/Covariance Modeling

View — Semivariogram | Covariance

γ ·10⁵
73.2
58.56
43.92
29.28
14.64
0

0.15 0.3 0.45 0.6 0.75 0.9 1.05 1.2
Distance, h ·10⁻⁵

Semivariogram/Covariance Surface
☐ Show Search Direction
Angle Direction: 0.0
Angle Tolerance: 45.0
Bandwidth (lags): 6.0
Semivariogram/Covariances:
Var1 & Var1

Models
☑ Model 1 ☐ Model 2 ☐ Model 3

Circular
Spherical
Tetraspherical
Pentaspherical
Exponential
Gaussian
Rational Quadratic
Hole Effect
K-Bessel
J-Bessel
Stable

Major Range 63283
☐ Anisotropy
Minor Range
Direction

Parameter   Partial Sill 0.00022996

☑ Nugget 0.000075418   ☐ Error Modeling
☑ Shifts
X: Y:

Lag Size: 12000   Number of Lags: 10

0.00022996*Spherical(63283)+0.000075418*Nugget

< Back   Next >   Finish   Cancel

The color scale, which represents the calculated semivariogram value, provides a direct link between the empirical semivariogram values on the graph and those on the semivariogram surface. The value of each "cell" in the semivariogram surface is color coded, with lower values blue and green and higher values orange and red. The average value for each cell of the semivariogram surface is plotted on the semivariogram graph. The x-axis on the semivariogram graph is the distance from the center of the cell to the center of the semivariogram surface. The

semivariogram values represent dissimilarity. For our example, the semivariogram starts low at small distances (things close together are more similar) and increases as distance increases (things get more dissimilar farther apart). Notice from the semivariogram surface that dissimilarity increases more rapidly in the southwest to northeast direction than in the southeast to northwest direction. Earlier, you removed a coarse-scale trend. Now it appears that there are directional components to the autocorrelation at finer scales, so we will model that next.

Directional semivariograms

A directional influence will affect the points of the semivariogram and the model that will be fit. In certain directions closer things may be more alike than in other directions. Directional influences are called anisotropy, and the Geostatistical Analyst can account for them. Anisotropy can be caused by wind, runoff, a geological structure, or a wide variety of other processes. The directional influence can be statistically quantified and accounted for when making your map.

You can explore the dissimilarity in data points for a certain direction with the Search Direction tool. This allows you to examine directional influences on the semivariogram chart. It does not affect the output surface. The following steps show you how to achieve this.

11. Check Show Search Direction. Note the reduction in the number of semivariogram values. Only those points in the direction of the search are displayed.

12. Click and hold the cursor on the center line in the Search Direction. Move the direction of the search tool. As you change the direction of the search, note how the semivariogram changes. Only the semivariogram surface values within the direction of the search are plotted on the semivariogram chart above.

To actually account for the directional influences on the semivariogram model for the surface calculations, you must calculate the anisotropical semivariogram or covariance model.

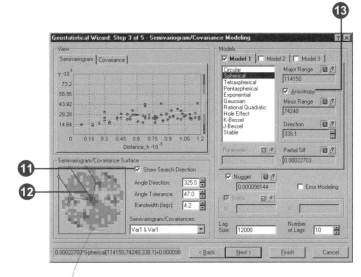

13. Check Anisotropy.

The blue ellipse on the semivariogram surface indicates the range of the semivariogram in different directions. In this case the major axis lies approximately in the NNW–SSE direction.

Anisotropy will now be incorporated into the model to adjust for the directional influence of autocorrelation in the output surface.

Range ————|

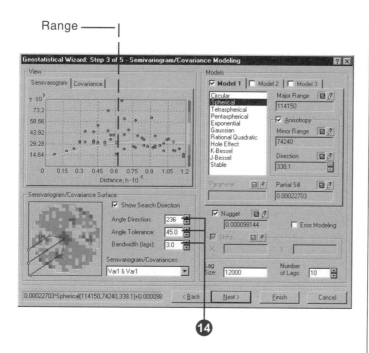

14. Type the following parameters for the Search direction to make the directional pointer coincide with the minor axis of the anisotropical ellipse:

Angle Direction: 236.0 *(336.6)*

Angle Tolerance: 45.0 ✓

Bandwidth (lags): 3.0 *(6.00)*

Note that the shape of the semivariogram curve increases more rapidly to its sill value. The x- and y-coordinates are in meters, so the range in this direction is approximately 74 km.

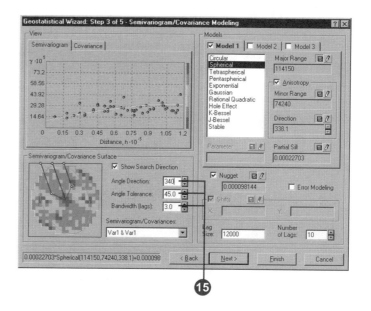

15. Type the following parameters for the Search direction to make the directional pointer coincide with the major axis of the anisotropical ellipse:

Angle Direction: 340.0

Angle Tolerance: 45.0

Bandwidth (lags): 3.0

The semivariogram model increases more gradually, then flattens out. The range in this direction is 114 km.

The plateau that the semivariogram models reach in both steps 14 and 15 is the same and is known as the sill. The range is the distance at which the semivariogram model reaches its limiting value (the sill). Beyond the range, the dissimilarity between points becomes constant with increased lag distance. The lag is defined by the distance

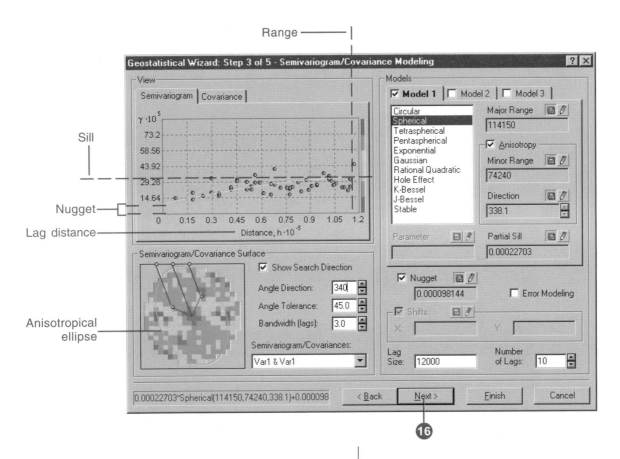

Range ——————|

Sill

Nugget

Lag distance

Anisotropical ellipse

Geostatistical Wizard: Step 3 of 5 - Semivariogram/Covariance Modeling

16

between pairs of points. Points separated by a lag distance greater than the range are spatially uncorrelated. The nugget represents measurement error and/or microscale variation (variation at spatial scales too fine to detect). It is possible to estimate the measurement error if you have multiple observations per location, or you can decompose the nugget into measurement error and microscale variation by checking the Nugget Error Modeling check box.

16. Click Next.

Now you have a fitted model to describe the spatial auto-correlation, taking into account detrending and directional influences in the data. This information, along with the configuration and measurements of locations around the prediction location, is used to make a prediction. But how should man-measured locations be used for the calculations?

Searching neighborhood

It is common practice to limit the data used by defining a circle (or ellipse) to enclose the points that are used to predict values at unmeasured locations.

Additionally, to avoid bias in a particular direction, the circle (or ellipse) can be divided into sectors from which an equal number of points are selected. By using the Searching Neighborhood dialog box, you can specify the number of points (a maximum of 200), the radius (or major/minor axis), and the number of sectors of the circle (or ellipse) to be used for prediction.

The points highlighted in the data view window give an indication of the weights that will be associated with each location in the prediction of unknown values. In this

example, four locations (red) have weights of more than 10 percent. The larger the weight, the more impact that location will have on the prediction of unknown values.

17. Click inside the graph view to select a prediction location (where the crosshairs meet). Note the change in the selection of data location (together with their associated weights) that will be used for calculating the value at the prediction location.

18. For the purpose of this tutorial, type the following coordinates in the Test Location input boxes:
X = -2044968 and Y = 208630.37.

19. Check the Shape check box and type 90 in the Angle input box. Notice how the shape changes. However, to account for the directional influences, change the angle back to 338.1.

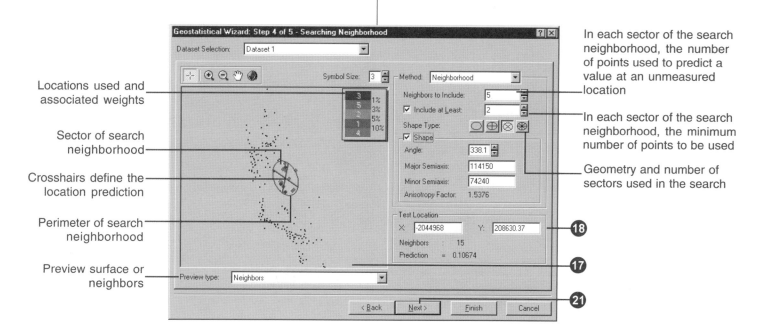

Locations used and associated weights

Sector of search neighborhood

Crosshairs define the location prediction

Perimeter of search neighborhood

Preview surface or neighbors

In each sector of the search neighborhood, the number of points used to predict a value at an unmeasured location

In each sector of the search neighborhood, the minimum number of points to be used

Geometry and number of sectors used in the search

20. Uncheck the Shape check box—Geostatistical Analyst will use the default values (calculated in the Semivariogram/Covariance dialog earlier).

21. Click Next on the Searching Neighborhood dialog box.

Before you actually create the surface, you next use the Cross-validation dialog to perform diagnostics on the parameters to determine "how good" your model will be.

Cross-validation

Cross-validation gives you an idea of "how well" the model predicts the unknown values.

For all points, cross-validation sequentially omits a point, predicts its value using the rest of the data, and then compares the measured and predicted values. The calculated statistics serve as diagnostics that indicate whether the model is reasonable for map production.

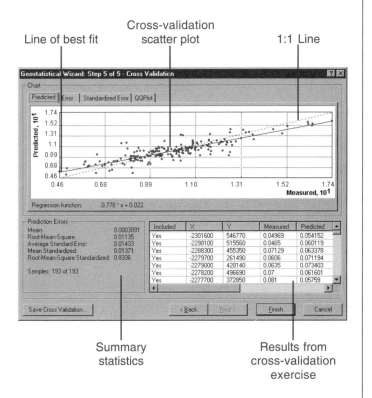

Line of best fit

Cross-validation scatter plot

1:1 Line

Summary statistics

Results from cross-validation exercise

In addition to visualizing the scatter of points around this 1:1 line, a number of statistical measures can be used to assess the model's performance. The objective of cross-validation is to help you make an informed decision about which model provides the most accurate predictions. For a model that provides accurate predictions, the mean error should be close to 0, the root-mean-square error and average standard error should be as small as possible (this is useful when comparing models), and the root-mean-square stardardized error should be close to 1.

Here the term "prediction error" is used for the difference between the prediction and the actual measured value. For a model that provides accurate predictions, the mean prediction error should be close to 0 if the predictions are unbiased, the root-mean-square standardized prediction error should be close to 1 if the standard errors are accurate, and the root-mean-square prediction error should be small if the predictions are close to the measured values.

The Cross Validation dialog box also allows you to display scatterplots that show the Error, Standardized Error, and QQPlot for each data point.

22. Click the QQPlot tab to display the QQPlot.

From the QQPlot you can see that some values fall slightly above the line and some slightly below the line, but most points fall very close to the straight dashed line, indicating that prediction errors are close to being normally distributed.

23. To highlight the location for a particular point, click on the row that relates to the point of interest in the table. The selected point is highlighted in green on the scattergram.

24. Optionally, click Save Cross Validation to save the table for further analysis of the results.

Selected point

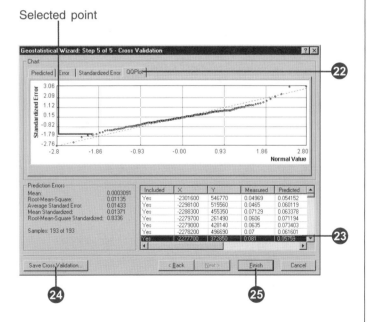

25. Click Finish.

The Output Layer Information dialog box provides a summary of the model that will be used to create a surface.

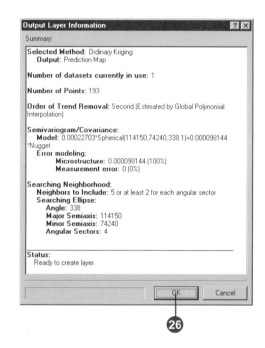

26. Click OK.

The predicted ozone map will appear as the top layer in ArcMap.

By default, the layer assumes the name of the kriging method used to produce the surface (e.g., Ordinary Kriging).

27. Click the layer name to highlight it, then click it again and change it to "Trend removed".

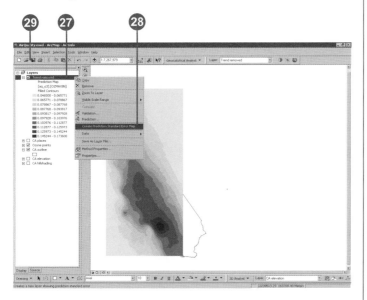

You can also create a Prediction Standard Error surface to examine the quality of the predictions.

28. Right-click on the "Trend removed" layer that you created and click on Create Prediction Standard Error Map.

29. Click Save on the Standard toolbar.

The Prediction Standard Errors quantify the uncertainty for each location in the surface that you created. A simple rule of thumb is that 95 percent of the time, the true value of the surface will be within the interval formed by the predicted value ± 2 times the prediction standard error if data are normally distributed. Notice in the Prediction Standard Error surface that locations near sample points generally have lower error.

The surface you created in Exercise 1 simply used the defaults of the Geostatistical Analyst, with no consideration of trends in the surface, of using smaller lag sizes, or of using an anisotropic semivariogram model. The prediction surface you created in this exercise took into consideration the global trends in the data, adjusted the lag size, and adjusted for the local directional influence (anisotropy) in the semivariogram.

In Exercise 4, you will compare the two models to see which one provides a better prediction of unknown values.

Note: Once again, you see that the interpolation continues into the ocean. You will learn in Exercise 6 how to restrict the prediction surface to stay within California.

Exercise 4: Comparing models

Using the Geostatistical Analyst, you can compare the results of two mapped surfaces. This allows you to make an informed decision as to which provides more accurate predictions of ozone concentration based on cross-validation statistics.

1. Right-click the "Trend removed" layer, point to Compare.... You will be comparing the "Trend removed" layer with the Default layer you created in Exercise 2.

Because the root-mean-square prediction error is smaller for the Trend removed layer, the root-mean-square standardized prediction error is closer to one for the Trend removed layer, and the mean prediction error is also closer to zero for the Trend removed layer, you can state with some evidence that the Trend removed model is better and more valid. Thus, you can remove the default layer since you no longer need it.

2. Click Close on the Cross Validation Comparison dialog box.

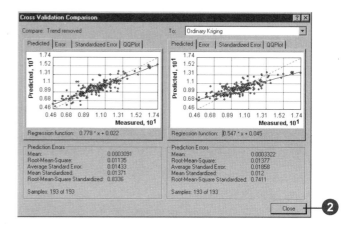

3. Right-click the Default layer and click Remove.

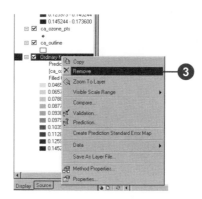

4. Click the Trend removed layer and move it to the bottom of the table of contents so that you can see the sample points and outline of California.

5. Click Save on the Standard toolbar.

You have now identified the best prediction surface, but there may be other types of surfaces that you might wish to create.

Exercise 5: Mapping the probability of ozone exceeding a critical threshold

In Exercises 1 and 3 you used ordinary kriging to map ozone concentration in California using different parameters. In the decision making process, care must be taken in using a map of predicted ozone for identifying unsafe areas because it is necessary to understand the uncertainty of the predictions. For example, suppose the critical threshold ozone value is 0.12 ppm for an eight-hour period, and you would like to decide if any locations exceed this value. To aid the decision making process, you can use the Geostatistical Analyst to map the probability that ozone values exceed the threshold.

While the Geostatistical Analyst provides a number of methods that can perform this task, for this exercise you will use the indicator kriging technique. This technique does not require the dataset to conform to a particular distribution. The data values are transformed to a series of 0s and 1s according to whether the values of the data are below or above a threshold. If a threshold above 0.12 ppm is used, any value below this threshold will be assigned a value of 0, whereas the values above the threshold will be assigned a value of 1. Indicator kriging then uses a semivariogram model that is calculated from the transformed 0–1 dataset.

1. Click the Geostatistical Analyst toolbar and click Geostatistical Wizard.

2. Click the Layer dropdown arrow and click ca_ozone_pts.

3. Click the Attribute dropdown arrow and click the OZONE attribute.

4. Click Kriging in the method box.

5. Click Next on the Choose Input Data and Method dialog box.

6. Click Indicator Kriging; notice that Probability Map is selected.

7. Set the Primary Threshold Value to 0.12.

8. Click the Exceed radial button to select it.

9. Click Next on the Geostatistical Method Selection dialog box.

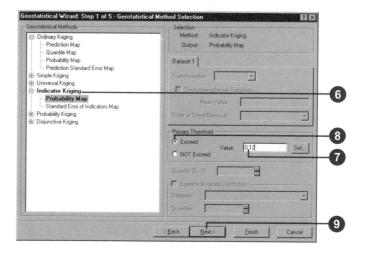

10. Click Next on the Additional Cutoffs Selection dialog box.

11. Click Anisotropy to account for the directional nature of the data.

12. Type 25000 for the lag size and 10 for the number of lags.

13. Click Next on the Semivariogram/Covariance Modeling dialog box.

14. Click Next on the Searching Neighborhood dialog box.

The blue line represents the threshold value (0.12 ppm). Points to the left have an indicator-transform value of 0, whereas points to the right have an indicator-transform value of 1.

15. Click and scroll right until the Measured, Indicator, and Indicator Prediction columns are displayed.

16. Click and highlight a row in the table with an indicator value of 0. That point will be highlighted in green on the scattergraph, to the left of the blue threshold line.

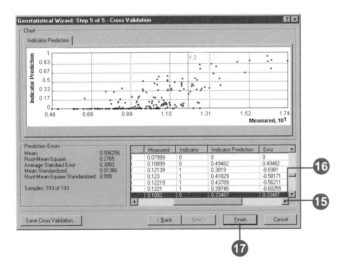

The measured and indicator columns display the actual and transformed values for each sample location. The indicator prediction values can be interpreted as the probability of exeeding the threshold. The indicator prediction values are calculated using the semivariogram modeled from the binary (0,1) data, created as indicator transformations of your original data. Cross-validation sequentially omits a point and then calculates indicator prediction values for each.

For example, the highest measured value is 0.1736. If this location had not actually been measured, a prediction of about an 85 percent chance that it was above the threshold based on the indicator kriging model would have been made.

17. Click Finish on the Cross Validation dialog box.

18. Click OK on the Output Layer Information dialog box.

The probability map will appear as the top layer in the ArcMap data view.

The map displays the indicator prediction values, interpreted as the probability that the threshold value of 0.12 ppm was exceeded on one or more days in the year 1996.

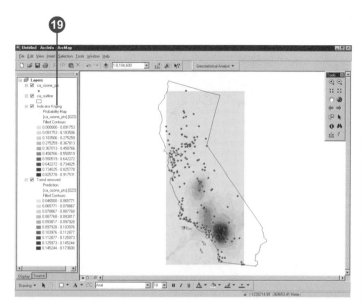

It is clear from the map that near Los Angeles the probability of values exceeding our threshold (staying, on average, below 0.12 ppm for every eight-hour period during the year) is likely.

19. Click and hold the Indicator Kriging layer. Drag the layer and reposition between the ca_outline and trend removed layers.

Click Save on the Standard toolbar to save your map. Exercise 6 will show you how you can use the functionality within ArcMap to produce a cartographically pleasing map of the prediction surface that you created in Exercise 3 and the probability surface that you created in this exercise.

Exercise 6: Producing the final map

You will now produce a final map for presentation. You will use ArcMap to produce a final output map in which the prediction and the probability surfaces will be displayed.

Displaying both surfaces

You can change the display of the probability map so you will be able to see both the prediction and the probability maps at the same time. The probability levels will be displayed as a contour map.

1. Right-click the Indicator Kriging layer. Click Properties.

2. Click the Symbology tab.

3. Uncheck the Filled Contours check box, then check the Contours check box.

4. Click the Color Ramp dropdown arrow and choose an alternative color ramp.

5. Click OK.

   You now see both the probability map (the contours) and the prediction map as the diagram to the right shows.

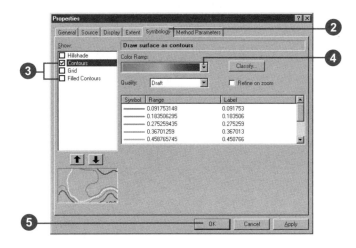

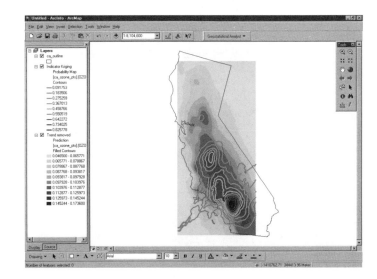

Extrapolating ozone values

By default, the Geostatistical Analyst interpolates the value of the selected variable at any location that lies within the area defined by the north–south and east–west limits of the sample point data. However, the map of predicted ozone does not cover the geographical extent of California (the ca_outline layer). To overcome this problem you will extrapolate values (predict values outside the default bounding box) for both surfaces.

1. Right-click the Indicator Kriging layer in the table of contents and click Properties. Click the Extent tab. In Set the extent to: select a custom extent entered below and type the following values for the Visible Extent, then click OK:

Left: -2400000   Right: -1600000

Top: 860000   Bottom: -400000

Repeat this step for the Trend removed layer.

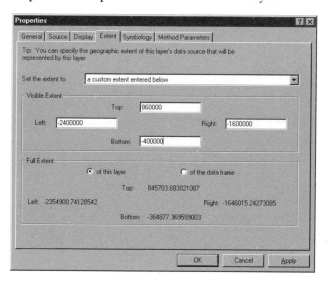

Clipping the layers to the California State outline

You will now clip the layers to the ca_outline layer as you are only interested in mapping the ozone levels within the State of California and this will produce a more appealing map.

1. Right-click Layers and click Properties.

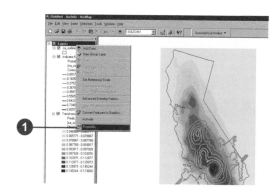

2. Click the Data Frame tab.

3. Check the Enable Clip to Shape check box.

4. Click Specify Shape.

5. Click Outline of Features.

6. Click the Layer dropdown and click ca_outline.

7. Click OK.

8. Click OK to close the Data Frame Properties dialog box.

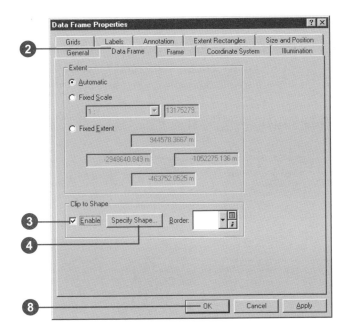

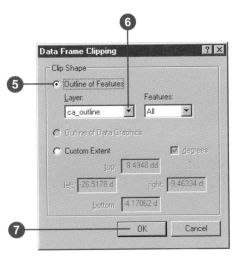

The clipped map should look like the following diagram.

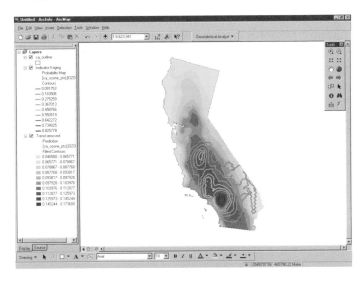

Locating the City of Los Angeles

1. Click the Add Data button on the Standard toolbar.

2. Navigate to the folder where you installed the tutorial data (the default installation path is C:\ArcGIS\ArcTutor\Geostatistics), then click ca_cities.

3. Click Add.

   A map of the location of cities in California will be displayed.

4. Right-click the ca_cities layer and click Open Attribute Table.

5. Scroll through the table and find the AreaName called Los Angeles. Click this row.

   The City of Los Angeles is highlighted on the map.

6. Click to close the attribute table.

7. Click the Zoom In tool on the Tools toolbar and zoom in on the City of Los Angeles.

Notice that the area with the highest ozone concentration is actually located just to the east of Los Angeles.

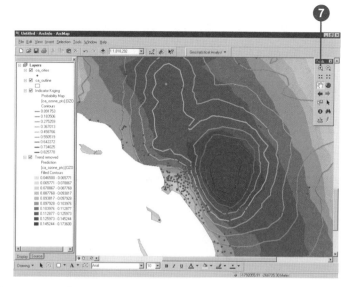

Create a layout

1. Click View on the Main menu and click Layout View.

2. Click the map to highlight it.

3. Click and drag the bottom-left corner of the Data Frame to resize the map.

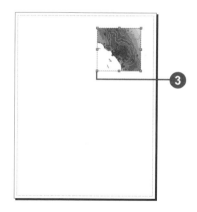

4. Click Insert on the Main menu and click Data Frame.

A new data frame is inserted on the map. You can now copy all the layers in the first data frame into this one in order to display a map of ozone values for the whole of California alongside the ozone map, which zooms in on the Los Angeles area.

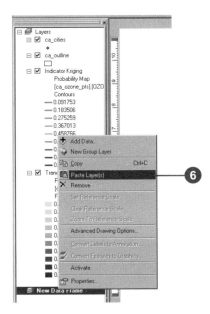

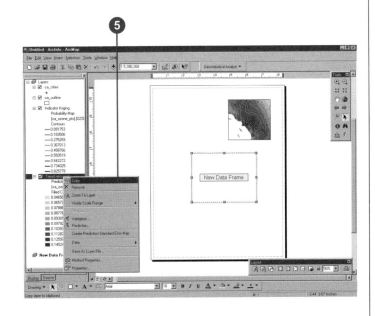

Follow steps 5 and 6 for all the other layers.

7. Click and drag the New Data Frame to fit the whole page.

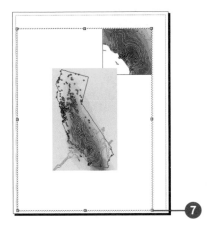

5. Right-click the Trend removed layer and click Copy.

6. Right-click the New Data Frame in the table of contents and click Paste Layer(s).

8. Click the Full Extent button on the Tools toolbar to view the full extent of the map in the New Data Frame.

9. Right-click the New Data Frame and click Properties.

10. Click the Data Frame tab and, as you did for the first Data Frame, check Enable Clip to Shape and click the Specify Shape button. Choose ca_outline as the layer to clip to, then click OK.

Adding a hillshade and transparency

1. Right-click the New Data Frame and click Add Data.

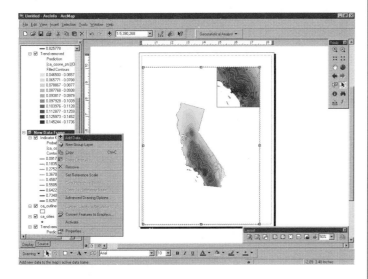

2. Navigate to the folder where you installed the tutorial data (the default installation path is C:\ArcGIS\ArcTutor\Geostatistics), then click ca_hillshade.

3. Click Add.

    A hillshade map of California will be displayed.

4. Click ca_hillshade and move it to the bottom of the table of contents.

5. Right-click the Trend removed layer in the New Data Frame table of contents and click Properties.

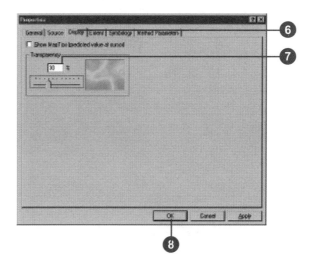

6. Click the Display tab.

7. Type 30 for the percentage of transparency.

8. Click OK.

    The hillshade should now partially display underneath the Trend removed layer.

Adding map elements

1. Click Insert on the Main menu and click Legend.

2. Move the legend to the bottom-left corner of the layout.

3. Optionally, click Insert and add a North arrow, a Scale bar, and Text.

The following diagram shows the type of finished map you could produce using the functionality of ArcMap. Refer to *Using ArcMap* if necessary to learn about inserting elements into the layout.

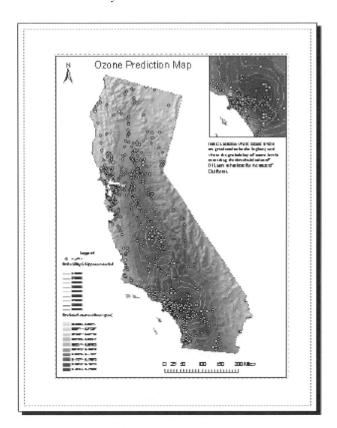

The map shows that the area east of Los Angeles has the highest predicted levels of ozone and the highest probability of exceeding the critical average threshold (0.12 ppm) on at least one eight-hour period during 1996. Since this is the case in the analysis (but remember the original data has been altered), you may wish to focus on these areas and analyze time series measurements of ozone to accurately identify the areas at potential risk.

The principles of geostatistical analysis

3

IN THIS CHAPTER

- **Understanding deterministic methods**

- **Understanding geostatistical methods**

- **Working through a problem**

- **Basic principles behind geostatistical methods**

- **Modeling a semivariogram**

- **Predicting unknown values with kriging**

- **The Geostatistical Analyst extension**

Geostatistical Analyst uses sample points taken at different locations in a landscape and creates (interpolates) a continuous surface. The sample points are measurements of some phenomenon such as radiation leaking from a nuclear power plant, an oil spill, or elevation heights. Geostatistical Analyst derives a surface using the values from the measured locations to predict values for each location in the landscape.

Geostatistical Analyst provides two groups of interpolation techniques: deterministic and geostatistical. All methods rely on the similarity of nearby sample points to create the surface. Deterministic techniques use mathematical functions for interpolation. Geostatistics relies on both statistical and mathematical methods, which can be used to create surfaces and assess the uncertainty of the predictions.

Geostatistical Analyst, in addition to providing various interpolation techniques, also provides many supporting tools. These tools allow you to explore and gain a better understanding of the data so that you create the best surfaces based on the available information.

This chapter will provide an overview of the theory behind deterministic and geostatistical interpolation techniques. The first part of the chapter will introduce you to the deterministic interpolation methods. You will then be exposed to geostatistical methods through an example, and then you will read about the principles, concepts, and assumptions that provide the foundation for geostatistics.

Mathmetical.

Understanding deterministic methods

Generating a continuous surface used to represent a particular measure is a key capability required in most GIS applications. Perhaps the most commonly used surface type is a digital elevation model of terrain. These datasets are readily available at small scales for various parts of the world. However, as you have read earlier, just about any measure taken at locations across a landscape, subsurface, or atmosphere can be used to generate a continuous surface. A major challenge facing most GIS modelers is to generate the most accurate possible surface from existing sample data as well as to characterize the error and variability of the predicted surface. Newly generated surfaces are used in further GIS modeling and analysis as well as in 3D visualization. Understanding the quality of this data can greatly improve the utility and purpose of GIS modeling. This is the role of the Geostatistical Analyst.

Analyzing the surface properties of nearby locations

Generally speaking, things that are closer together tend to be more alike than things that are farther apart. This is a fundamental geographic principal (Tobler, 1970). Suppose you are a town planner, and you need to build a scenic park in your town. You have several candidate sites, and you may want to model their viewsheds at each location. This will require a more detailed elevation surface dataset for your study area. Suppose you have preexisting elevation data for 1,000 locations throughout the town. You can use this to build a new elevation surface.

When trying to build the elevation surface, you can assume that the sample values closest to the prediction location will be similar. But how many sample locations should you consider? And should all of the sample values be considered equally?

As you move farther away from the prediction location, the influence of the points will decrease. Considering a point too far away may actually be detrimental because the point may be located in an area that is dramatically different from the prediction location.

One solution is to consider enough points to give a good sample but small enough to be practical. The number will vary with the amount and distribution of the sample points and the character of the surface. If the elevation samples are relatively evenly distributed and the surface characteristics do not change across your landscape, you can predict surface values from nearby points with reasonable accuracy. To account for the distance relationship, the values of closer points are weighted more heavily than those farther away.

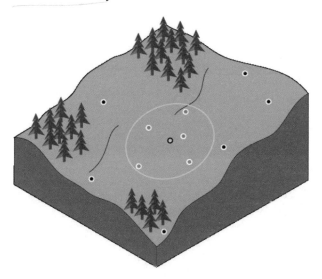

This is the basis for the Inverse Distance Weighting (IDW) interpolation technique. As its name implies, the weight of a value decreases as the distance increases from the prediction location.

Visualizing global polynomial interpolation

There are other solutions for predicting the values for unmeasured locations. Another proposed site for the observation area is on the face of a gently sloping hill. The face of the hill is a sloping plane. However, the locations of the samples are in slight depressions or on small mounds (local variation). Using the local neighbors to predict a location may over or underestimate because of the influence of depressions and mounds. Further, you may pick up the local variation and may not capture the overall sloping plane (referred to as the trend). The ability to identify and model local structures and surface trends can increase the accuracy of your predicted surface.

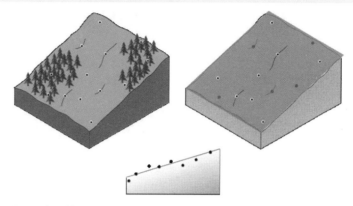

To base your prediction on the overriding trend, you can fit a plane between the sample points. A plane is a special case of a family of mathematical formulas called polynomials. You then determine the unknown height from the value on the plane for the prediction location. The plane may be above certain points and below others. The goal for interpolation is to minimize error. You can measure the error by subtracting each measured point from its predicted value on the plane, squaring it, and adding the results together. This sum is referred to as a least-squares fit. This process is the theoretical basis for the first-order global polynomial interpolation.

But what if you were trying to fit the plane to a landscape that is a valley? You will have a difficult task obtaining a good surface from a plane. However, if you are allowed one bend in the plane (see image below), you may be able to obtain a better fit (get closer to more values). To allow one bend is the basis for second-order global polynomial interpolation. Two bends in the plane would be a third-order polynomial, and so forth. The bends can occur in both directions, possibly resulting in a "bowl-shaped" surface.

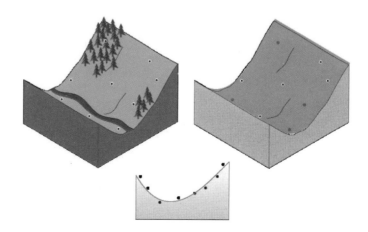

Visualizing local polynomial interpolation

Now what happens if the area slopes, levels off, and then slopes again? Asking you to fit a flat plane through this study site would give poor predictions for the unmeasured values. However, if you are permitted to fit many smaller overlapping planes, and then use the center of each plane as the prediction for each location in the study area, the resulting surface will be more flexible and perhaps more accurate. This is the conceptual basis for local polynomial interpolation.

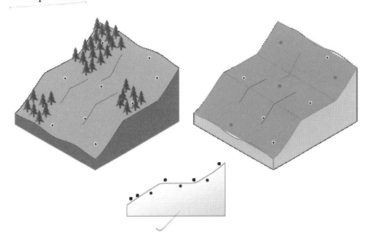

Visualizing radial basis functions

Radial basis functions enable you to create a surface that captures global trends and picks up the local variation. This helps in cases where fitting a plane to the sample values will not accurately represent the surface.

To create the surface, suppose you have the ability to bend and stretch the predicted surface so that it passes through all of the measured values. There are many ways you can predict the shape of the surface between the measured points. For example, you can force the surface to form nice curves (thin-plate spline), or you can control how tightly you pull on the edges of the surface (spline with tension). This is the conceptual framework for interpolators based on radial basis functions.

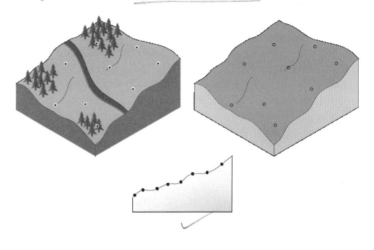

Understanding geostatistical methods

Geostatistical solutions

So far, the techniques that we have discussed are referred to as deterministic interpolation methods because they are directly based on the surrounding measured values or on specified mathematical formulas that determine the smoothness of the resulting surface. A second family of interpolation methods consists of geostatistical methods that are based on statistical models that include autocorrelation (statistical relationships among the measured points). Not only do these techniques have the capability of producing a prediction surface, but they can also provide some measure of the certainty or accuracy of the predictions.

The following example will guide you through the basic steps of geostatistics using ordinary kriging.

Kriging is similar to IDW in that it weights the surrounding measured values to derive a prediction for each location. However, the weights are based not only on the distance between the measured points and the prediction location but also on the overall spatial arrangement among the measured points. To use the spatial arrangement in the weights, the spatial autocorrelation must be quantified.

To solve the geostatistical example, you will walk through a series of steps.

Calculate the empirical semivariogram—kriging, like most interpolation techniques, is built on the assumption that things that are close to one another are more alike than those farther away (quantified here as spatial autocorrelation). The empirical semivariogram is a means to explore this relationship. Pairs that are close in distance should have a smaller measurement difference than those farther away from one another. The extent that this assumption is true can be examined in the empirical semivariogram.

Fit a model—this is done by defining a line that provides the best fit through the points in the empirical semivariogram cloud graph. That is, you need to find a line such that the (weighted) squared difference between each point and the line is as small as possible. This is referred to as the (weighted) least-squares fit. This line is considered a model that quantifies the spatial autocorrelation in your data.

Create the matrices—the equations for ordinary kriging are contained in matrices and vectors that depend on the spatial autocorrelation among the measured sample locations and prediction location. The autocorrelation values come from the semivariogram model described above. The matrices and vectors determine the kriging weights that are assigned to each measured value.

Make a prediction—from the kriging weights for the measured values, you can calculate a prediction for the location with the unknown value.

Working through a problem

Suppose you have gone out and collected five elevation points in your landscape. The configuration of the points is displayed in orange on the map below. Beside each point, the spatial coordinates are given as (X,Y).

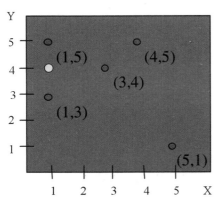

Values:
at (1,5) observe = 100
at (3,4) observe = 105
at (1,3) observe = 105
at (4,5) observe = 100
at (5,1) observe = 115

The kriging equations

You will use ordinary kriging to predict a value for location $X = 1$ and $Y = 4$, coordinate (1,4), which is called the prediction location (yellow point on the map). The ordinary kriging model is

$$Z(\mathbf{s}) = \mu + \varepsilon(\mathbf{s})$$

where $\mathbf{s} = (X,Y)$ is a location; one of the sample locations is $\mathbf{s} = (1,5)$, and $Z(\mathbf{s})$ is the value at that location; for example, $Z(1,5) = 100$. The model is based on a constant mean μ for the data (no trend) and random errors $\varepsilon(\mathbf{s})$ with spatial dependence. Assume that the random process $\varepsilon(\mathbf{s})$ is intrinsically stationary. These assumptions are discussed in the next sections. The predictor is formed as a weighted sum of the data,

$$\hat{Z}(\mathbf{s}_0) = \sum_{i=1}^{N} \lambda_i Z(\mathbf{s}_i)$$

where

$Z(\mathbf{s}_i)$ is the measured value at the ith location, for example, $Z(1,5) = 100$;

λ_i is an unknown weight for the measured value at the ith location;

$\mathbf{s}_0$ is the prediction location, for example, (1,4); and

$N = 5$ for the five measured values.

This is the same type of predictor as for IDW interpolation. However, in IDW, the weight, λ_i, depends solely on the distance to the prediction location. In ordinary kriging, the weight, λ_i, depends on the semivariogram, the distance to the prediction location, and the spatial relationships among the measured values around the prediction location.

When making predictions for several locations, expect some of the predictions to be above the actual values and some below. On average, the difference between the predictions and the actual values should be zero. This is referred to as making the prediction unbiased. To ensure the predictor is unbiased for the unknown measurement, the sum of the weight λ_i must equal one. Using this constraint, make sure the difference between the true value, $Z(\mathbf{s}_0)$, and the predictor, $\Sigma \lambda_i Z(\mathbf{s}_i)$, is as small as possible. That is, minimize the statistical expectation of the following formula,

$$\left(Z(\mathbf{s}_0) - \sum_{i=1}^{N} \lambda_i Z(\mathbf{s}_i) \right)^2$$

from which the kriging equations were obtained. By minimizing its expectation, on average, the kriging predictor is as close as possible to the unknown value. The solution to the minimization, constrained by unbiasedness, gives the kriging equations,

$$\Gamma \quad * \quad \lambda \quad = \quad g$$

or

$$\begin{pmatrix} \gamma_{11} & \cdots & \gamma_{1N} & 1 \\ \vdots & \ddots & \vdots & \vdots \\ \gamma_{N1} & \cdots & \gamma_{NN} & 1 \\ 1 & \cdots & 1 & 0 \end{pmatrix} * \begin{pmatrix} \lambda_1 \\ \vdots \\ \lambda_N \\ m \end{pmatrix} = \begin{pmatrix} \gamma_{10} \\ \vdots \\ \gamma_{N0} \\ 1 \end{pmatrix}$$

These equations will also become more understandable when the values are filled in for the matrix and vectors in the following section. Remember, the goal is to solve the equations for all of the λ_is (the weights), so the predictor can be formed by using $\sum_i \lambda_i Z(s_i)$.

Most of the elements can be filled in if you know the semivariogram. In the next few sections, you will see how to calculate the semivariogram values. The gamma matrix Γ contains the modeled semivariogram values between all pairs of sample locations, where γ_{ij} denotes the modeled semivariogram values based on the distance between the two samples identified as the ith and jth locations. The vector g contains the modeled semivariogram values between each measured location and the prediction location, where γ_{i0} denotes the modeled semivariogram values based on the distance between the ith sample location and the prediction location. The unknown m in the vector λ is also estimated and it arises because of the unbiasedness constraint.

Calculating the empirical semivariogram

To compute the values for the Γ matrix, we must examine the structure of the data by creating the empirical semivariogram. In a semivariogram, half the difference squared between the pairs of locations (the y-axis) is plotted relative to the distance that separates them (the x-axis).

The first step in creating the empirical semivariogram is to calculate the distance and squared difference between each pair of locations. The distance between two locations is calculated by using the Euclidean distance:

$$d_{ij} = \sqrt{(x_i - x_j)^2 + (y_i - y_j)^2}$$

The empirical semivariance is 0.5 times the difference squared 0.5 * average[(value at location i - value at location j)^2].

Locations	Distance Cal.	Distances	Difference^2	Semivariance
(1,5),(3,4)	sqrt[(1-3)^2 + (5-4)^2]	2.236	25	12.5
(1,5),(1,3)	sqrt[0^2 + 2^2]	2	25	12.5
(1,5),(4,5)	sqrt[3^2 + 0^2]	3	0	0
(1,5),(5,1)	sqrt[4^2 + 4^2]	5.657	225	112.5
(3,4),(1,3)	sqrt[2^2 + 1^2]	2.236	0	0
(3,4),(4,5)	sqrt[1^2 + 1^2]	1.414	25	12.5
(3,4),(5,1)	sqrt[2^2 + 3^2]	3.606	100	50
(1,3),(4,5)	sqrt[3^2 + 2^2]	3.606	25	12.5
(1,3),(5,1)	sqrt[4^2 + 2^2]	4.472	100	50
(4,5),(5,1)	sqrt[1^2 + 4^2]	4.123	225	112.5

As you can see, with larger datasets (more measured samples) the number of pairs of locations will increase rapidly and will quickly become unmanageable. Therefore, you can group the pairs of locations, which is referred to as binning. In this example, a bin is a specified range of distances. That is, all points that are within 0 to 1 meter apart are grouped into the first bin, those that are within 1+ to -2 meters apart are grouped into the second bin, and so forth. The average empirical semivariance of all pairs of points is taken. In the following example, the data is placed into five bins.

Binning the Empirical Semivariogram

Lag Distance	Pairs Distance	Av. Distance	Semivariance	Average
1+-2	1.414, 2	1.707	12.5, 12.5	12.5
2+-3	2.236, 2.236, 3	2.491	12.5, 0, 0	4.167
3+-4	3.606, 3.606	3.606	50, 12.5	31.25
4+-5	4.472, 4.123	4.298	50, 112.5	81.25
5+	5.657	5.657	112.5	112.5

Fitting a model

Now you can plot the average semivariance versus average distance of the bins onto a graph—the empirical semivariogram. But the empirical semivariogram values cannot be used directly in the Γ matrix because you might get negative standard errors for the predictions; instead, you must fit a model to the empirical semivariogram. Once the model is fit, you will use the fitted model when determining semivariogram values for various distances.

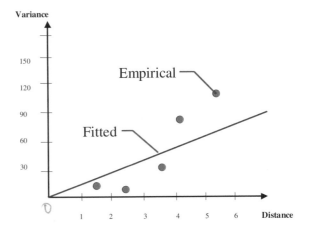

For simplicity, the model that you will fit is a least-squares regression line, and you will force it to have a positive slope and pass through zero. In the Geostatistical Analyst, there are many more models that could be fit.

The formula to determine the semivariance at any given distance in this example is:

$$\text{Semivariance} = \text{Slope} * \text{Distance}$$

Slope is the slope of the fitted model. Distance is the distance between pairs of locations and is symbolized as h. In the example, the semivariance for any distance can be determined by:

$$\text{Semivariance} = 13.5 * h$$

Now create the Γ matrix. For example, γ_{i2} for the locations (1,5) and (3,4) in the equation is:

$$\text{Semivariance} = 13.5 * 2.236 = 30.19$$

		(1, 5)	(3, 4)	(1, 3)	(4, 5)	(5, 1)	
	Γ Matrix (Gamma)						
(1, 5)		0	30.19	27.0	40.5	76.37	1
(3, 4)		30.19	0	30.19	19.09	48.67	1
(1, 3)		27.0	30.19	0	48.67	60.37	1
(4, 5)		40.5	19.09	48.67	0	55.66	1
(5, 1)		76.37	48.67	60.37	55.66	0	1
		1	1	1	1	1	0

In the example above, for pair (1,5) and (3,4), the lag distance was calculated using the distance between the two locations (see the previous table). The semivariogram value is found by multiplying the slope 13.5 times the distance. The 1s and 0 in the bottom row and the rightmost column arise due to unbiasedness constraints.

The matrix formula for ordinary kriging is:

$$\Gamma * \lambda = g$$

Now the Γ matrix has been produced, but it is necessary to solve for λ, which contains the weights to assign to the measured values surrounding the prediction location. Thus, perform simple matrix algebra and get the following formula:

$$\lambda = \Gamma^{-1} * g$$

where Γ^{-1} is the inverse matrix of Γ. By performing basic linear algebra, the inverse of Γ is obtained.

Inverse of Γ Matrix (Gamma)					
-0.02575	0.00704	0.0151	0.00664	-0.00303	0.3424
0.00704	-0.04584	0.01085	0.02275	0.0052	-0.22768
0.0151	0.01085	-0.02646	-0.00471	0.00522	0.17869
0.00664	0.02275	-0.00471	-0.02902	0.00433	0.28471
-0.00303	0.0052	0.00522	0.00433	-0.01173	0.42189
0.3424	-0.22768	0.17869	0.28471	0.42189	-41.701

Next, the **g** vector is created for the unmeasured location that we wish to predict. For example, use location (1,4). Calculate the distance from (1,4) to each of the measured points (1,5), (3,4), (1,3), (4,5), and (5,1). From these distances, determine the fitted semivariance using the formula Semivariance = 13.5* h, which was derived earlier. The **g** vector for (1,4) is given in the following table.

Point	Distance	g Vector for (1,4)
(1,5)	1	13.5
(3,4)	2	27.0
(1,3)	1	13.5
(4,5)	3.162	42.69
(5,1)	5	67.5
		1

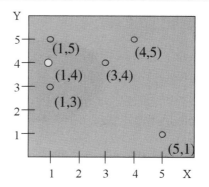

Now that the Γ matrix and the **g** vector have been created, solve for the kriging weights vector: $\lambda = \Gamma^{-1} * g$. Use linear algebra to do so. The weights are given in the table below.

Making a prediction

Now that you have the weights, multiply the weight for each measured value times the value. Add the products together and, finally, you have the final prediction for location (1,4).

Weights	Values	Product	
0.46757	100	46.757	
0.09834	105	10.3257	
0.46982	105	49.3311	
-0.02113	100	-2.113	
-0.0146	115	-1.679	
-0.18281		102.6218	**Kriging Predictor**

Next, examine the results. The following figure shows the weights (in parentheses) of the measured locations for predicting the unmeasured location (1,4).

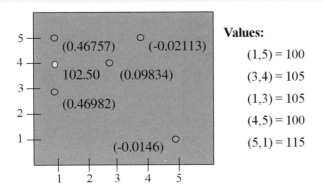

Values:

$(1,5) = 100$

$(3,4) = 105$

$(1,3) = 105$

$(4,5) = 100$

$(5,1) = 115$

the prediction location. In the example, the prediction interval ranges from 95.49 to 109.75 ($102.62 \pm 1.96 * 3.64$).

G Vector	Weights (λ)	g Vector Times Weights
13.5	0.46757	6.312195
27.0	0.09834	2.65518
13.5	0.46982	6.34257
42.69	-0.02113	-0.90204
67.5	-0.0146	-0.9855
1	-0.18281	-0.18281
	Kriging Variance	13.2396
	Kriging Std Error	3.6386

As expected, the weights decrease with distance but are more refined than a straight distance weighting since they account for the spatial arrangement of the data. The prediction appears to be reasonable.

Kriging variance

One of the strengths of using a statistical approach is that it is possible to also calculate a statistical measure of uncertainty for the prediction. To do so, multiply each entry in the λ vector times each entry in the **g** vector and add them together to obtain what is known as the predicted kriging variance. The square root of the kriging variance is called the kriging standard error.

In this case, the kriging standard error value is 3.6386. If it is assumed that the errors are normally distributed, 95 percent prediction intervals can be obtained in the following way:

Kriging Predictor $\pm 1.96*$**sqrt**(kriging variance)

The value 1.96 comes from the standard normal distribution where 95 percent of the probability is contained from -1.96 to 1.96. The prediction interval can be interpreted as follows. If predictions are made again and again from the same model, in the long run 95 percent of the time the prediction interval will contain the value at

Basic principles behind geostatistical methods

Random processes with dependence

Unlike the deterministic interpolation approaches, geostatistics assumes that all values in your study area are the result of a random process. A random process does not mean that all events are independent as with each flip of a coin. Geostatistics is based on random processes with dependence. For an example, flip three coins and determine if they are heads or tails. The fourth coin will not be flipped. The rule to determine how to lay the fourth coin is if the second and third coins are heads, then lay the fourth coin the same as the first; otherwise, lay the fourth coin opposite to the first.

In a spatial or temporal context, such dependence is called autocorrelation.

Prediction for random processes with dependence

How does this relate to geostatistics and predicting unmeasured values? In the coin example, the dependence rules were given. In reality, the dependency rules are unknown. In geostatistics there are two key tasks: (1) to uncover the dependency rules and (2) to make predictions. As you can see from the example, the predictions come from first knowing the dependency rules.

Kriging is based on these same two tasks: (1) semivariogram and covariance functions (spatial autocorrelation) and (2) prediction of unknown values. Because of these two distinct tasks, it has

been said that geostatistics uses the data twice: first to estimate the spatial autocorrelation and second to make the predictions.

Understanding stationarity

Consider again the coin example. There is a unique dependence rule among the coins. With only one set of measured values, there is no hope of knowing the dependence rules without being told what they are. However, through continued observations of numerous samples, dependencies become apparent. In general, statistics relies on some notion of replication, where it is believed estimates can be derived and the variation and uncertainty of the estimate can be understood from repeated observations.

In a spatial setting, the idea of stationarity is used to obtain the necessary replication. Stationarity is an assumption that is often reasonable for spatial data. There are two types of stationarity. One is called mean stationarity. Here it is assumed that the mean is constant between samples and is independent of location.

The second type of stationarity is called second-order stationarity for covariance and intrinsic stationarity for semivariograms. Second-order stationarity is the assumption that the covariance is the same between any two points that are at the same distance and direction apart no matter which two points you choose. The covariance is dependent on the distance between any two values and not on their locations. For semivariograms, instrinsic stationarity is the assumption that the variance of the difference is the same between any two points that are at the same distance and direction apart no matter which two points you choose.

Second-order and intrinsic stationarity are assumptions necessary to get the necessary replication to estimate the dependence rules, which allows us to make predictions and assess uncertainty in the predictions. Notice that it is the spatial information (similar distance between any two points) that provides the replication. The coin example is dependent (the first and second coins are independent, but the first and fourth are dependent), so this random process does not have second-order stationarity.

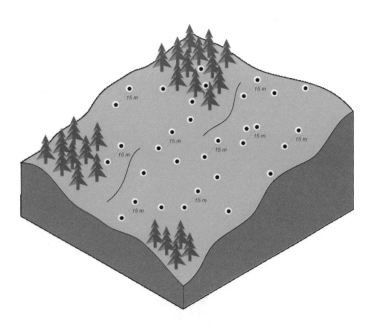

Modeling a semivariogram

The following sections will further discuss how a semivariogram is created. Assuming stationarity, the autocorrelation can be examined and quantified. In geostatistics this is called spatial modeling, also known as structural analysis or variography. In spatial modeling of the semivariogram, begin with a graph of the empirical semivariogram, computed as,

Semivariogram(distance h) = 0.5 * average [(value at location i - value at location j)^2]

for all pairs of locations separated by distance h. The formula involves calculating half the difference squared between the values of the paired locations. To plot all pairs quickly becomes unmanageable. Instead of plotting each pair, the pairs are grouped into lag bins. For example, compute the average semivariance for all pairs of points that are greater than 40 meters but less than 50 meters apart. The empirical semivariogram is a graph of the averaged semivariogram values on the y-axis and distance (or lag) on the x-axis (see diagram below).

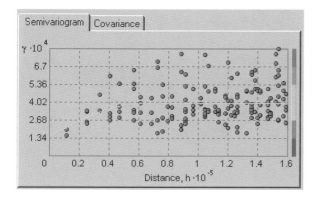

Again, note that it is the intrinsic stationarity assumption that allows replication. Thus it is possible to use "averaging" in the semivariogram formula above.

Once you've created the empirical semivariogram, you can fit a line to the points forming the empirical semivariogram model. The modeling of a semivariogram is similar to fitting a least-squares line in regression analysis. Some function is selected that serves as the model, for example, a spherical type that rises at first and then levels off for larger distances beyond a certain range.

The basic goal is to calculate the parameters of the curve to minimize the deviations from the points according to some criterion. There are a lot of different semivariogram models to choose from. See Chapter 7 for more details and recommendations on how to choose a model. Now you will go through each of these steps in detail.

Creating the empirical semivariogram

To create an empirical semivariogram, determine the squared difference between the values for all pairs of locations. When these are plotted, with half the squared difference on the y-axis and the distance that separates the locations on the x-axis, it is called the semivariogram cloud. The scene below shows the pairings of one location (the red point) with 11 other locations.

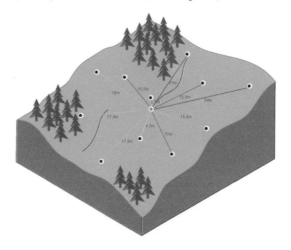

One of the main goals of variography is to explore and quantify the spatial dependence, also called the spatial autocorrelation. Spatial autocorrelation quantifies the assumption that things that are closer are more alike than things farther apart. Thus, pairs of locations that are closer (far left on the x-axis of the semivariogram cloud) would have more similar values (low on the y-axis of the semivariogram cloud). As pairs of locations become farther apart (moving to the right on the x-axis of the semivariogram cloud), they should become more dissimilar and have a higher squared difference (move up on the y-axis of the semivariogram cloud).

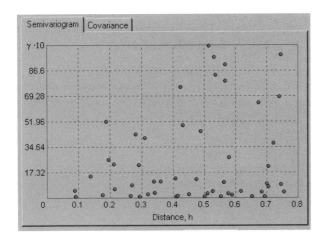

Binning the empirical semivariogram

As you can see from the landscape of locations in the previous page and the semivariogram cloud above, plotting each pair of locations quickly becomes unmanageable. There are so many points that the plot becomes congested, and little can be interpreted from it. To reduce the number of points in the empirical semivariogram, the pairs of locations will be grouped based on

their distance from one another. This grouping process is known as binning.

Binning is a two-stage process. First, form pairs of points, and second, group the pairs so that they have a common distance and direction. In the landscape scene of 12 locations, you can see the pairing of all the locations with one location, the red point. Similar colors for the links between pairs indicate similar bin distances.

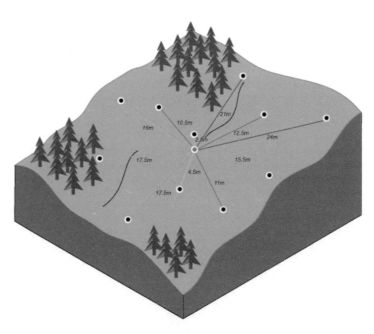

This process continues for all possible pairs. You can see that in the pairing process the number of pairs increases rapidly with the addition of each location. This is why, for each bin, only the average distance and semivariance for all the pairs in that bin are plotted as a single point on the empirical semivariogram cloud graph.

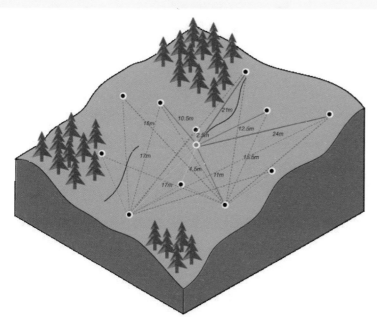

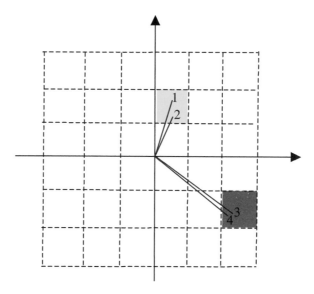

In the second stage of the binning process, pairs are grouped based on common distances and directions. Imagine a graph so each point has a common origin. This property makes the empirical semivariogram symmetric. Always put the links to the right of the vertical axis.

The figure below shows all possible pairwise links among all 12 locations. The points are rotated to orient north to the top.

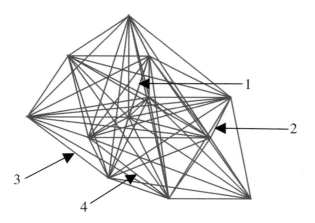

Now, you can see that links 1 and 2 have a fairly similar distance and direction. Each cell in the grid forms a bin. Links 1 and 2 fall into the same bin, which is colored yellow. For link 1 form the squared difference from the values at the two locations that are linked, and do likewise for link 2. Then these are averaged and multiplied by 0.5 to give one empirical semivariogram value for the bin.

Perform the same process for another bin, the one colored green, with links 3 and 4. To keep things simple, only four links are shown, but of course there are many, many more.

For each bin, form the squared difference from the values for all pairs of locations that are linked, and these are then averaged and multiplied by 0.5 to give one empirical semivariogram value per bin. In the Geostatistical Analyst, you can control the lag size and number of bins. The empirical semivariogram value in each bin is color coded and is called the semivariogram surface.

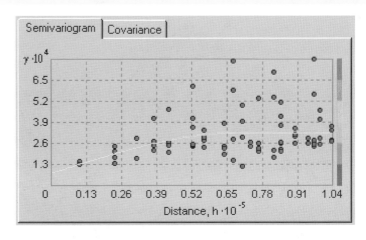

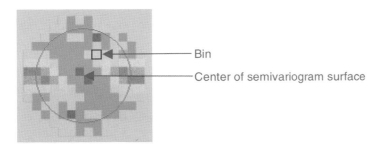

In the figure above, there are seven bins horizontally and vertically from the center of the semivariogram surface. For the bins, the "cool" colors (blue and green) are lower values, and the "warm" colors (red and orange) are higher values. As you can see, in general, the empirical semivariogram values increase as the bins get farther away from the origin. This indicates that values are more dissimilar with increasing distance. Also notice the symmetry that we described earlier.

The Geostatistical Analyst also gives a plot of the empirical semivariogram.

In the graph above, the empirical semivariogram value for each bin for each direction is plotted as a red dot, where the y-axis is the empirical semivariogram value and the x-axis is the distance from the center of the bin to the origin (center of semivariogram surface). The color bar on the right matches the colors on the semivariogram surface. By binning and averaging the semivariogram cloud values, it is much more obvious that dissimilarity increases with distance. The yellow line in the figure above is a fitted semivariogram model, which will be discussed shortly.

An alternative method that is often used for grouping the pairs into bins is based on radial sectors (see the figure below). The Geostatistical Analyst does not use this method.

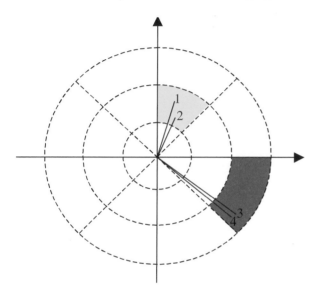

Empirical semivariograms for different directions

Sometimes the values for the measured locations will contain a directional influence that can be statistically quantified but perhaps cannot be explained by any known identifiable process. This directional influence is known as anisotropy. The angle of tolerance will determine the angle in which close points will be included or excluded until it reaches the bandwidth. The band-width specifies how wide the search should be when determining which pairs of points will be plotted in the semivariogram. The points in the bins are pairs of locations that are within certain distances and directions apart. You can conceptually view directional binning either by limiting the pairs of points that will

be graphed in the grouping process or by graphing all pairs and considering only the portion of the graph representing a certain direction. The scene below depicts a directional binning of 90 degrees, a bandwidth of five meters, an angle tolerance of 45 degrees, and a lag distance of five meters from a single sample point (in blue).

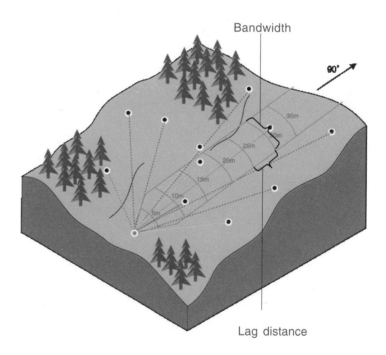

The directional search continues for each sample point and direction on the surface.

The scene below shows the directional binning of three points. Notice that fewer pairs of locations will be included in the grouping process than with the omnidirectional semivariogram in the previous example.

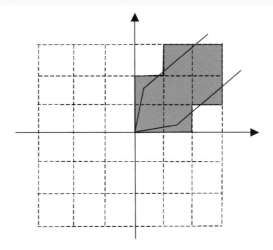

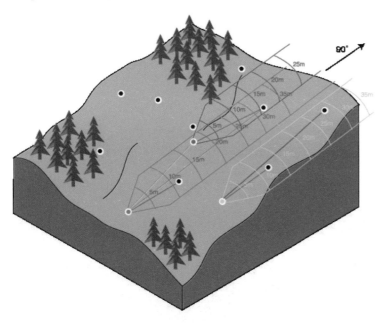

The pairs are then binned according to common distances and directions, the bins are averaged, and the average of the pairs for each bin is plotted on the semivariogram.

Alternatively, in the grid method of binning described earlier, all of the pairs can be binned, and you can make directional subsets as illustrated below. The bin will be plotted on the semivariogram cloud graph if the center of the cell on the semivariogram surface is included in the search direction.

Choosing the lag size

The selection of a lag size has important effects on the empirical semivariogram. For example, if the lag size is too large, short-range autocorrelation may be masked. If the lag size is too small, there may be many empty bins, and sample sizes within bins will be too small to get representative "averages" for bins.

When samples are located on a sampling grid, the grid spacing is usually a good indicator for lag size. However, if the data is acquired using an irregular or random sampling scheme, the selection of a suitable lag size is not so straightforward. A rule of thumb is to multiply the lag size times the number of lags, which should be about half of the largest distance among all points. Also, if the range of the fitted semivariogram model is very small, relative to the extent of the empirical semivariogram, then you can decrease the lag size. Conversely, if the range of the fitted semivariogram model is large, relative to the extent of the empirical semivariogram, you can increase the lag size. Semivariogram models are discussed next.

Fitting a model to the empirical semivariogram

Semivariogram/Covariance modeling is a key step between spatial description and spatial prediction. Earlier, it was described how to fit a semivariogram model and how it is used in the kriging equations (gamma matrix, Γ, and $\mathbf{g}$ vector). The main application of geostatistics is the prediction of attribute values at unsampled locations (kriging).

So far, you've read how the empirical semivariogram and covariance provide information on the spatial autocorrelation of datasets. However, they do not provide information for all possible directions and distances. For this reason and to ensure that kriging predictions have positive kriging variances, it is necessary to fit a model (i.e., a continuous function or curve) to the empirical semivariogram/covariance.

Abstractly, this is similar to regression analysis, where a continuous line or a curve of various types is fit.

Different types of semivariogram models

The Geostatistical Analyst provides the following functions to choose from to model the empirical semivariogram: Circular, Spherical, Tetraspherical, Pentaspherical, Exponential, Gaussian, Rational Quadratic, Hole Effect, K-Bessel, J-Bessel, and Stable. The selected model influences the prediction of the unknown values, particularly when the shape of the curve near the origin differs significantly. The steeper the curve near the origin, the more influence the closest neighbors will have on the prediction.

As a result, the output surface will be less smooth. Each model is designed to fit different types of phenomena more accurately.

The diagrams below show two common models and identify how the functions differ:

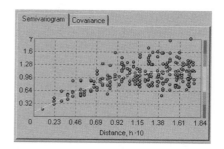

- The Spherical model

This model shows a progressive decrease of spatial autocorrelation (equivalently, an increase of semivariance) until some distance, beyond which autocorrelation is zero. The spherical model is one of the most commonly used models.

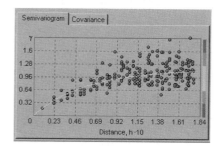

- The Exponential model

This model is applied when spatial autocorrelation decreases exponentially with increasing distance, disappearing completely only at an infinite distance. The exponential model is also commonly used.

Understanding a semivariogram—the range, sill, and nugget

As previously discussed, the semivariogram depicts the spatial autocorrelation of the measured sample points. Once each pair of locations is plotted (after binning), a model is fit through them. There are certain characteristics that are commonly used to describe these models.

The range and sill

When you look at the model of a semivariogram, you will notice that at a certain distance the model levels out. The distance where the model first flattens out is known as the range. Sample locations separated by distances closer than the range are spatially autocorrelated, whereas locations farther apart than the range are not.

The value that the semivariogram model attains at the range (the value on the y-axis) is called the sill. The partial sill is the sill minus the nugget.

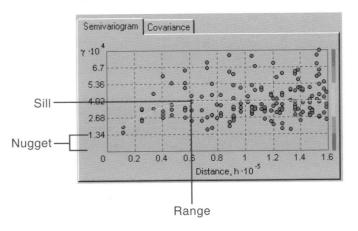

The nugget

Theoretically, at zero separation distance (i.e., lag = 0), the semivariogram value should be zero. However, at an infinitesimally small separation distance, the difference between measurements often does not tend to zero. This is called the nugget effect. For example, if the semivariogram model intercepts the y-axis at 2, then the nugget is 2.

The nugget effect can be attributed to measurement errors or spatial sources of variation at distances smaller than the sampling interval (or both). Measurement error occurs because of the error inherent in measuring devices. Natural phenomena can vary spatially over a range of scales. Variation at micro scales smaller than the sampling distances will appear as part of the nugget value. Before collecting data, it is important to gain some understanding of the scales of spatial variation that interest you.

Accounting for directional influences—trend and anisotropy

There are two types of directional components that can affect the predictions in your output surface: global trends and directional influences on the semivariogram/covariance (known as anisotropy). A global trend is an overriding process that affects all measurements in a deterministic manner. The global trend can be represented by a mathematical formula (e.g., a polynomial) and removed from the analysis of the measured points but added back in before predictions are made. This process is referred to as detrending (see Chapter 7, 'Using analytical tools when generating surfaces').

An example of a global trend can be seen in the effects of the prevailing winds on a smoke stack at a factory (right). In the image, the higher concentrations of pollution are depicted in the warm colors (reds and yellows) and the lower concentrations in the cool colors (greens and blues). Notice that the values of the pollutant change more slowly in the east–west direction than in the north–south direction. This is because east–west is aligned with the wind while north–south is perpendicular to the wind.

The shape of the semivariogram/covariance curve may also vary with direction (anisotropy) after the global trend is removed or if no trend exists. Anisotropy differs from the global trend discussed above because the global trend can be described by a physical process (in the example above, the prevailing winds) and modeled by a mathematical formula. The cause of the anisotropy (directional influence) in the semivariogram is not usually known, so it is modeled as random error. Even without knowing the cause, anisotropic influences can be quantified and accounted for.

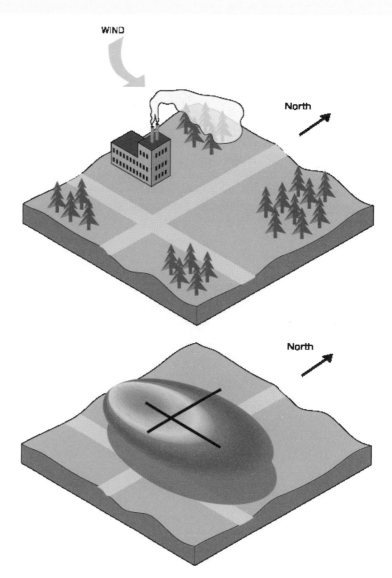

Anisotropy is usually not a deterministic process that can be described by a single mathematical formula. It does not have a single source or influence that predictably affects all measured points. Anisotropy is a characteristic of a random process that shows higher autocorrelation in one direction than in another. The following image shows conceptually how the process might look. Once again, the higher concentrations of pollution are depicted in the warm colors (reds and yellows) and the lower concentrations in the cool colors (greens and blues). The random process shows undulations that are shorter in one direction than another. These undulations could be the result of some unknown or unmeasurable physical process but are modeled as a random process with directional autocorrelation.

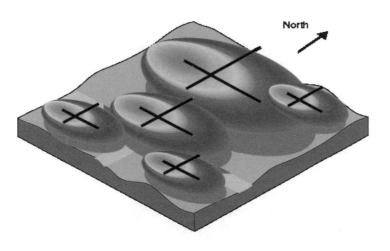

In this example, because of anisotropy, when the empirical semivariogram for the measured points is plotted, you can see that the spatial relationship is different for two directions. In the north–south direction the shape of the semivariogram curve increases more rapidly before leveling out.

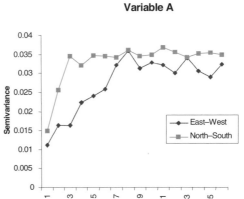

For anisotropy, the shape of the semivariogram may vary with direction. Isotropy exists when the semivariogram does not vary according to direction.

Combining variogram models

Many times there are two or more processes that will dictate the spatial distribution of some phenomenon. For instance, the quantity of vegetation (the biomass) may be related to elevation and soil moisture. If this relationship is known, it is possible to use cokriging to predict biomass. You could use the measured values of biomass as dataset one, elevation as dataset two, and soil moisture as dataset three (see Chapter 6, 'Creating a surface with geostatistical techniques'). You might fit different variogram models to each dataset because each exhibits different spatial structure. That is, the spherical model might fit elevation best, the exponential model might fit soil moisture best, and a combination of the models might fit biomass best. The models can then be combined in a way that best fits the structure of the data.

However, sometimes you do not know the causal relationships of the factors that are determining the spatial structure in some phenomenon. Using the same example of biomass above, you may only have the sample points measuring the biomass. When you examine the variogram, you notice distinct inflection points.

The points go up, straighten out, and then bend again to level off to the sill. You suppose that there are two distinct structures in the data and a single model will not capture it. You may model the semivariogram with two separate models (e.g., spherical and exponential) and combine them into a single model.

Representing multiple distinct random processes through a single variogram is discouraged, and it is best to separate the spatial processes whenever possible. However, the causal relationships are not always understood. The choice of multiple models adds more parameters to estimate and is a subjective exercise that you perform by eye and then quantify by cross-validation and validation statistics (see Chapter 7, 'Using analytical tools when generating surfaces').

The Geostatistical Analyst allows you to select up to three models in addition to a nugget effect model. In the example above, the model consists of three components: a nugget effect model and two spherical models with different ranges.

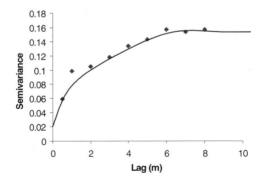

Using the Geostatistical Analyst to fit a model to a semivariogram

The example that was presented earlier in this chapter was simplified to make it easier to understand. To demonstrate the concept of modeling a semivariogram, more sample points will be used.

Ten measured sample points have been taken of elevation.

Point Number	X-Coordinate	Y-Coordinate	Value
1	1	3	105
2	1	5	100
3	1	6	95
4	3	4	105
5	3	6	105
6	4	5	100
7	5	1	115
8	6	3	120
9	6	6	110
10	7	1	120

In this example, a value for the location x = 2.75, y = 2.75 will be predicted where the value is currently unknown (the yellow point in the image below).

The spatial configuration of the measured points, their values, and the prediction location are displayed in ArcMap below.

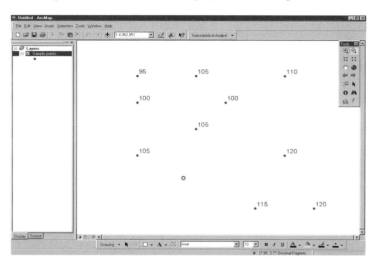

In the first two panels of the Geostatistical Wizard, you specify the dataset, the prediction field, and the kriging method (in this case, Ordinary Kriging). The third panel contains the semivari-ogram modeling dialog box. Here our goal is to fit a semivariogram model to the empirical semivariogram. You can see the list of available models below. In the previous example, a simple straight line is fitted, but you can see there are many more choices. Each model is slightly different so that you can fit the best one possible. Chapter 7, 'Using analytical tools when generating surfaces', provides more information on the models.

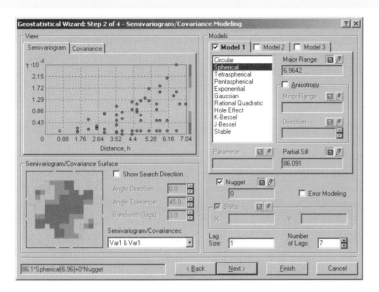

$$\gamma(\mathbf{h}) = \begin{cases} \theta_s \left[\dfrac{3}{2} \dfrac{h}{\theta_r} - \dfrac{1}{2} \left(\dfrac{h}{\theta_r} \right)^3 \right] & \text{for} \quad 0 \le h \le \theta_r \\ \theta_s & \text{for} \quad \theta_r < h \end{cases}$$

where

θ_s is the sill value,

h is the lag vector, and h is the length of **h** (distance between 2 locations),

θ_r is the range of the model.

Note the parameters of the spherical model are in blue lettering at the bottom left of the dialog box. This indicates a spherical model is being used with a sill value of 86.1, a range of 6.96, and zero nugget. Therefore, the calculated semivariogram values using the selected spherical model will be:

$\gamma(\mathbf{h}) = 86.1*(1.5*(h/6.96)-0.5(h/6.96)^3)$, for all lag values ≤ 6.96

and

$\gamma(\mathbf{h}) = 86.1$, for all lag values > 6.96

This is similar to finding the semivariogram value for a given distance, h, on the fitted line in our previous example, once the line was fitted, the values for the matrix and vectors were determined for the ordinary kriging equation from the line. Here the same can be done using the fitted spherical model.

In this example, the spherical model will be fitted to the empirical semivariogram. The formula for the spherical model is given here. As you can see, the formula is more involved than the simple line used in the previous example in this chapter. However, the two serve the same purpose with differing results.

Kriging

Like IDW interpolation, kriging forms weights from surrounding measured values to predict values at unmeasured locations. As with IDW interpolation, the closest measured values have the most influence. However, the kriging weights for the surrounding measured points are more sophisticated than those of IDW. IDW uses a simple algorithm based on distance, but kriging weights come from a semivariogram that was developed by looking at the spatial structure of the data. To create a continuous surface or map of the phenomenon, predictions are made for locations in the study area based on the semivariogram and the spatial arrangement of measured values that are nearby.

Searching neighborhood

It can be assumed that as the locations get farther from the prediction location, the measured values will have less spatial autocorrelation with the prediction location. Thus, it is possible to eliminate locations that are farther away that demonstrate little influence using search neighborhoods. Not only is there less relationship with locations that are farther away, but it is possible that the locations that are farther away may have a detrimental influence if they are located in an area much different than the prediction location. Another reason to use search neighborhoods is for computational speed. Recall from the first example that a 5-x-5 matrix was inverted. If you had 2,000 data locations, the matrix would be too large to invert. The smaller the search neighborhood, the faster the predictions can be made. As a result, it is common practice to limit the number of points used in a prediction by specifying a search neighborhood.

The specified shape of the neighborhood restricts how far and where to look for the measured values to be used in the prediction. Other neighborhood parameters restrict the locations that will be used within that shape.

The shape of the neighborhood is influenced by the input data and the surface that you are trying to create. If there are no directional influences on the spatial autocorrelation of your data, then you will want to consider points equally in all directions. To do so, you will probably want the shape of your neighborhood to be a circle. However, if there is directional autocorrelation in your data, then you may want the shape of your neighborhood to be an ellipse with the major axis parallel with the direction of long-range autocorrelation.

The searching neighborhood can be specified in Step 3 of the Geostatistical Wizard. Once a neighborhood shape is specified, you can also restrict which locations within the shape should be used. You can define the maximum and minimum number of neighbors to include. You can also divide the neighborhood into sectors to ensure you get values from all directions. If you divide the neighborhood into sectors, the specified maximum and minimum number of neighbors will be applied to each sector.

There are several different sector types that can be used (below).

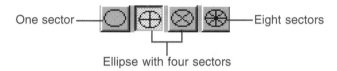

One sector ——— Eight sectors

Ellipse with four sectors

Using the data configuration within the specified neighborhood, in conjunction with the fitted semivariogram model, the weights for the measured locations can be determined. From the weights and the values, a prediction can be made for the unknown value for the prediction location. This process is performed for each spatial location to create a model of the continuous surface.

Creating a prediction surface using neighborhood searching

As the datasets get larger and cover more area, you will want to limit which measured points you consider when predicting. If you consider points too far away, they may be in areas much different than the prediction location. You will want to include enough points in your calculations for a good sampling, but you do not want to include those that are too far away from the prediction location because either they contribute very little or they come from an area unlike the area in which you are predicting (below). In the dialog box below a circular neighborhood with a radius of 3 is specified, and the maximum number of neighbors to include is 5.

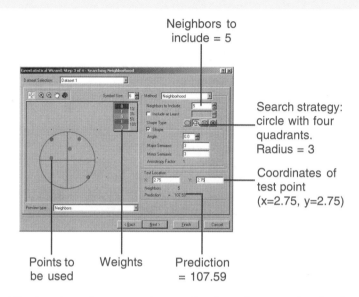

Neighbors to include = 5

Search strategy: circle with four quadrants. Radius = 3

Coordinates of test point (x=2.75, y=2.75)

Points to be used   Weights   Prediction = 107.59

The locations that are used to predict the unknown value for the desired location (2.75, 2.75) are highlighted and color coded (according to percentage size of coefficients λ_i)in the dialog view box. The points in the neighborhood are:

Neighborhood Point Number	Original Point Number	x-coordinate	y-coordinate	Value
1	1	1	3	105
2	2	1	5	100
3	4	3	4	105
4	6	4	5	100
5	7	5	1	115

The predicted value for the desired location (x = 2.75, y = 2.75) is 107.59. The Geostatistical Analyst predicted the value by solving the ordinary kriging equations.

$$\Gamma * \lambda = g \text{ and solving for the weights } \lambda = \Gamma^{-1} * g$$

With the spherical semivariogram model and with the trimmed down set of measured values identified through the neighborhood search, it is possible to solve for λ in the equation above. First, create the Γ matrix. This is done by calculating the distances between the pairs of points and substituting them into the fitted spherical model,

$$\gamma(h) = 86.1*(1.5*(h/6.96)-0.5(h/6.96)^3), \text{ for } 0 < h < 6.96$$

The distances between the measured points are:

Points	Distance	Points	Distance
1,2	2.000	2,4	3.000
1,3	2.236	2,5	5.657
1,4	3.605	3,4	1.414
1,5	4.472	3,5	3.606
2,3	2.236	4,5	4.124

If the distance (h) between points 1 and 3 is substituted, where h = 2.236, the semivariogram value is:

$$\gamma(h) = 86.1*(1.5*(2.236/6.96)-0.5(2.236/6.96)^3) = 40.065$$

Repeat this process for each pair of points to produce the Γ matrix. To keep the notation clear in the matrices, the points have been renumbered as shown in the top left.

i	1	2	3	4	5	6
1	0.000	36.091	40.065	60.920	71.564	1.000
2	36.091	0.000	40.065	52.221	81.855	1.000
3	40.065	40.065	0.0000	25.881	60.920	1.000
4	60.920	52.221	25.881	0.000	67.559	1.000
5	71.564	81.855	60.920	67.559	0.000	1.000
6	1.000	1.000	1.000	1.000	1.000	0.000

Next find the inverse Γ^{-1}.

i	1	2	3	4	5	6
1	-0.0191	0.01005	0.00776	-0.0021	0.00336	0.2114
2	0.01005	-0.0187	0.00472	0.00402	-0.0001	0.24891
3	0.00776	0.00472	-0.0317	0.01619	0.00304	-0.1038
4	-0.0021	0.00402	0.01619	-0.0214	0.00324	0.27739
5	0.00336	-0.0001	0.00304	0.00324	-0.0095	0.36607
6	0.2114	0.24891	-0.1038	0.27739	0.36607	-47.922

Now it is necessary to create the g vector to solve the ordinary kriging equation, $\lambda = \Gamma^{-1} * g$. To do so, calculate the distance of each of the five measured locations in our neighborhood to the prediction location (2.75, 2.75). The distances are:

From   x = 2.75, y = 2.75

Points	Distance
1	1.768
2	2.850
3	1.275
4	2.574
5	2.850

The **g** vector is created by substituting each of the distances into the fitted spherical model.

From   x = 2.75, y = 2.75

Points	Fitted Semivariance
1	32.097
2	49.936
3	23.390
4	45.584
5	49.936
6	1.000

The extra row in the **g** vector (and the extra row and column in the Γ matrix) has been added to ensure the weights sum to 1 (i.e., using the Lagrange multiplier explained further in Appendix A).

Now solve for the weights of the λ vector. An example of solving for the weight of point 1 is:

$$\lambda_1 = (-0.019*32.097 + 0.01005*49.936 + 0.00776*23.390$$
$$-0.0021*45.584 + 0.00336*49.936 + 0.2114*1.000)$$
$$= 0.355$$

The weights for all of the points and the Lagrange multiplier (entry number 6) are:

Points	λ_i
1	0.355
2	-0.073
3	0.529
4	-0.022
5	0.211
6	-0.210

Finally, predict the value of the location (2.75, 2.75) by multiplying the weights of the measured points (dropping entry number 6) by their values and then adding them together.

Prediction = 0.355 * 105 − 0.073 * 100 + 0.529 * 105
− 0.022 * 100 + 0.211 * 115

Prediction = 107.59

i	λ_i	Value$_i$
1	0.355	105
2	-0.073	100
3	0.529	105
4	-0.022	100
5	0.211	115

Repeating this for many prediction locations and mapping the results produces the prediction surface shown below.

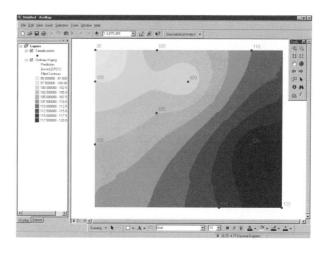

Output surfaces can be created with the Geostatistical Analyst in a number of formats. These include a shapefile of contour lines, a shapefile of filled contour polygons, and a grid representing a continuous surface and hillshade.

A guide to the Geostatistical Analyst extension

In this last section, you will learn more about the Geostatistical Analyst extension to ArcMap.

The software is accessed via the Geostatistical Analyst dropdown menu on the ArcMap toolbar. There are three main components to the Geostatistical Analyst: (1) Explore Data, (2) Geostatistical Wizard, and (3) Create Subsets.

Explore data

Before using the interpolation techniques, you can explore your data with these tools. ESDA tools allow you to gain insight into your data, enabling you to select the appropriate parameters for interpolation model. For example, when using ordinary kriging to produce a quantile map, you should examine the distribution of the data because it is assumed that the data is normally distributed. Alternatively, you may explore for a trend in your data with the ESDA tools, and you may wish to remove it in the prediction process.

The following tools are provided:

- Histogram—Explore the univariate distribution of a dataset.

- Voronoi Map—Analyze stationarity and spatial variability of a dataset.

- Normal QQPlot—Check for normality of a dataset.

- Trend Analysis—Identify global trends in a dataset.

- Semivariogram/Covariance Cloud—Analyze the spatial dependencies in a dataset.

- General QQPlot—Explore whether two datasets have the same distributions.

- Crosscovariance Cloud—Understand crosscovariance between two datasets.

Geostatistical Wizard

The Geostatistical Analyst provides a number of interpolation techniques that use sample points to produce surfaces of the phenomena of interest. The interpolation techniques in the Geostatistical Analyst are divided into two main types: deterministic and geostatistical.

Deterministic

Deterministic techniques are based on parameters that control either (i) the extent of similarity (e.g., Inverse Distance Weighted) of the values or (ii) the degree of smoothing (e.g., radial basis functions) in the surface. These techniques do not use a model of random spatial processes.

Geostatistics

Geostatistics assume that at least some of the spatial variation of natural phenomena can be modeled by random processes with spatial autocorrelation.

Geostatistical techniques can be used to:

- Describe and model spatial patterns—variography.

- Predict values at unmeasured locations—kriging.

- Assess the uncertainty associated with a predicted value at the unmeasured locations—kriging.

Kriging can be used to produce the following surfaces:

- Maps of kriging predicted values

- Maps of kriging standard errors associated with predicted values

- Maps of probability, indicating whether or not a predefined critical level was exceeded

- Maps of quantiles for a predetermined probability level

Create subsets

The most rigorous way to assess the quality of an output surface is to compare the predicted values with those measured in the field. It is often not possible to go back to the study area to collect an independent validation dataset. One solution is to divide the original dataset into two parts. One part can be used to model the spatial structure and produce a surface. The other part can be used to compare and validate the quality of the predictions. The Create Subsets dialog box enables you to produce both test and training datasets.

Processing data

The software includes many tools for analyzing data and producing a variety of output surfaces.

While the aim of the investigation may vary, you are encouraged to adopt the following approach when analyzing/mapping spatial processes:

Represent the data	Add layers and display in ArcMap.
Explore the data	Investigate the statistical and spatial properties of your data.
Fit a model	Choose a model to create a surface. The Geostatistical Wizard is used in the definition and refinement of an appropriate model.
Perform diagnostics	Assess the quality of the output surface using Cross-Validation and Validation tools. This will help you understand how well the model predicts the values at unmeasured locations.
Compare the models	More than one surface can be produced. The surface can be compared using cross-validation statistics.

Exploratory Spatial Data Analysis 4

IN THIS CHAPTER

- **What is Exploratory Spatial Data Analysis?**

- **The Exploratory Spatial Data Analysis tools**

- **Examining the distribution of the data**

- **Looking for global and local outliers**

- **Looking for global trends**

- **Examining spatial autocorrelation and directional variation**

- **Understanding covariation among multiple datasets**

Exploratory Spatial Data Analysis allows you to examine your data in different ways. Before creating a surface, ESDA enables you to gain a deeper understanding of the phenomena you are investigating so that you can make better decisions on issues relating to your data. The ESDA environment is composed of a series of tools, each allowing a view into the data. Each view can be manipulated and explored, allowing different insights about the data. Each view is interconnected with all other views as well as with ArcMap. That is, if a bar is selected in the histogram, the points comprising the bar are also selected on the QQPlot (if opened), on any other open ESDA view, and on the ArcMap map.

The ESDA environment is designed to explore, as its name implies. However, there are certain tasks that are useful in most explorations. Exploring the distribution of the data, looking for global and local outliers, looking for global trends, examining spatial autocorrelation, and understanding the covariation among multiple datasets are all useful tasks to perform on your data. The ESDA tools can assist you with these tasks as well as many others.

What is Exploratory Spatial Data Analysis?

The ESDA environment allows you to graphically investigate your dataset to gain a better understanding of it. Each ESDA tool provides a different view of the data and is displayed in a separate window. The different views are Histogram, Voronoi Map, Normal QQPlot, Trend Analysis, Semivariogram/Covariance Cloud, General QQPlot, and Crosscovariance Cloud. All views interact with one another and with the ArcMap map.

Working with selections; brushing and linking

The views in ESDA are interconnected by selecting (brushing) and highlighting the selected points on all maps and graphs (linking). Brushing is a graphical way to perform a selection in either the ArcMap data view or in an ESDA tool. Any selection that occurs in an ESDA view or in the ArcMap data view will be selected in all ESDA windows as well as on the ArcMap map (see the diagram on the following page); this is called linking. When brushing in some ESDA tools (Histogram, Voronoi map, QQPlot, and Trend analysis), the selected points in the view are linked to the ArcMap map, and the corresponding points are highlighted. Because points in the semivariogram/covariance plots represent pairs of locations, when brushing in the Semivariogram/Covariance Cloud tool, the pairs are highlighted in the ArcMap data view and a line connects each pair. When pairs of points in the ArcMap data view are selected, the points in the semivariogram/covariance plot are also highlighted.

Layer interaction between ArcMap and ESDA

The ESDA tools interact with the layers in ArcMap in the following ways:

1. ESDA tools work on point feature and polygon feature (i.e., census, epidemiology, or demographic data) layers.

2. The layer that is highlighted in the ArcMap table of contents prior to initiating an ESDA tool will be the default layer for the tool.

3. If the highlighted point feature layer is not checked as selectable, the default layer in the tool will be the first layer in the TOC.

4. Only selectable point feature layers will be in a dropdown list of layers that can be explored by the tool.

5. The query definition for any layer will be honored.

6. The layer that is being explored in ESDA does not have to be displayed in the ArcMap data view, but if it is not the different brushings will not be visible on the map.

7. If only one point feature layer is highlighted in the ArcMap table of contents and an ESDA tool requiring multiple layers is selected, the highlighted layer will be the default for the first input dataset for that tool.

8. If two or more point feature layers are highlighted in the ArcMap table of contents and an ESDA tool requiring multiple layers is selected, the first highlighted point feature layer in the table of contents is the first input dataset for that ESDA tool, and the second highlighted layer is the second dataset.

Transformations

Several methods in the Geostatistical Analyst require that the data is normally distributed. When the data is skewed (the distribution is lopsided), you may want to transform your data to make it normal. In ESDA, the Histogram and Normal QQPlot allow you to explore the effects of different transformations on the distribution of the dataset. If you choose to transform your data before creating a surface using geostatistics, the predictions will be transformed back to the original scale for your interpolated surface.

Exploratory Spatial Data Analysis

Selection of Data Points

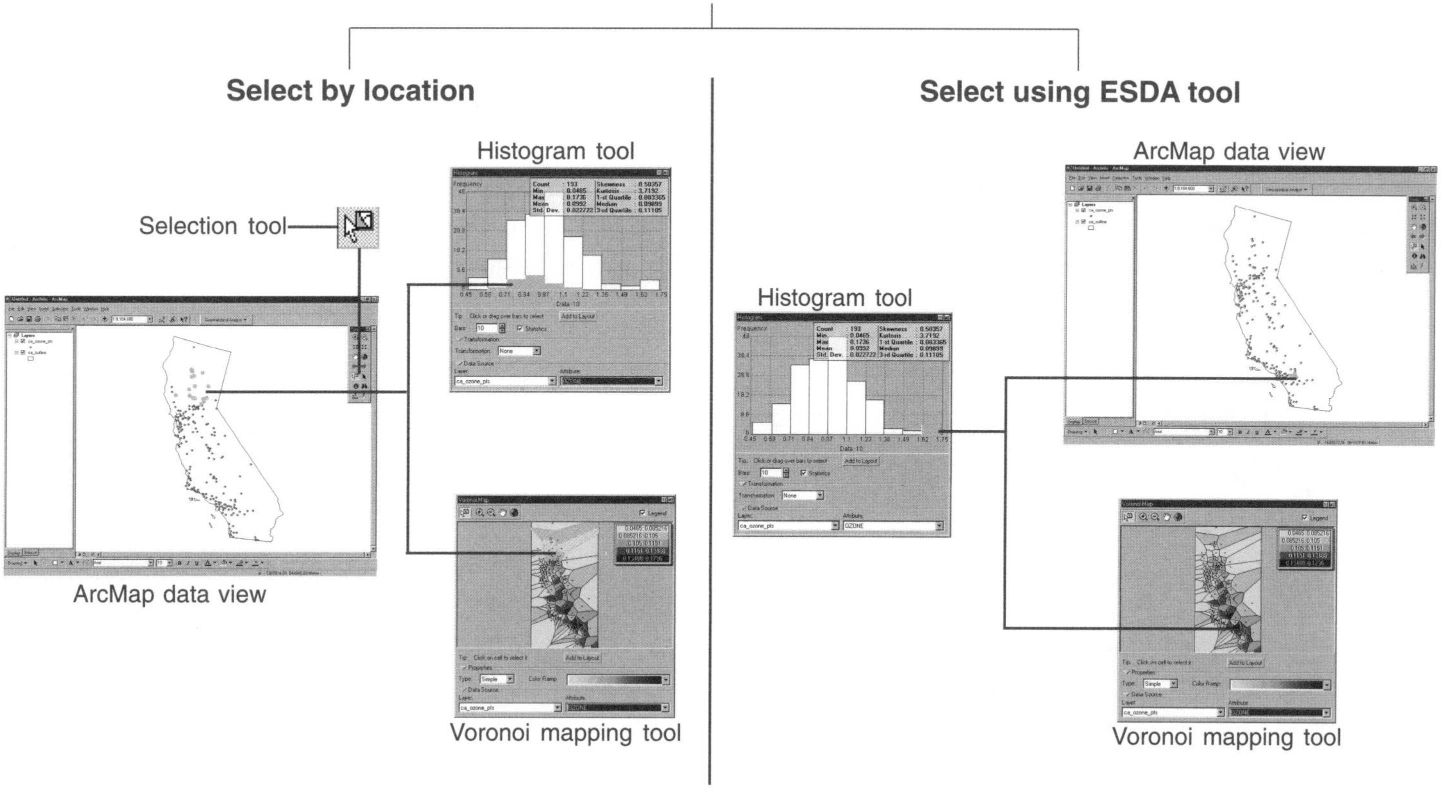

Select by location

Selection tool

Histogram tool

ArcMap data view

Voronoi mapping tool

Select using ESDA tool

ArcMap data view

Histogram tool

Voronoi mapping tool

Select points of interest in the ArcMap data view. The ESDA tools will display the selected points in the context of all points (e.g., partitioned histogram).

Select a feature of interest (e.g., the tail of a histogram) in an ESDA window. The locations of the selected points are displayed in the ArcMap data view. When you initiate a new ESDA tool it will also display the associated properties of the selected points (e.g., location of Voronoi cells).

Exploratory Spatial Data Analysis tools

Each ESDA tool provides you with the capability to examine your data in different views. Each view is displayed in a separate window and fully interacts with the ArcMap display as well as with other ESDA windows. The tools available are Histogram, Voronoi Map, Normal QQPlot, Trend Analysis, Semivariogram/Covariance Cloud, General QQPlot, and Crosscovariance Cloud.

Histogram

The histogram tool in ESDA provides a univariate (one-variable) description of your data. The tool displays the frequency distribution for the dataset of interest and calculates summary statistics.

Frequency distribution

The frequency distribution is a bar graph that displays how often observed values fall within certain intervals or classes. You specify the number of classes of equal width that should be used in the histogram. The relative proportion of data that falls in each

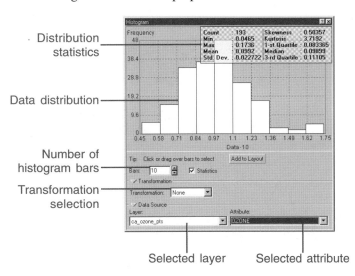

Distribution statistics

Data distribution

Number of histogram bars

Transformation selection

Selected layer   Selected attribute

class is represented by the height of each bar. For example, the histogram above shows the frequency distribution (10 classes) for an ozone dataset.

Summary statistics

The important features of a distribution can be summarized by a few statistics that describe its location, spread, and shape.

Measures of location

Measures of location provide you with an idea of where the center and other parts of the distribution lie.

The mean is the arithmetic average of the data. The mean provides a measure of the center of the distribution.

The median value corresponds to a cumulative proportion of 0.5. If the data was arranged in increasing order, 50 percent of the values would lie below the median, and 50 percent of the values would lie above the median. The median provides another measure of the center of the distribution.

The first and third quartiles correspond to a cumulative proportion of 0.25 and 0.75, respectively. If the data was arranged in increasing order, 25 percent of the values would lie below the first quartile, and 25 percent of the values would lie above the third quartile. The first and third quartiles are special cases of quantiles. The quantiles are calculated as follows:

$$\text{quantile} = (i) - 0.5 / N$$

where (i) is the ith rank of the ordered data values and N is the number of data.

Measures of spread

The spread of points around the mean value is another characteristic of the displayed frequency distribution. The variance of the data is the average squared deviation of all values from the mean. The units are the square of the units of the original measurements and, because it involves squared differences, the calculated variance is sensitive to unusually high or low values.

The standard deviation is the square root of the variance. It describes the spread of the data about the mean in the same units as the original measurements. The smaller the variance and standard deviation, the tighter the cluster of measurements about the mean value.

The diagram below shows two distributions with different standard deviations. The frequency distribution given by the black line is more variable (wider spread) than the frequency distribution given by the red line. The variance and standard deviation for the black frequency distribution are greater than those for the red frequency distribution.

Measures of shape

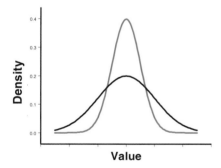

The frequency distribution is also characterized by its shape.

The coefficient of skewness is a measure of the symmetry of a distribution. For symmetric distributions, the coefficient of skewness is zero. If a distribution has a long right tail of large values, it is positively skewed, and if it has a long left tail of small values, it is negatively skewed. The mean is larger than the median for positively skewed distributions, and vice versa for negatively skewed distributions. The figure below shows a positively skewed distribution.

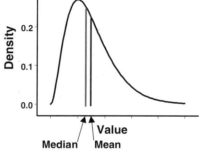

The kurtosis is based on the size of the tails of a distribution and provides a measure of how likely the distribution will produce outliers. The kurtosis of a normal distribution is 3. Distributions with relatively thick tails are "leptokurtic" and have kurtosis greater than 3. Distributions with relatively thin tails are "platykurtic" and have a kurtosis less than 3. In the figure below, a normal distribution is given in red, and a leptokurtic (thick-tailed) distribution is given in black.

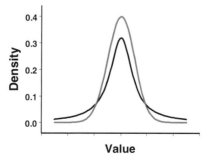

Voronoi map

Voronoi maps are constructed from a series of polygons formed around the location of a sample point.

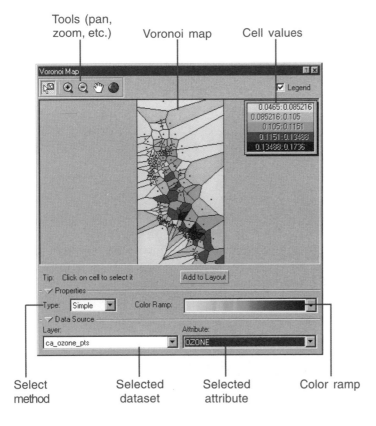

Tools (pan, zoom, etc.)   Voronoi map   Cell values

Select method   Selected dataset   Selected attribute   Color ramp

Voronoi polygons are created so that every location within a polygon is closer to the sample point in that polygon than any other sample point. After the polygons are created, neighbors of a sample point are defined as any other sample point whose

polygon shares a border with the chosen sample point. For example, in the following figure, the bright green sample point is enclosed by a polygon, given as red. Every location within the red polygon is closer to the bright green sample point than any other sample point (given as small dark blue dots). The blue polygons all share a border with the red polygon, so the sample points within the blue polygons are neighbors of the bright green sample point.

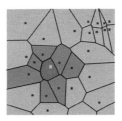

Using this definition of neighbors, a variety of local statistics can be computed. For example, a local mean is computed by taking the average of the sample points in the red and blue polygons. This average is then assigned to the red polygon. After this is repeated for all polygons and their neighbors, a color ramp shows the relative values of the local means, which helps visualize regions of high and low values.

The Voronoi Mapping tool provides a number of methods for assigning or calculating values to polygons.

Simple: The value assigned to a cell is the value recorded at the sample point within that cell.

Mean: The value assigned to a cell is the mean value that is calculated from the cell and its neighbors.

Mode: All cells are placed into five class intervals. The value assigned to a cell is the mode (most frequently occurring class) of the cell and its neighbors.

Cluster: All cells are placed into five class intervals. If the class interval of a cell is different from each of its neighbors, the cell is colored grey to distinguish it from its neighbors.

Entropy: All cells are placed into five classes based on a natural grouping of data values (i.e., smart quantiles, refer to Chapter 8, 'Displaying and managing geostatistical layers'). The value assigned to a cell is the entropy that is calculated from the cell and its neighbors, that is,

$$\text{Entropy} = -\Sigma (p_i * \text{Log} \, p_i)$$

where p_i is the proportion of cells that are assigned to each class.

For example, consider a cell surrounded by four neighbors (a total of five cells). The values are placed into the corresponding classes:

Class	Frequency	p_i
1	3	3/5
2	0	0
3	1	1/5
4	0	0
5	1	1/5

The entropy assigned to the cell will be:

$$E = -[0.6*\log_2 (0.6) + 0.2*\log_2 (0.2) + 0.2*\log_2 (0.2)] = 1.371$$

Minimum entropy occurs when the cell values are all located in the same class. Then,

$$E_{min} = -[1 * \log_2 (1)] = 0$$

Maximum entropy occurs when each cell value is located in a different class interval. Then,

$$E_{max} = -[0.2 * \log_2 (0.2) + 0.2 * \log_2 (0.2) + 0.2 * \log_2 (0.2) + 0.2 \\ * \log_2 (0.2) + 0.2 * \log_2 (0.2)] = 2.322$$

Median: The value assigned to a cell is the median value calculated from the frequency distribution of the cell and its neighbors.

Standard deviation: The value assigned to a cell is the standard deviation that is calculated from the cell and its neighbors.

Interquartile range: The first and third quartiles are calculated from the frequency distribution of a cell and its neighbors. The value assigned to the cell is calculated by subtracting the value of the first quartile from the value of the third quartile.

The different Voronoi statistics are used for different purposes. The statistics can be grouped into the following general functional categories:

Local Smoothing

Mean

Mode

Median

Local Variation

Standard deviation

Interquartile range

Entropy

Local Outliers

Cluster

Local Influence

Simple

Normal QQPlot and General QQPlot

QQPlots are graphs on which quantiles from two distributions are plotted relative to each other.

Constructing a Normal QQPlot

For the data, a cumulative distribution is produced by ordering the data and producing a graph of the ordered values versus cumulative distribution values calculated as $(i - 0.5)/n$ for the ith ordered value out of n total values (the percent of the data below a value). Linear interpolation is used between values. The Normal QQPlot is created by plotting data values versus the value of a standard normal where their cumulative distributions are equal; see the figure below.

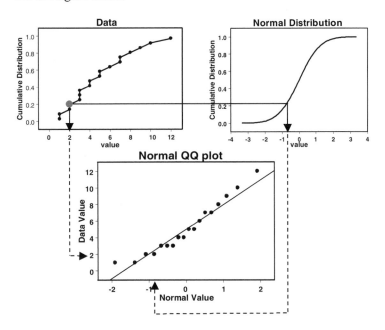

Constructing a General QQPlot

The General QQPlot is used to assess the similarity of the distributions of two datasets. A General QQPlot is created by plotting data values for two datasets where their cumulative distributions are equal; see figure below.

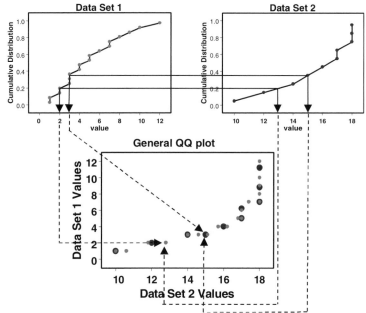

Normal QQPlot

Transformation to apply

Plot of the quantiles of the input dataset versus quantiles of the standard normal distribution

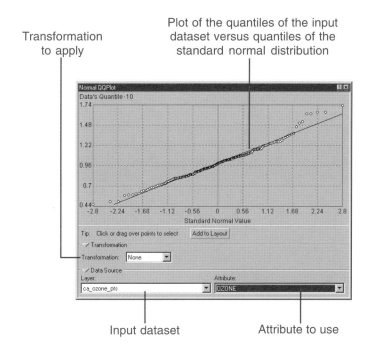

Input dataset   Attribute to use

General QQPlot

Plot of the quantiles of two datasets

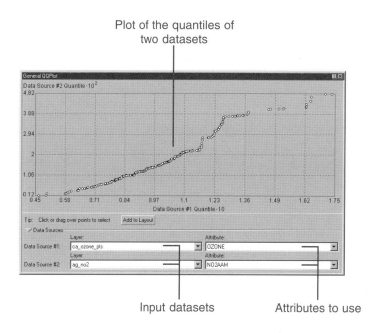

Input datasets   Attributes to use

Trend analysis

You may be interested in mapping a trend, or you may wish to remove a trend from the dataset before using kriging. The Trend Analysis tool can help identify global trends in the input dataset.

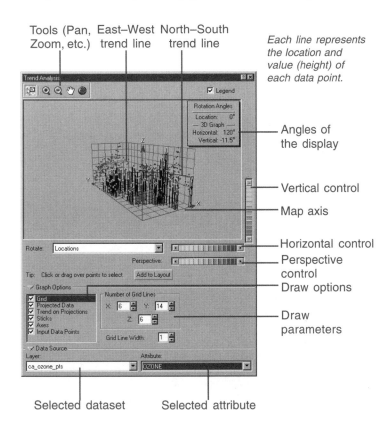

Tools (Pan, Zoom, etc.)
East–West trend line
North–South trend line

Each line represents the location and value (height) of each data point.

Angles of the display

Vertical control

Map axis

Horizontal control

Perspective control

Draw options

Draw parameters

Selected dataset

Selected attribute

The Trend Analysis tool provides a three-dimensional perspective of the data. The locations of sample points are plotted on the x,y plane. Above each sample point, the value is given by the height of a stick in the z dimension. The unique feature of the Trend Analysis tool is that the values are then projected onto the x,z plane and the y,z plane as scatter plots. This can be thought of as sideways views through the three-dimensional data. Polynomials are then fit through the scatter plots on the projected planes. An additional feature is that you can rotate the data to isolate directional trends through the values. There are a host of other features that allow you to rotate and vary the perspective of the whole image, change size and color of points and lines, remove planes and points, and select the order of the polynomial that is fit to the scatter plots. In the diagram below, the data was rotated 25 degrees clockwise, and second-order polynomials were fit to the scatter plots. There appears to be a strong quadratic trend on the back panel (given by the green line), with values starting low, rising up, and then dropping back down. The trend on the right panel (given by the blue line) appears more linear and gradual.

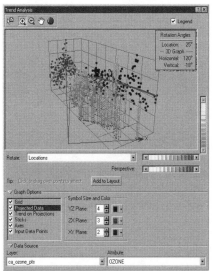

Semivariogram/Covariance cloud

The semivariogram/covariance cloud shows the empirical semivariogram (half of the difference squared) and covariance for all pairs of locations within a dataset and plots them as a function of the distance between the two locations.

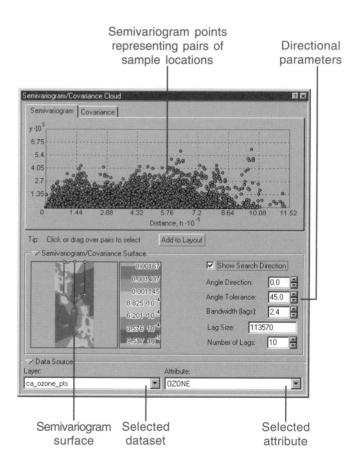

Semivariogram points representing pairs of sample locations

Directional parameters

Semivariogram surface

Selected dataset

Selected attribute

Let $z(s_i)$ denote the value at the ith location in a dataset.

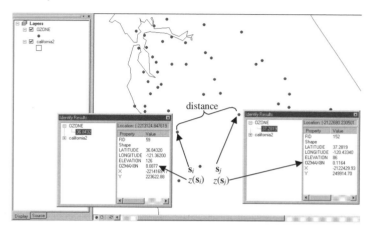

Then the empirical semivariogram for the **(i,j)**th pair is simply $0.5*$ $(z(\mathbf{s}_i) - z(\mathbf{s}_j))^2$, and the empirical covariance is the cross-product $(z(\mathbf{s}_i) - \bar{z})(z(\mathbf{s}_j) - \bar{z})$, where $\bar{z}$ is the average of the data. The semivariogram/covariance cloud can be used to examine the local characteristics of spatial autocorrelation within a dataset and look for outliers. The semivariogram cloud looks like this:

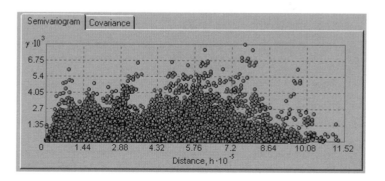

where each red dot is the empirical semivariogram (half of the difference squared plotted relative to the separation distance) between a pair of locations in the dataset. You can brush dots and see the linked pairs in ArcMap.

A Semivariogram Surface with Search Direction capabilities is also given. The values in the semivariogram cloud are put into bins based on the direction and distance between a pair of locations. These bin values are then averaged and smoothed to produce a surface of the semivariogram. On the right, a color ramp is given along with the values on the borders between color transitions. The extent of the semivariogram surface is controlled by Lag Size and Number of Lags. (See Chapter 3, 'The principles of geostatistical analysis', for additional discussions on the semivariogram surface, bins, and lags.)

You can view subsets of values in the semivariogram cloud by clicking on search direction and then clicking on the direction controller to resize it or change its orientation. You can also click on the arrow to temporarily hide this part of the tool.

where OZONE is the attribute field containing the ozone concentration. You can click on the arrow to temporarily hide this part of the tool.

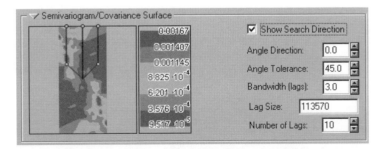

You select the dataset and attribute using the following:

The crosscovariance cloud

The crosscovariance cloud shows the empirical crosscovariance for all pairs of locations between two datasets and plots them as a function of the distance between the two locations.

Crosscovariance points representing pairs of sample locations between datasets

Directional parameters

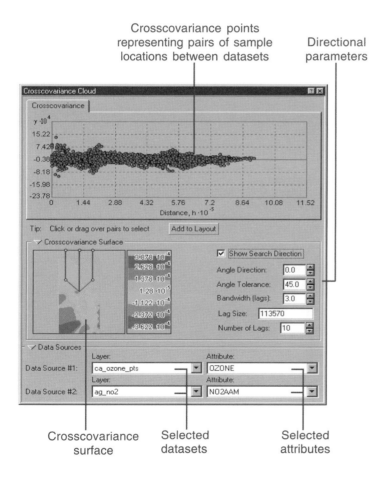

Crosscovariance surface

Selected datasets

Selected attributes

Let $z(\mathbf{s}_i)$ denote the value at the ith location in dataset 1, and let $y(\mathbf{t}_j)$ denote the value at the jth location in dataset 2.

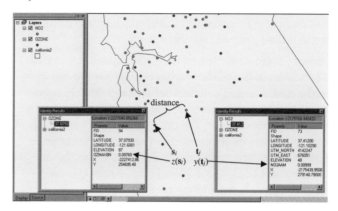

Then the empirical crosscovariance for the (i,j)th pair is simply the cross-product, $(z(\mathbf{s}_i) - \bar{z})(y(\mathbf{t}_j) - \bar{y})$,

where $\bar{z}$ and $\bar{y}$ are the averages of the first and second datasets, respectively. The crosscovariance cloud can be used to examine the local characteristics of spatial correlation between two datasets, and it can be used to look for spatial shifts in correlation between two datasets. The crosscovariance cloud looks like this:

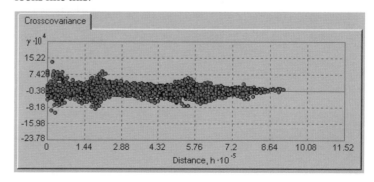

where each red dot is the empirical crosscovariance between a pair of locations in each dataset. You can brush dots and see the linked pairs in ArcMap. (In order to differentiate which of the pairs came from which dataset, set a different selection color in the properties dialog box of each dataset.)

A Covariance Surface with Search Direction capabilities is also given. The values in the crosscovariance cloud are put into bins based on the direction and distance between a pair of locations. These bin values are then averaged and smoothed to produce a surface of the crosscovariance. On the right, a color ramp is given along with the values on the borders between color transitions. The extent of the crosscovariance surface is controlled by Lag Size and Number of Lags. (See Chapter 3, 'The principles of geostatistical analysis', for additional discussions on the semivariogram surface, bins, and lags.)

You can view subsets of values in the crosscovariance cloud by checking Show Search Direction and then clicking on the direction controller to resize it or change its orientation. You can also click the arrow to temporarily hide this part of the tool.

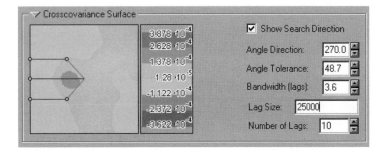

Examining the distribution of the data

Certain kriging methods work best if the data is approximately normally distributed (a bell-shaped curve), which has a probability density function that looks like this:

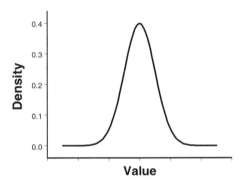

In particular, quantile and probability maps using ordinary, simple, and universal kriging assume that the data comes from a normal distribution.

As we discussed in Chapter 3, kriging also relies on the assumption of stationarity. This assumption requires, in part, that all data values come from distributions that have the same variability. We often observe in nature that when the values increase, so does their variability. Transformations can be used to make your data normally distributed and satisfy the assumption of equal variability for your data.

The histogram and Normal QQPlot allow the use of several transformations including the Box–Cox (also known as power transformation), logarithmic, and arcsine (see Chapter 7, 'Using analytical tools when generating surfaces', for more details). The Box–Cox transformation is $Y(\mathbf{s}) = (Z(\mathbf{s})^{\lambda} - 1)/\lambda$ for $\lambda \neq 0$. For an instance when you would use this transformation, suppose that your data is composed of counts of some phenomenon. For these types of data, the variance is often related to the mean. That is, if you have small counts in part of your study area, the variability in that local region will be smaller than the variability in another region where the counts are larger. In this case, it is well known that if you first take the square root transformation of all of your data, it will help to make the variances more constant throughout your study area, and it often makes the data appear normally distributed as well. The square root transformation occurs when $\lambda = \frac{1}{2}$. The log transformation, which is usually considered part of the Box–Cox transformations when $\lambda = 0$, $Y(\mathbf{s}) = \ln(Z(\mathbf{s}))$ for $Z(\mathbf{s}) > 0$, and 'ln' is the natural logarithm. The log transformation is often used where the data has a positively skewed distribution and there are some very large values. These large values may be localized in your study area, and the log transformation will help to make the variances be more constant and normalize your data. A positively skewed distribution looks like this:

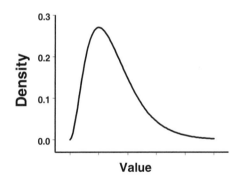

The arcsine transformation is $Y(\mathbf{s}) = \sin^{-1}(Z(\mathbf{s}))$ for $Z(\mathbf{s})$ between 0 and 1. The arcsine transformation can be used for data that is a proportion (or percentage). Often, when data is a proportion, the variance is smallest near 0 and 1 and largest near 0.5. The arcsine transformation will help to make the variances more constant throughout your study area and often makes the data appear normally distributed as well.

You can use the histogram and Normal QQPlots to see what transformations, if any, are needed to make your data more normally distributed. The same transformation will likely equalize variances as well, helping to satisfy the stationarity assumption.

Using the Histogram tool to examine distributions

With the Histogram tool you can easily examine the shape of the distribution by direct observation. By looking at the mean and median statistics, you can also determine the center location of the distribution. Notice in the image below that the shape of the histogram looks bell shaped, and since the mean and median values are very close, this distribution is close to normal. You can also highlight the extreme values in the tail of the histogram and see how they are spatially distributed in the landscape. In the image below for ozone data, the high values are located in urban areas, as expected.

If your data is highly skewed, you can test the effects of a transformation on your data. The diagram below shows a skewed distribution before a transformation is applied.

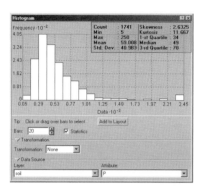

A log transform is applied to the skewed data and, in this case, the transformation makes the distribution close to normal.

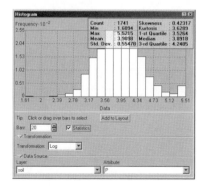

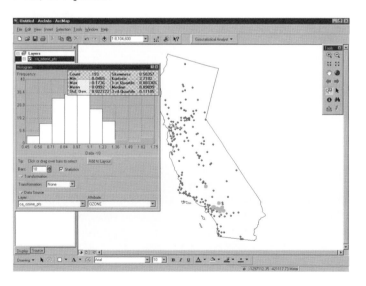

Understanding distributions with the QQPlot

For two identical distributions, the General QQPlot will be a straight line. Therefore, comparing this line with the points on the Normal QQPlot provides an indication of univariate normality. If the data is asymmetric (i.e., far from normal), the points will deviate from the line.

In the diagram below, the quantiles of the standard normal distribution are plotted in the Normal QQPlot on the x-axis, and the quantiles of the dataset are plotted on the y-axis. You can see that the plot is close to a straight line. The main departure from this line occurs at high values of ozone concentration. The Normal QQPlot tool allows you to select the points that do not fall on a straight line. The locations of the selected points are then highlighted in the ArcMap data view. (They are seen here to concentrate in one small area around Los Angeles.)

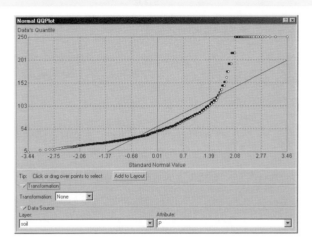

However, as can be seen in the image below, when the log transformation is applied to the dataset, the points lie close to the straight line.

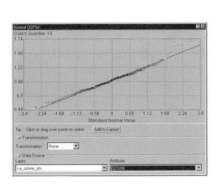

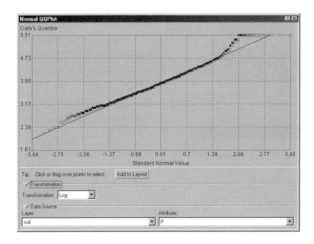

The same dataset that was transformed in the previous histogram example is also transformed in the Normal QQPlot in the images below. Notice in the first image how the points stray greatly from the straight line.

Examining the distribution of your data

The ESDA tools help you examine the distribution of your data.

You are looking to see if your data is normally distributed (a bell-shaped curve). The mean and median will be similar in a normal distribution, the skewness should be near zero, and the kurtosis should be near 3.

If the data is highly skewed, you may choose to transform it to see if you can make it normal. Care should be taken while transforming data when creating a surface because the predictions will be back-transformed, and this back transformation gives approximately unbiased predictions with an approximate kriging standard error.

Tip

The QQPlot

The points will be close to a straight line if the data is normally distributed.

Examining the distribution with the Histogram tool

1. Click on the point feature layer in the ArcMap table of contents that you wish to explore.

2. Click on the Geostatistical Analyst toolbar, click Explore Data, then click Histogram.

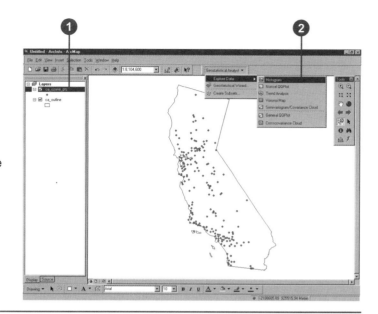

Exploring the distribution through the QQPlot

1. Click on the point feature layer in the ArcMap table of contents that you wish to explore.

2. Click on the Geostatistical Analyst toolbar, click Explore Data, then click Normal QQPlot.

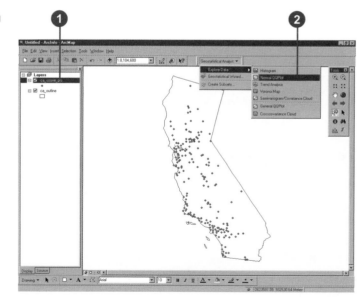

Looking for global and local outliers

A global outlier is a measured sample point that has a very high or a very low value relative to all of the values in a dataset. For example, if 99 out of 100 points have values between 300 and 400, but the 100th point has a value of 750, the 100th point may be a global outlier.

A local outlier is a measured sample point that has a value that is within the normal range for the entire dataset, but if you look at the surrounding points, it is unusually high or low. For example, the diagram below is a cross section of a valley in a landscape. However, there is one point in the center of the valley that has an unusually high value relative to its surroundings, but it is not unusual compared to the entire dataset.

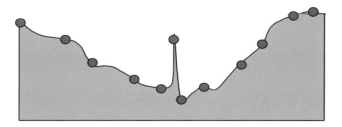

It is important to identify outliers for two reasons: they may be real abnormalities in the phenomenon, or the value might have been measured or recorded incorrectly.

If an outlier is an actual abnormality in the phenomenon, this may be the most significant point of the study and for understanding the phenomenon. For instance, a sample on the vein of a mineral ore might be an outlier and the location that is most important to a mining company.

If outliers are caused by errors during data entry that are clearly incorrect, they should either be corrected or removed before creating a surface. Outliers can have several detrimental effects on your prediction surface including effects on semivariogram modeling and the influence of neighboring values.

Looking for outliers through the histogram

The histogram tool enables you to select points on the tail of the distribution. The selected points are displayed in the ArcMap data view. If the extreme values are isolated locations (i.e., surrounded by very different values), then they may require further investigation and, if necessary, be removed.

In the example above, the high ozone values are not outliers and, therefore, they should not be removed from the dataset.

Identifying outliers through the semivariogram/ covariance cloud

If you have a global outlier with an unusually high value in your dataset, all pairings of points with that outlier will have high values in the semivariogram cloud, no matter the distance. This can be seen in the semivariogram cloud in the image below. Notice that there are two main strata of points in the semivariogram. If you brush points in the upper strata, as demonstrated in the image below, you can see in the ArcMap view that all of these high values come from pairings with a single location—the global outlier. Thus, the upper stratum of points has been created by all of the locations pairing with the single outlier, and the lower stratum is comprised of the pairings among the rest of the locations. When you look at the histogram, which is also in the image below, you can see one high value on the right tail of the histogram, again identifying the global outlier. This value was probably entered incorrectly and should be removed or corrected.

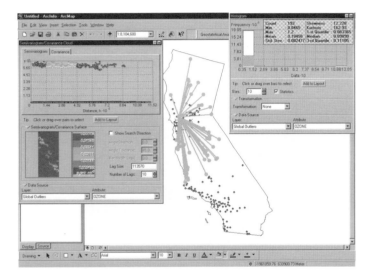

When there is a local outlier, the value will not be out of the range of the entire distribution but will be unusual relative to the surrounding values. In the image below, you can see that a group of pairs of locations that are close together have a high semivariogram value (they are to the far left on the x-axis, indicating that they are close together, and high on the y-axis, indicating that the semivariogram values are high). When these points are brushed, you can see that all of these points are pairing to a single location. When you look at the histogram, you can see that the distribution is normal and that there is no single value that is unusual. The location that is in question is highlighted in the lower tail of the histogram and is pairing with

higher surrounding values (see the highlighted points in the histogram). This location may be a local outlier. Further investigation must be made.

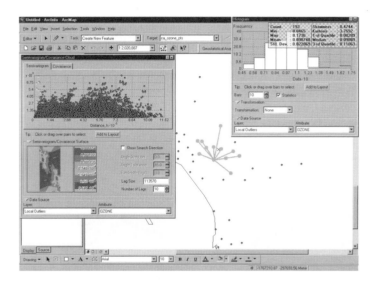

Looking for outliers through Voronoi mapping

Voronoi maps created using the cluster and entropy methods can be used to help identify possible outliers.

Entropy values provide a measure of dissimilarity between neighboring cells. In nature you would expect that things closer together are more likely to be more similar than things farther apart. Therefore, local outliers may be identified by areas of high entropy.

The cluster method identifies those cells that are dissimilar to their surrounding neighbors. You would expect the value recorded in a particular cell to be similar to at least one of its neighbors. Therefore, this tool may be used to identify possible local outliers.

Identifying global and local outliers

To identify a global outlier, look for unusual high or low values in the histogram and two distinct horizontal groupings of points in the semivariogram cloud. For local outliers, there will be high semivariogram values associated with a single point at close distances in the semivariogram cloud.

Both global and local outliers can have detrimental effects on your prediction surface by changing the semivariogram model and influencing the prediction values.

See Also

See Chapter 3, 'The principles of geostatistical analysis', for an additional discussion on outliers.

Identifying global outliers using the Histogram tool

1. Click on the point or polygon feature layer in the ArcMap table of contents that you wish to explore.

2. Click on the Geostatistical Analyst toolbar, click Explore Data, then click Histogram.

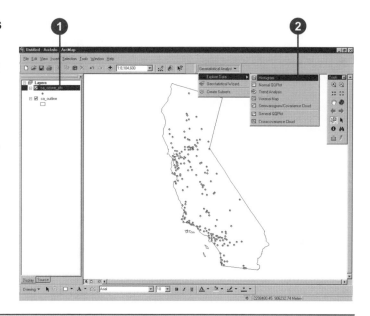

Looking for global outliers through the Semivariogram/ Covariance Cloud

1. Click on the point or polygon feature layer in the ArcMap table of contents that you wish to explore.

2. Click on the Geostatistical Analyst toolbar, click Explore Data, then click Semivariogram/Covariance Cloud.

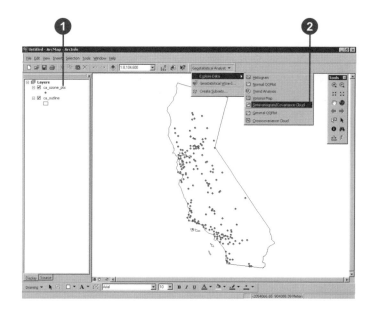

Finding local outliers using Voronoi map

1. Click on the point or polygon feature layer in the ArcMap table of contents that you wish to explore.

2. Click on the Geostatistical Analyst toolbar, click Explore Data, then click Voronoi Map.

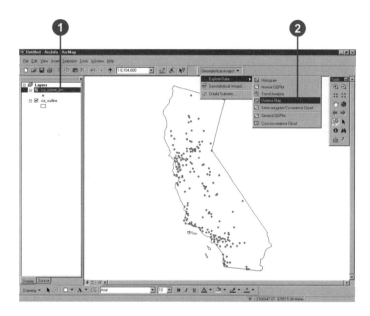

Looking for global trends

A surface may be made up of two main components: a fixed global trend and random short-range variation. The global trend is sometimes referred to as the fixed mean structure. Random short-range variation (sometimes referred to as random error) can be modeled in two parts: spatial autocorrelation and the nugget effect.

If you decide a global trend exists in your data, then you must decide how to model it. Whether you use a deterministic method or a geostatistical method to create a surface usually depends on your objective. If you wish to model just the global trend and create a smooth surface, you may use a global or local polynomial interpolation method to create a final surface (see Chapter 3, 'The principles of geostatistical analysis', and Chapter 5, 'Deterministic methods for spatial interpolation'). However, you may wish to incorporate the trend in a geostatistical method, remove it, and then model the remaining component as random short-range variation. The main reason to remove a trend in geostatistics is to satisfy stationarity assumptions (see Chapter 3, 'The principles of geostatistical analysis').

If you remove the trend in a geostatistical method, you will be modeling the random short-range variation in the residuals. The trend will be automatically added back so that you obtain reasonable predictions.

If you decompose your data into trend plus short-range variation, you are assuming that the trend is fixed and that the short-range variation is random. Here, random does not mean "unpredictable", but rather that it is governed by rules of probability that include dependence on neighboring values, which is called autocorrelation. The final surface is the sum of the fixed and random surfaces. That is, think of adding two layers: one that never changes, while the other changes randomly. For example, suppose that you are studying biomass. If you were to go back in time, say 1,000 years, and start over to the present day,

the global trend part of the biomass surface would be unchanged. However, the short-range variation part of the biomass surface would change. The unchanging global trend could be due to fixed effects such as topography. Short-range variation could be caused by less permanent features that could not be observed through time, such as precipitation, so it is assumed it is random and likely to be autocorrelated.

If you can identify and quantify the trend, you will gain a deeper understanding of your data and thus make better decisions. If you remove the trend, you will be able to more accurately model the random short-range variation because the global trend will not be influencing your spatial analysis.

Examining the global trend through trend analysis

The Trend tool raises the points above a plot of the study site to the height of the values of the attribute of interest in a three-dimensional plot of the study area. The points are then projected in two directions (by default, north and east) onto planes that are perpendicular to the map plane. A polynomial curve is fit to each projection. The entire map surface can be rotated in any direction, which also changes the direction represented by the projected planes. If the curve through the projected points is flat, no trend exists, as is shown with the blue line in the right projected plane in the image below.

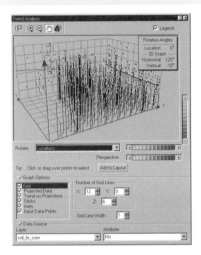

If you rotate the sample points 30 degrees in the example below, the trend is accentuated and demonstrates a strong upside-down "U" shape (see image below). This suggests that a second-order polynomial can be fit to the data (see Chapter 3, 'The principles of geostatistical analysis', and Chapter 5, 'Deterministic methods for spatial interpolation'). Through the refinement allowed in the Trend Analysis tool, the true direction of the trend can be identified. In this case, its strongest influence is from the southeast to the northwest.

If there is a definite pattern to the polynomial, such as an upward curving model as shown with the green line in the back-left projected plane in the diagram below, this suggests a global trend in the data.

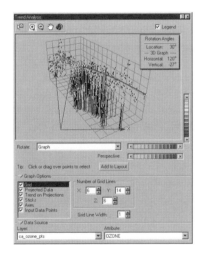

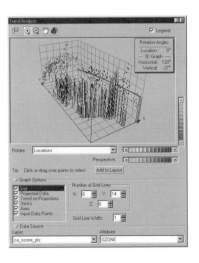

Looking for global trends

To identify a global trend in your data, look for a curve that is not flat on the projected plane.

If you have a global trend in your data, you may want to create a surface using one of the deterministic interpolation methods (e.g., global or local polynomial), or you may wish to remove the trend before modeling the semivariogram/covariance for kriging.

See Also

See Chapter 5, 'Deterministic methods for spatial interpolation', for discussions on the deterministic interpolation techniques and Chapter 7, 'Using analytical tools when generating surfaces', for additional information on trends.

Identifying global trends with the Trend Analysis tool

1. Click on the point or polygon feature layer in the ArcMap table of contents that you wish to explore.

2. Click on the Geostatistical Analyst toolbar, click Explore Data, then click Trend Analysis.

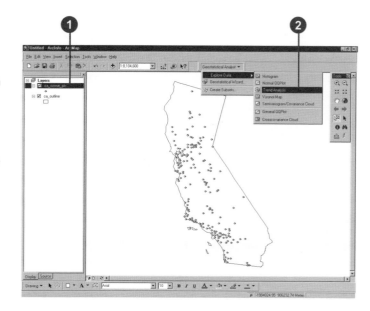

Examining spatial autocorrelation and directional variation

By exploring your data, you will gain a better understanding of the spatial autocorrelation among the measured values. This understanding can be used to make better decisions when choosing models for spatial prediction.

Spatial autocorrelation

You can explore the spatial autocorrelation that is present in your data by examining the different pairs of sample locations. By measuring the distance between two locations and then plotting half the difference squared between the values at the locations, a semivariogram cloud is created. On the x-axis is the distance between the locations, and on the y-axis is the difference of their values squared. Each dot in the semivariogram represents a pair of locations, not the individual locations on the map.

If data is spatially dependent, pairs of points that are close together (on the far left of the x-axis) should have less difference (be low on the y-axis). As points become farther away from each other (moving right on the x-axis), in general, the difference squared should be greater (moving up on the y-axis). Often there is a certain distance beyond which the squared difference levels out. Pairs of locations beyond this distance are considered to be uncorrelated.

A fundamental assumption for geostatistical methods is that any two locations that are a similar distance and direction from each other should have a similar difference squared. This relationship is called stationarity (see Chapter 3, 'The principles of geostatistical analysis', and Chapter 7, 'Using analytical tools when generating surfaces').

Spatial autocorrelation may depend only on the distance between two locations, which is called isotropy. However, it is possible that the same autocorrelation value may occur at different distances when considering different directions. Another way to think of this is that things are more alike for longer distances in

some directions than in other directions. This directional influence is seen in semivariograms and covariances and is called anisotropy.

It is important to explore for anisotropy so that if you detect directional differences in the autocorrelation, you can account for them in the semivariogram or covariance models. This, in turn, has an effect on the geostatistical prediction method.

Exploring spatial structure through the Semivariogram/Covariance Cloud tool

The Semivariogram/Covariance Cloud tool can be used to investigate autocorrelation in your dataset. Let us consider the Ozone dataset. Notice in the following figure that you can select all pairs of locations that are a certain distance apart by brushing all points at that distance in the semivariogram cloud.

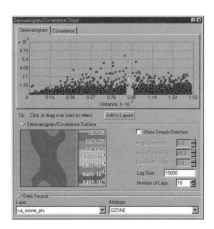

Looking for directional influences with the Semivariogram/Covariance Cloud tool

In the previous example you used the Semivariogram/Covariance Cloud tool to look at the general autocorrelation of the data. However, looking at the variogram surface, it appears that there might be directional differences in the semivariogram values. When you click on the Search Direction and set the angles and bandwidths as in the following figure, you can see that the locations linked together have very similar values because the semivariogram values are relatively low.

Now, if you change the direction of the links, as in the following figure, you can see that some linked locations have values that are quite different, which result in the higher semivariogram values. This indicates that locations separated by a distance of about 0.9×10^5 meters in the 70/250-degree orientation are, on average, more different than locations in the 160/340-degree orientation. Recall that when variation changes more rapidly in one direction than another it is termed anisotropy. When interpolating a surface using the Geostatistical Analyst Wizard, you can use semivariogram models that account for anisotropy.

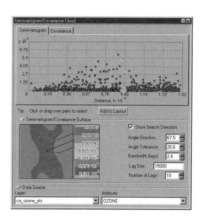

Examining spatial structure and directional variation

Examining spatial structure allows you to investigate the spatial autocorrelation of the sample points and explore if there are any directional influences.

Look for pairs of points that are close together (to the left on the x-axis in the semivariogram), which should be more alike (low on the y-axis). As the pairs are farther apart (moving to the right on the x-axis), the variance should be greater (higher on the y-axis).

If the pairs of points in the semivariogram produce a horizontal straight line, there may be no spatial correlation in the data, thus it would be meaningless to create a surface.

See Also

See Chapter 7, 'Using analytical tools when generating surfaces', for further discussion on semivariogram modeling and directional trends.

Understanding spatial structure

1. Click on the point or polygon feature layer in the ArcMap table of contents that you wish to explore.

2. Click on the Geostatistical Analyst toolbar, click Explore Data, then click Semivariogram/Covariance Cloud.

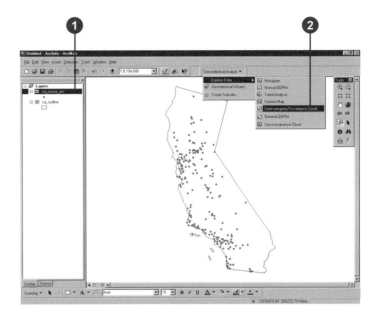

Understanding covariation among multiple datasets

Exploring covariation among multiple datasets

The Crosscovariance Cloud tool can be used to investigate cross-correlation between two datasets. Consider the Ozone (dataset 1) and NO$_2$ (dataset 2) datasets. Notice that the cross-correlation between NO$_2$ and Ozone seems to be asymmetric. The dark red area shows that the highest correlation occurs when taking NO$_2$ values that are shifted to the west of the Ozone values. The Search Direction tool will help identify the reasons for this. When it is pointed toward the west, the following is obtained:

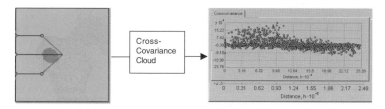

and when it is pointed toward the east, the following is obtained:

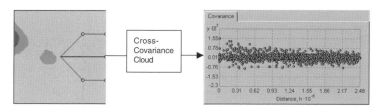

It is clear that there are higher covariance values when the Search Direction is pointed toward the west. Now you can examine which pairs contribute the high values to the crosscovariance. The Crosscovariance Cloud tool and Histogram tool are used in the figure below to explore these features. If you use the Search Direction tool pointed in the west direction and brush some of the

high crosscovariance points in the cloud, you see that most of the pairs of data are located in the Los Angeles area. You also can see that the values of NO$_2$ are shifted to the west of the ozone values. From the histograms, you can see that the high covariance values occur because, for all pairs of data, both NO$_2$ (blue bars in NO$_2$ histogram) and Ozone (orange bars in Ozone histogram) are above their respective means. So you have learned that much of the asymmetry in the crosscovariance is due to a shift in the high values for NO$_2$ to the west of the high values of Ozone in the Los Angeles area. Notice that you could also obtain high crosscovariance values whenever selected pairs from both datasets have values that are below their respective means. In fact, in general, you would expect to see high crosscovariance values from pairs of locations that are both above their respective means and below their respective means, and these would come from several regions in the study area. By exploring this data, you have identified that the crosscovariance in the Los Angeles area seems to be different from that in the rest of the State (see the following page). Using this information, you might decide that the results of the crosscovariance cloud are due to a nonconstant mean in the data and try to remove trends from both NO$_2$ and Ozone, or you might stratify the study area into regions and do kriging and cokriging within regions.

Exploring the correlation between two datasets

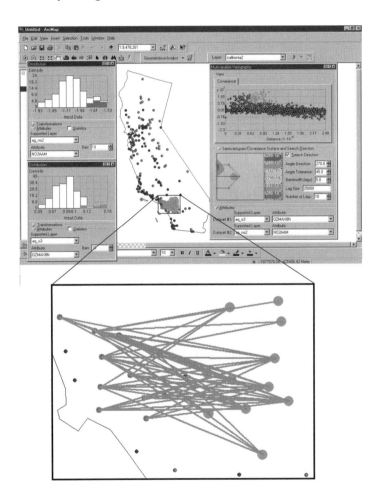

Data pairing for the Los Angeles area with high cross-correlation between ozone and nitrogen dioxide

Understanding spatial covariation among multiple datasets

The tool allows you to examine the crosscovariance cloud between two datasets.

Check if the Covariance Surface is symmetric and use the Search Direction tool to see if the crosscovariance cloud is similar in all directions.

If you see that there is a spatial shift in the values of two datasets, or unusually high crosscovariance values, you can investigate where these occur. If you note that unusual crosscovariance values occur for isolated locations or within restricted areas in your study site, you may want to take some action such as investigating certain data values, detrending data, or stratifying your data.

Understanding spatial covariation using the Crosscovariance Cloud

1. Right-click on the point feature layer in the ArcMap table of contents identifying the first layer in the crosscovariance analysis and click Properties.

2. Click on Selection.

3. Click on the symbol radio button.

4. Click on the symbol.

5. Choose a color and size for the selection.

   Repeat steps 1–5 for the second layer to be used in the crosscovariance analysis, but choose different selection sizes and colors.

6. Highlight the layers in the ArcMap table of contents by holding down the Ctrl key while left-clicking on the two layers.

7. Click on Geostatistical Analyst, click Explore Data, and click Crosscovariance Cloud. ▶

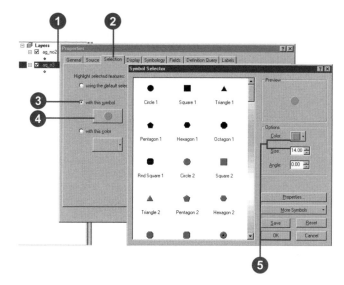

8. Click on the appropriate attribute for each layer in the Attribute dropdown list.

9. Input the Lag Size and Number of Lags.

10. Check Search Direction.

11. Click on the center blue line in the Covariance Surface and spin the search direction until it points to the angle where you believe there is a shift; in this example it is 270 degress (given in the angle direction box).

12. Brush some points in the covariance cloud by holding down the left mouse button and dragging it over some of the points. Examine where, on the ArcMap map, the pairs of points are that were brushed.

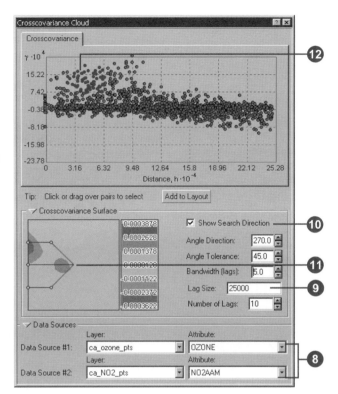

Deterministic methods for spatial interpolation 5

IN THIS CHAPTER

- **How Inverse Distance Weighted interpolation works**

- **Creating a surface using Inverse Distance Weighted interpolation**

- **How global polynomial interpolation works**

- **Creating a map using global polynomial interpolation**

- **How local polynomial interpolation works**

- **Creating a surface using local polynomial interpolation**

- **How radial basis functions interpolation works**

- **Creating a surface using radial basis functions interpolation**

There are two main groupings of interpolation techniques: deterministic and geostatistical. Deterministic interpolation techniques create surfaces from measured points, based on either the extent of similarity (e.g., Inverse Distance Weighted) or the degree of smoothing (e.g., radial basis functions). Geostatistical interpolation techniques (e.g., kriging) utilize the statistical properties of the measured points. The geostatistical techniques quantify the spatial autocorrelation among measured points and account for the spatial configuration of the sample points around the prediction location. Geostatistical techniques will be discussed in Chapter 6, 'Creating a surface with geostatistical techniques'.

Deterministic interpolation techniques can be divided into two groups: global and local. Global techniques calculate predictions using the entire dataset. Local techniques calculate predictions from the measured points within neighborhoods, which are smaller spatial areas within the larger study area. Geostatistical Analyst provides the global polynomial as a global interpolator and the Inverse Distance Weighted, local polynomial, and radial basis functions as local interpolators.

A deterministic interpolation can either force the resulting surface to pass through the data values or not. An interpolation technique that predicts a value identical to the measured value at a sampled location is known as an exact interpolator. An inexact interpolator predicts a value that is different from the measured value. The latter can be used to avoid sharp peaks or troughs in the output surface. Inverse Distance Weighted and radial basis functions are exact interpolators, while global and local polynomial are inexact.

How Inverse Distance Weighted interpolation works

Inverse Distance Weighted interpolation explicitly implements the assumption that things that are close to one another are more alike than those that are farther apart. To predict a value for any unmeasured location, IDW will use the measured values surrounding the prediction location. Those measured values closest to the prediction location will have more influence on the predicted value than those farther away. Thus, IDW assumes that each measured point has a local influence that diminishes with distance. It weights the points closer to the prediction location greater than those farther away, hence the name inverse distance weighted.

The general formula is:

$$\hat{Z}(s_0) = \sum_{i=1}^{N} \lambda_i Z(s_i)$$

where:

$\hat{Z}(s_0)$ is the value we are trying to predict for location s_0.

N is the number of measured sample points surrounding the prediction location that will be used in the prediction.

λ_i are the weights assigned to each measured point that we are going to use. These weights will decrease with distance.

$Z(s_i)$ is the observed value at the location s_i.

The formula to determine the weights is the following:

$$\lambda_i = d_{i0}^{-p} / \sum_{i=1}^{N} d_{i0}^{-p} \quad \sum_{i=1}^{N} \lambda_i = 1,$$

As the distance becomes larger, the wight is reduced by a factor of p.

The quantity d_{i0} is the distance between the prediction location, s_0, and each of the measured locations, s_i.

The power parameter p influences the weighting of the measured location's value on the prediction location's value; that is, as the distance increases between the measured sample locations and the prediction location, the weight (or influence) that the measured point will have on the prediction will decrease exponentially.

The weights for the measured locations that will be used in the prediction are scaled so that their sum is equal to 1.

The power function

The optimal p value is determined by minimizing the root-mean-square prediction error (RMSPE). The RMSPE is the statistic that is calculated from cross-validation (see Chapter 7, 'Using analytical tools when generating surfaces'). In cross-validation, each measured point is removed and compared to the predicted value for that location. The RMSPE is a summary statistic quantifying the error of the prediction surface. The Geostatistical Analyst tries several different powers for IDW to identify the power that produces the minimum RMSPE. The diagram below shows how the Geostatistical Analyst calculates the optimal power. The RMSPE is plotted for several different powers for the same dataset. A curve is fit to the points (a quadratic local polynomial equation), and from the curve the power that provides the smallest RMSPE is determined as the optimal power.

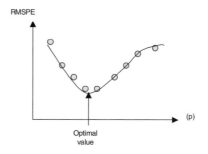

Weights are proportional to the inverse distance raised to the power p. As a result, as the distance increases, the weights decrease rapidly. How fast the weights decrease is dependent on the value for p. If $p = 0$, there is no decrease with distance, and because each weight λ_i will be the same, the prediction will be the mean of all the measured values. As p increases, the weights for distant points decrease rapidly as can be seen in the diagram below. If the p value is very high, only the immediate few surrounding points will influence the prediction.

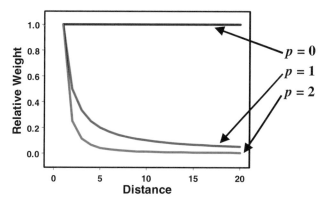

The Geostatistical Analyst uses power functions greater than 1. A $p = 2$ is known as the inverse distance squared weighted interpolation.

The search neighborhood

Because things that are close to one another are more alike than those farther away, as the locations get farther away, the measured values will have little relationship with the value of the prediction location. To speed calculations we can discount to zero these points that are farther away with little influence. As a result, it is common practice to limit the number of measured values that are used when predicting the unknown value for a location by specifying a search neighborhood. The specified shape of the neighborhood restricts how far and where to look for the measured values to be used in the prediction. Other neighborhood parameters restrict the locations that will be used within that shape. In the following image, five measured points (neighbors) will be used when predicting a value for the location without a measurement, the yellow point.

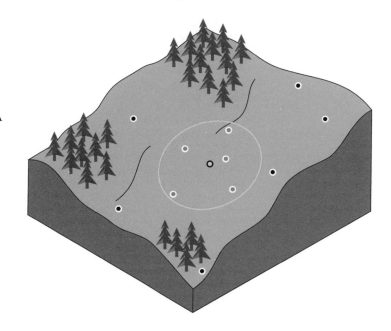

The shape of the neighborhood is influenced by the input data and the surface you are trying to create. If there are no directional influences on the weighting of your data, then you will want to consider points equally in all directions. To do so, you will probably want the shape of your neighborhood to be a circle. However, if there is a directional influence on your data, such as a prevailing wind, then you may want to adjust for it by changing the shape of your neighborhood to be an ellipse with the major axis parallel with the wind. The adjustment for this directional influence is justified because you know that locations upwind from a prediction location are going to be more similar at distances farther away than locations that are perpendicular to the wind.

Once a neighborhood shape is specified, you can also restrict which locations within the shape should be used. You can define the maximum and minimum number of locations to use, and you can divide the neighborhood into sectors. If you divide the neighborhood into sectors, then the maximum and minimum constraints will be applied to each sector. There are several different sectors that can be used and are displayed below.

The points highlighted in the data view of the Searching Neighborhood dialog box identify the locations and the weights that will be used for predicting a location at the center of the ellipse. The neighborhood is contained within the displayed ellipse. In the following example, two points (red) in the sector to the west and one point in the southern sector will be weighted more than 10 percent. In the northern sector, one point (yellow) will be weighted between 3 percent and 5 percent.

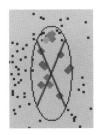

One sector 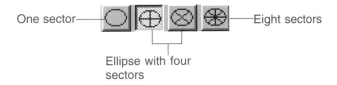 Eight sectors

Ellipse with four sectors

The surface calculated using IDW depends on the selection of a power parameter (p) and the neighborhood search strategy. IDW is an exact interpolator, where the maximum and minimum values (see diagram above) in the interpolated surface can only occur at sample points. The output surface is sensitive to clustering and the presence of outliers. IDW assumes that the surface is being driven by the local variation, which can be captured through the neighborhood.

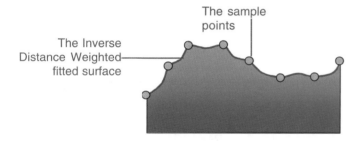

The sample points

The Inverse Distance Weighted fitted surface

Creating a map using IDW

IDW assumes that the surface is being driven by local variation. It works better if sample points are evenly distributed throughout the area and if they are not clustered. The important parameters are the search neighborhood specifications, the power parameter 'p', and the anisotropy (see Chapter 3, 'The principles of geostatistical analysis') factor if one exists.

Tip

Using a database file instead of a point layer

A database file can be used in place of an ArcMap layer by clicking the Browse button and navigating to the desired database file on the Choose Input Data and Method dialog box.

See Also

For additional information on setting the parameters for the Searching Neighborhood dialog box and understanding the Cross Validation dialog box, see Chapter 7, 'Using analytical tools when generating surfaces'.

Creating a prediction map

1. Click on the point layer on which to perform IDW in the ArcMap table of contents.

2. Start the Geostatistical Analyst.

3. Click the Attribute dropdown menu and click the attribute on which to perform IDW in the Choose Input Data and Method dialog box.

4. Click the Inverse Distance Weighting method.

5. Click Next.

6. Specify the desired parameters in the IDW Set Parameters dialog box and click Next.

7. Examine the results on the Cross Validation dialog box and click Finish.

8. Click on the Output Layer Information dialog box and click OK.

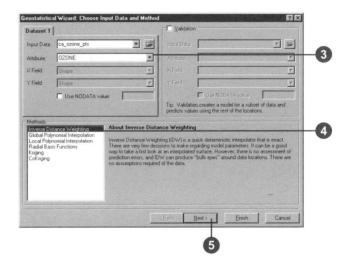

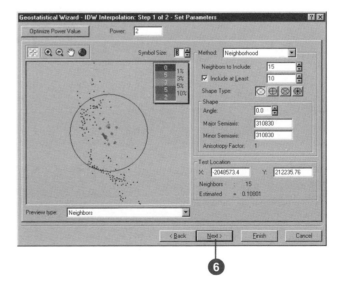

Tip

Creating training and test datasets

When performing validation, two datasets are used: a training dataset and a test dataset. The training dataset contains the measured locations that will be used to create an interpolation model. The test dataset will be used to validate the predictions. The training dataset is entered as Dataset 1 and the test dataset as the Validation dataset. See 'Performing validation on a geostatistical layer created from a subset', in Chapter 9, to obtain additional information on creating subsets.

Tip

Using validation

Make sure that there are enough data samples in the training set to portray an accurate representation of the surface. If the training set is too small, abnormal data values can skew the model parameters and the output results.

See Also

For additional information on setting the parameters for the Searching Neighborhood dialog box and understanding the Cross Validation dialog box, see Chapter 7, 'Using analytical tools when generating surfaces'.

Creating a prediction map using validation

1. Click on the point layer on which to perform IDW in the ArcMap table of contents.

2. Start Geostatistical Analyst.

3. Click the Attribute dropdown menu and specify the field on which to perfom IDW in the Choose Input Data and Method dialog box.

4. Check Validation.

5. Pick a point layer file in the Input Data dropdown menu or browse for the desired layer.

6. Click the Attribute dropdown menu and specify the field on which to validate the IDW interpolation within the Choose Input Data and Method dialog box.

7. Click the Inverse Distance Weighting method.

8. Click Next.

9. Specify the desired parameters in the IDW Set Parameters dialog box and click Next.

10. Examine the results on the Cross Validation and Validation dialog boxes and click Finish.

11. Click on the Output Layer Information dialog box and click OK.

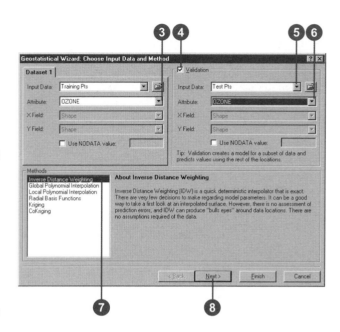

How global polynomial interpolation works

Global polynomial interpolation fits a smooth surface that is defined by a mathematical function (a polynomial) to the input sample points. The global polynomial surface changes gradually and captures coarse-scale pattern in the data.

Conceptually, global polynomial interpolation is like taking a piece of paper and fitting it between the raised points (raised to the height of value). This is demonstrated in the diagram below for a set of sample points of elevation taken on a gently sloping hill (the piece of paper is magenta).

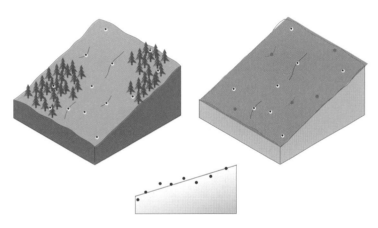

But a flat piece of paper will not accurately capture a landscape containing a valley. However, if you are allowed to bend the piece of paper once, you will get a much better fit. Adding a term to the mathematical formula produces a similar result, a bend in the plane. A flat plane (no bend in the piece of paper) is a first-order polynomial (linear). Allowing for one bend is a second-order polynomial (quadratic), two bends a third-order (cubic), and so forth, up to 10 in the Geostatistical Analyst. The following image conceptually demonstrates a second-order polynomial fitted to a valley.

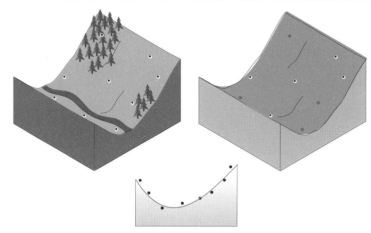

Rarely will the piece of paper pass through the actual measured points, thus making global polynomial interpolation an inexact interpolator. Some points will be above the piece of paper, and others will be below. However, if you add up how much higher each point is above the piece of paper and add up how much lower each point is below the piece of paper, the two sums should be similar. The surface, given in magenta, is obtained by using a least-squares regression fit. The resulting surface minimizes the squared differences among the raised values and the sheet of paper.

When to use global polynomial interpolation

The result from global polynomial interpolation is a smooth mathematical surface that represents gradual trends in the surface over the area of interest.

Global interpolation is used for:

1. Fitting a surface to the sample points when the surface varies slowly from region to region over the area of interest (e.g., pollution over an industrial area).

2. Examining and/or removing the effects of long-range or global trends. In such circumstances the technique is often referred to as trend surface analysis.

Global polynomial interpolation creates a slowly varying surface using low-order polynomials that possibly describe some physical process (e.g., pollution and wind direction). However, it should be noted that the more complex the polynomial, the more difficult it is to ascribe physical meaning to it. Furthermore, the calculated surfaces are highly susceptible to outliers (extremely high and low values, especially at the edges).

Creating a map using global polynomial interpolation

Use global polynomial interpolation when producing a prediction map. It is best used to fit a surface when the attribute varies slowly over the area of interest and for examining the effects of global trends or trend surface analysis. The surface is sensitive to outliers, especially at the edges. The attribute being modeled should vary slowly over the area of interest.

Creating a prediction map

1. Click on the point layer on which to perform Global Polynomial Interpolation in the ArcMap table of contents.

2. Start the Geostatistical Analyst.

3. Click the Attribute dropdown menu and click the attribute on which to perform Global Polynomial Interpolation in the Choose Input Data and Method dialog box.

4. Click the Global Polynomial Interpolation method and click Next.

5. Specify the desired order of polynomial in the Global Polynomial Interpolation Set Parameters dialog box and click Next.

6. Examine the results on the Cross Validation dialog box and click Finish.

7. On the Output Layer Information dialog box click OK.

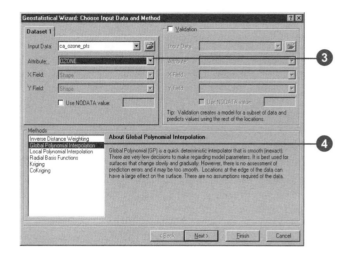

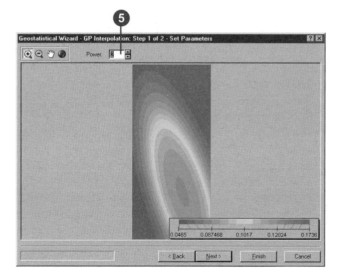

How local polynomial interpolation works

Global polynomial interpolation fits a polynomial to the entire surface. Local polynomial interpolation fits many polynomials, each within specified overlapping neighborhoods. The search neighborhood can be defined using the Searching Neighborhood dialog box (see the Inverse Distance Weighted discussion earlier in this chapter and discussions in Chapter 7, 'Using analytical tools when generating surfaces'). The shape, maximum and minimum number of points to use, and the sector configuration can be specified. Alternatively, a slider can be used to define the width of the neighborhood in conjunction with a power parameter that will, based on distance, decrease the weights of the sample points within the neighborhood. Thus, local polynomial interpolation produces surfaces that account for more local variation.

A first-order global polynomial fits a single plane through the data; a second-order global polynomial fits a surface with a bend in it, allowing surfaces representing valleys; a third-order global polynomial allows for two bends; and so forth. However, when a surface has a different shape, such as is the case of a landscape that slopes, levels out, and then slopes again, a single global polynomial will not fit well. Multiple polynomial planes would be able to represent the surface more accurately (see diagram below).

Local polynomial interpolation fits the specified order (e.g., zero, first, second, and third) polynomial using all points only within the defined neighborhood. The neighborhoods overlap, and the value used for each prediction is the value of the fitted polynomial at the center of the neighborhood.

In the image below, a cross section of sample elevation data is taken (a transect). In the first image, three neighbors are used (the red points) to fit a first-order polynomial, a line (the red line), to predict the unknown value for the location identified by the blue point. A second location (the yellow point) is predicted by another first-order polynomial in the right image below. It is very close to the first location, and the same measured points are used in the predictions; but the weights will be a little different, thus the polynomial fit (the blue line) is slightly different.

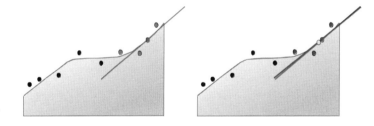

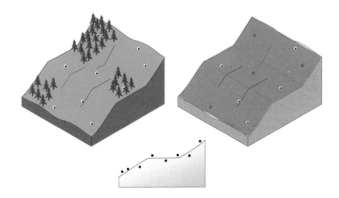

This process continues, centering on subsequent prediction locations, fitting local polynomials to predict the values. The two images below show two more arbitrary points being predicted to create the final surface. The orange point is predicted from the fitted polynomial (the green line) using the green measured sample points. And the brown point is predicted from the light purple polynomial.

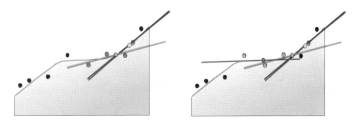

In the two images below, two more polynomials are fit (the yellow and gray lines) to predict two more locations (the bluish green and green points).

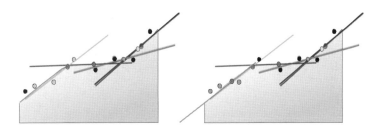

This process continues for each location. You can see how the surface is created (the purple surface line) for the sample points below.

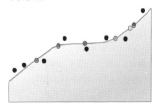

The model is optimized by iteratively cross-validating the output surfaces that are calculated using different parameters. The optimal parameter is chosen to minimize the RMSPE similar to the selection of the 'p' value in IDW.

When to use local interpolation

Global polynomial interpolation is good for creating smooth surfaces and for identifying long-range trends in the dataset. However, in earth sciences the variable of interest usually has short-range variation in addition to long-range trend. When the dataset exhibits short-range variation, local polynomial interpolation maps can capture the short-range variation.

Local polynomial interpolation is sensitive to the neighborhood distance. For this reason, you can preview the surface before producing the output layer.

As with IDW, you can define a model that accounts for anisotropy (refer to the IDW discussion earlier in this chapter).

Creating a map using local polynomial interpolation

Local polynomial interpolation is not an exact interpolator. It will produce a smooth surface. It is best if the data exhibits short-range variation.

See Also

For additional information on setting the parameters for the Searching Neighborhood dialog box and understanding the Cross Validation dialog box, see Chapter 7, 'Using analytical tools when generating surfaces'.

Creating a prediction map

1. Click on the point layer on which to perform Local Polynomial Interpolation in the ArcMap table of contents.

2. Start Geostatistical Analyst.

3. Click the Attribute dropdown menu and click the attribute on which to perform Local Polynomial Interpolation in the Choose Input Data and Method dialog box.

4. Click the Local Polynomial Interpolation method.

5. Click Next.

6. Specify the desired parameters in the LP Interpolation Set Parameters dialog box and click Next.

7. Examine the results on the Cross Validation dialog box and click Finish.

8. On the Output Layer Information dialog box, click OK.

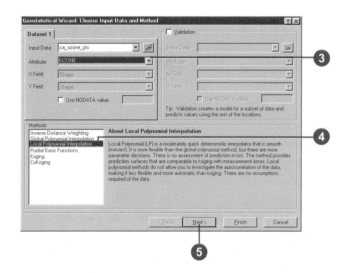

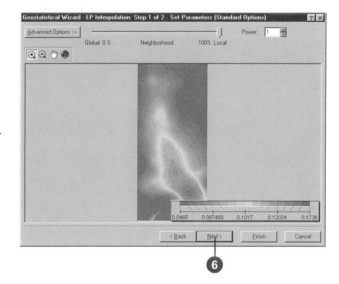

How radial basis functions work

Radial basis functions (RBF) methods are a series of exact interpolation techniques, that is, the surface must go through each measured sample value. There are five different basis functions: thin-plate spline, spline with tension, completely regularized spline, multiquadric function, and inverse multiquadric spline. Each basis function has a different shape and results in a different interpolation surface. RBF methods are a form of artificial neural networks.

RBFs are conceptually similar to fitting a rubber membrane through the measured sample values while minimizing the total curvature of the surface. The selected basis function determines how the rubber membrane will fit between the values. The diagram below demonstrates conceptually how an RBF surface fits through a series of elevation sample values. Notice in the cross section that the surface passes through the data values.

Being exact interpolators, RBF methods differ from the global and local polynomial interpolators, which are both inexact interpolators that do not require the surface to pass through the measured points. When comparing RBF to the IDW method, another exact interpolator, IDW will never predict values above the maximum measured value or below the minimum measured value, as you can see in the cross section of a transect of sample data below.

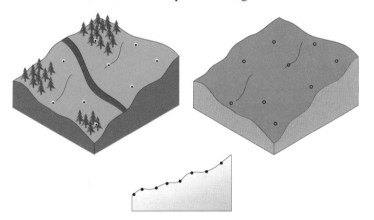

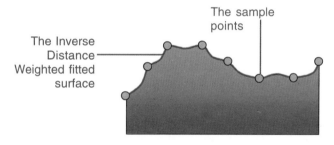

The sample points

The Inverse Distance Weighted fitted surface

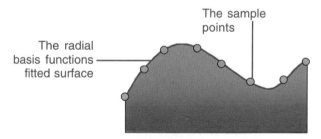

The sample points

The radial basis functions fitted surface

However, RBFs can predict values above the maximum and below the minimum measured values as in the cross section below.

The optimal parameter is determined using cross-validation in a similar manner, as shown for IDW and local polynomial interpolation (see the IDW discussion earlier in this chapter).

When to use RBFs

The RBFs are used for calculating smooth surfaces from a large number of data points. The functions produce good results for gently varying surfaces such as elevation.

The techniques are inappropriate when there are large changes in the surface values within a short horizontal distance and/or when you suspect the sample data is prone to error or uncertainty.

The concepts behind RBFs

In Geostatistical Analyst, RBFs are formed over each data location. An RBF is a function that changes with distance from a location. For example, in the following figure there are three locations, and the RBF for each location is given in a different color.

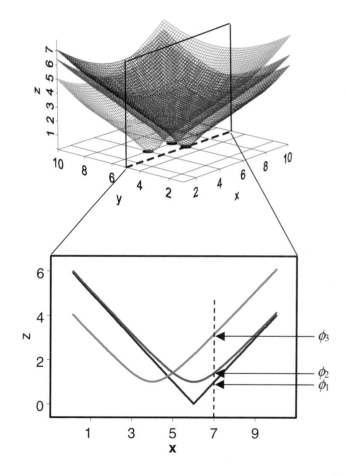

In this example, the RBF is simply the distance from each location, so it forms an inverted cone over each location. If you take a cross section of the x,z plane for y = 5 (the second figure above), you will see a slice of each RBF. Now suppose that you want to predict a value at y = 5 and x = 7. The value of each RBF at the prediction location can be taken from the figure above, given by the values ϕ_1, ϕ_2, and ϕ_3, which simply depend on the distance from each data location. The predictor is formed by taking the weighted average $w_1\phi_1 + w_2\phi_2 + w_3\phi_3 + ...$. Now, the question is, how to determine the weights? So far, you have not used the data values at all! The weights w_1, w_2, w_3, and so on, are found by requiring that, when the prediction is moved to a location with a measured value, the data value is predicted exactly. This forms N equations in N unknowns and can be solved uniquely. Thus, the surface passes through the data values, making predictions exact. The RBF shown above is a special case of the multiquadric RBF. Geostatistical Analyst also allows you to use other RBFs such as completely regularized splines, thin-plate splines, splines with tension, and inverse multiquadric RBFs. Often, the difference between these is not great, but you may have reasons to choose one, or you can try several and use validation to pick one. Each RBF has a parameter that controls the "smoothness" of the surface.

For all methods except the inverse multiquadric, the higher the parameter value, the smoother the map; the opposite is true for the inverse multiquadric.

Creating a map using RBFs

RBFs are exact interpolators that create smooth surfaces. They produce good results for gently varying surfaces. Because predictions are exact, RBFs can be locally sensitive to outliers.

See Also

For additional information on setting the parameters for the Searching Neighborhood dialog box and understanding the Cross Validation dialog box, see Chapter 7, 'Using analytical tools when generating surfaces'.

Creating a prediction map using RBFs

1. Click on the point layer on which to perform Radial Basis Functions in the ArcMap table of contents.

2. Start Geostatistical Analyst.

3. Click the Attribute dropdown menu and click the attribute on which to perfom Radial Basis Functions in the Choose Input Data and Method dialog box.

4. Click the Radial Basis Functions method.

5. Click Next.

6. Click on the Kernel Functions dropdown menu and click the desired Radial Basis Function in the RBF Interpolation Set Parameters dialog box.

7. Specify the desired parameters in the RBF Set Parameters dialog box and click Next.

8. Examine the results on the Cross Validation dialog box and click Finish.

9. On the Output Layer Information dialog box, click OK.

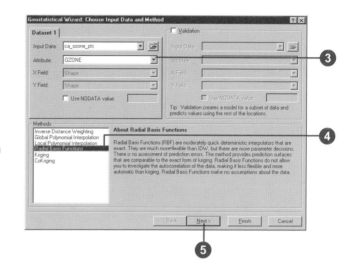

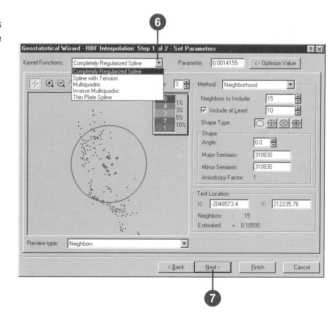

Creating a surface with geostatistical techniques

6

IN THIS CHAPTER

- **What are geostatistical interpolation techniques?**

- **Understanding kriging models**

- **Understanding output surfaces**

- **Creating a map using defaults**

- **Understanding transformations and trends**

- **Understanding and mapping with:**

  - **Ordinary kriging**

  - **Simple kriging**

  - **Universal kriging**

  - **Indicator kriging**

  - **Probability kriging**

  - **Disjunctive kriging**

  - **Cokriging**

In the previous chapter, you learned about deterministic techniques for interpolation. Deterministic techniques used the existing configuration of the sample points to create a surface (Inverse Distance Weighted) or fit a mathematical function to the measured points (global and local polynomial and radial basis functions). In this chapter, you will get an overview of the different geostatistical interpolation techniques. As their name implies, geostatistical techniques create surfaces incorporating the statistical properties of the measured data. Because geostatistics is based on statistics, these techniques produce not only prediction surfaces but also error or uncertainty surfaces, giving you an indication of how good the predictions are.

Many methods are associated with geostatistics, but they are all in the kriging family. Ordinary, simple, universal, probability, indicator, and disjunctive kriging along with their counterparts in cokriging are available in Geostatistical Analyst. Not only do these kriging methods create prediction and error surfaces, but they can also produce probability and quantile output maps depending on your needs.

Kriging is divided into two distinct tasks: quantifying the spatial structure of the data and producing a prediction. Quantifying the structure, known as variography, is where you fit a spatial-dependence model to your data. To make a prediction for an unknown value for a specific location, kriging will use the fitted model from variography, the spatial data configuration, and the values of the measured sample points around the prediction location. Geostatistical Analyst provides many tools to help you determine which parameters to use, but it also provides reliable defaults that you can use to make a surface quickly.

What are geostatistical interpolation techniques?

Geostatistics, in its original usage, referred to statistics of the "earth" such as in geography and geology. Now geostatistics is widely used in many fields and comprises a branch of spatial statistics. Originally, in spatial statistics, geostatistics was synonymous with "kriging", which is a statistical version of interpolation. The current definition has widened to not only include kriging but also many other interpolation techniques including the deterministic methods discussed in Chapter 5, 'Deterministic methods for spatial interpolation'. The Geostatistical Analyst is a realization of this wider definition of geostatistics. One of the essential features of geostatistics is that the phenomenon being studied takes values (not necessarily measured) everywhere within your study area, for example, the amount of nitrogen in a field or the concentration of ozone in the atmosphere. It is important to identify the types of data that can be analyzed appropriately using geostatistics. Think of the following rectangle as the study area of interest. Spatial locations within the study area are indexed by the letters s_i, where each particular location is indexed by the subscript i.

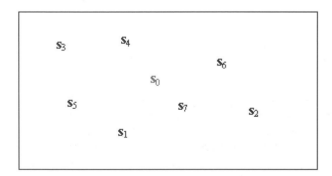

In the above example, suppose you have collected data at the locations s_1 through s_7, and you wish to predict the value at the location s_0, colored in red. This is an example of interpolation. Kriging assumes that you could put s_0 anywhere in the study area, and you assume that there is some real value at location s_0. For example, if the data consists of the concentration of nitrogen s_1, ..., s_7, then there is also some concentration at s_0 that you have not observed but would like to predict. Notice that the data is collected as point events, but values actually occur everywhere; so they are said to be spatially continuous.

In statistics, these values are often described as being one of the following types:

- Continuous; any real number, for example, -1.4789, 10965.6891, and so on

- Integer; for example, ... -2, -1, 0, 1, 2, ...

- Ordered Categorical; for example, worst, medium, best

- Unordered Categorical; for example, forest, agricultural, urban

- Binary; for example, 0 or 1

The word "continuous" can cause some confusion here. If the data is spatially continuous, and continuous in value with a multivariate normal distribution, and if you know the autocorrelation of the multivariate distribution, then kriging is an optimal predictor. However, if different forms of kriging have been developed to accommodate all the types of data above, then kriging is an approximate method that works well in practice.

Understanding the different kriging models

Kriging methods depend on mathematical and statistical models. The addition of a statistical model, which includes probability, separates kriging methods from the deterministic methods described in Chapter 5, 'Deterministic methods for spatial interpolation'. For kriging, you associate some probability with your predictions; that is, the values are not perfectly predictable from a statistical model. Consider the example of a sample of measured nitrogen values in a field. Obviously, even with a large sample, you will not be able to predict the exact value of nitrogen at some unmeasured location. Therefore, you not only try to predict it, but you assess the error of the prediction.

Kriging methods rely on the notion of autocorrelation. Correlation is often thought of as the tendency for two types of variables to be related. For example, the stock market tends to make positive changes with lower interest rates, so it is said that they are negatively correlated. However, it can also be said the stock market is positively autocorrelated, which means it has correlation within itself. In the stock market, two values will tend to be more similar if they are only one day apart, as opposed to being one year apart. The rate at which the correlation decays can be expressed as a function of distance.

In the figure that follows, the (auto)correlation is shown as a function of distance. This is a defining feature of geostatistics. In classical statistics, observations are assumed to be independent; that is, there is no correlation between observations. In geostatistics, the information on spatial locations allows you to compute distances between observations and to model autocorrelation as a function of distance.

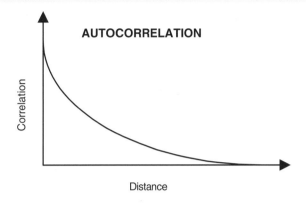

Also notice that, in general, the stock market goes up with time, and this is termed "trend". For geostatistical data, you have the same terms, and they are expressed in a simple mathematical formula,

$$Z(\mathbf{s}) = \mu(\mathbf{s}) + \varepsilon(\mathbf{s}),$$

where $Z(\mathbf{s})$ is the variable of interest, decomposed into a deterministic trend $\mu(\mathbf{s})$, and random, autocorrelated errors form $\varepsilon(\mathbf{s})$. The symbol $\mathbf{s}$ simply indicates the location; think of it as containing the spatial x- (longitude) and y- (latitude) coordinates. Variations on this formula form the basis for all of the different types of kriging, and it is worth a little effort to become familiar with it. Let us start on the right and move left.

No matter how complicated the trend in the model is, $\mu(s)$ still will not predict perfectly. In this case, some assumptions are made about the error term $\varepsilon(\mathbf{s})$; namely, they are expected to be 0 (on average) and that the autocorrelation between $\varepsilon(\mathbf{s})$ and $\varepsilon(\mathbf{s+h})$ does not depend on the actual location $\mathbf{s}$ but on the displacement **of h** between the two. This is necessary to ensure replication so the autocorrelation function can be estimated. For example, in the following figure, random errors at location pairs connected by the arrows are assumed to have the same autocorrelation.

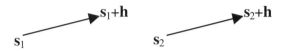

Next, examine the trend. It can be a simple constant; that is, $\mu(\mathbf{s}) = \mu$ for all locations $\mathbf{s}$, and if μ is unknown, then this is the model on which ordinary kriging is based. It can also be composed of a linear function of the spatial coordinates themselves, for example,

$$\mu(s) = \beta_0 + \beta_1 x + \beta_2 y + \beta_3 x^2 + \beta_4 y^2 + \beta_5 xy,$$

where this is a second-order polynomial trend surface and is just linear regression on the spatial x- and y-coordinates. Trends that vary, and where the regression coefficients are unknown, form models for universal kriging. Whenever the trend is completely known (i.e., all parameters and covariates known), whether constant or not, it forms the model for simple kriging.

Now look at the left side of the decomposition, $Z(\mathbf{s}) = \mu(\mathbf{s}) + \varepsilon(\mathbf{s})$. You can perform transformations on $Z(\mathbf{s})$. For example, you can change it to an indicator variable, where it is 0 if $Z(\mathbf{s})$ is below some value (e.g., 0.12 ppm for ozone concentration) or 1 if it is above some value. Then you may wish to predict the probability that $Z(\mathbf{s})$ is above the threshold value, and predictions based on this model form indicator kriging. You can make general unspecified transformations of the $Z(\mathbf{s})$, calling them $f_i(Z(\mathbf{s}_i))$ for the ith variable. You can form predictors of functions of variables; for example, if you want to predict at location $\mathbf{s}_0$, then you form the disjunctive kriging predictor of $g(Z(\mathbf{s}_0))$ using data $f_i(Z(\mathbf{s}_i))$. In the Geostatistical Analyst, the function g is either the indicator transformation or no transformation at all.

Finally, consider the case where you have more than one variable type and you form the models $Z_j(\mathbf{s}) = \mu_j(\mathbf{s}) + \varepsilon_j(\mathbf{s})$ for the jth variable type. Here, you can consider a different trend for each variable, and besides autocorrelation for the errors $\varepsilon_j(\mathbf{s})$, you also have crosscorrelation between the errors $\varepsilon_j(\mathbf{s})$ and $\varepsilon_k(\mathbf{s})$ for the two variable types. For example, you can consider the crosscorrelation between two variables such as ozone concentration and particulate matter, and they need not be measured at the same locations. Models based on more than one variable of interest form the basis of cokriging. You can form an indicator variable of $Z(\mathbf{s})$ and, if you predict it using the original untransformed data $Z(\mathbf{s})$ in a cokriging model, you obtain probability kriging. If originally you have more than one variable of interest, then you can consider ordinary cokriging, universal cokriging, simple cokriging, indicator cokriging, probability cokriging, and disjunctive cokriging as multivariate extensions of the different types of kriging described earlier.

Understanding output surface types

Kriging and cokriging are prediction methods, and the ultimate goal is to produce a surface of predicted values. You would also like to know, "How good are the predictions?" Three different types of prediction maps can be produced, and two of them have standard errors associated with them. On the previous pages, the kriging methods were organized by the models that they used; here they are organized by their goals. Consider the following figure, where predictions at three locations are assumed normally distributed.

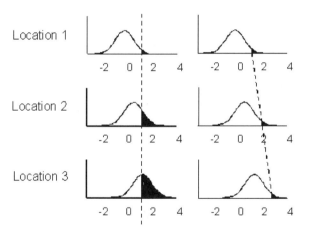

Then the prediction will be in the center of each curve, and a prediction map can be produced for the whole surface. Looking at the three figures on the left, if you want to predict the probability that the value is greater than a threshold value of, say, 1, it will be the area under the curve to the right of the dashed line. The prediction distribution changes for each location. Thus, when holding the threshold value constant, a probability map is produced for the whole surface. Looking at the three figures on the right, if you want to predict the quantile with 5 percent of the

probability to the right, then it will be the value at the dashed line (taken from the x-axis). Again, the prediction distribution changes for each location. Thus, when holding the probability constant, a quantile map is produced for the whole surface. Standard error maps can be produced for prediction and probability maps. The various methods and output maps, along with major assumptions, are given in the following table.

Kriging and Cokriging	Predictions	Prediction Standard Errors	Quantile Maps	Probability Maps	Standard Errors of Indicators
Ordinary	√	√	√ *	√ *	
Universal	√	√	√ *	√ *	
Simple	√	√	√ *	√ *	
Indicator				√	√
Probability				√	√
Disjunctive	√ +	√ +		√ +	√ +

* Requires assumption of multivariate normal distribution

+ Requires assumption of pairwise bivariate normality

Creating a kriging map using defaults

An output surface is created using the ordinary kriging method with default parameters.

Use this method when you are not familiar with geostatistics and the many parameters in the wizard dialog boxes; second, when you wish to visually explore your data in the map representation; and, finally, when you want to create an initial surface to compare how the refinement of the parameters may affect the output surface.

The data points need to be sampled from a phenomenon that is continuous in space.

Tip

Using the Finish button

Once the data and the method have been identified in the initial dialog box, you can click the Finish button and a surface will be created using the default options for the method.

Using the defaults

1. Click the point layer on which you wish to perform kriging in the ArcMap table of contents.

2. Start the Geostatistical Wizard.

3. Click the Attribute dropdown menu, and click the attribute on which you wish to perform kriging.

4. Click the Kriging method.

5. Click Next.

6. On all subsequent dialog boxes, click Next.

7. On the Cross Validation dialog box, click Finish.

8. On the Output Layer Information dialog box, click OK.

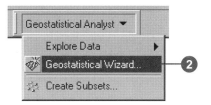

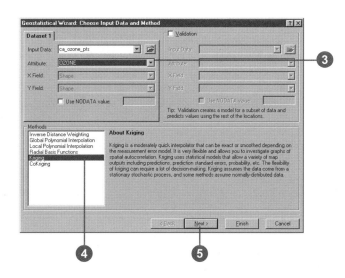

Understanding transformations and trends

Kriging as a predictor does not require that your data have a normal distribution. However, as you saw in the previous section, normality is necessary to obtain quantile and probability maps for ordinary, simple, and universal kriging. When considering only predictors that are formed from weighted averages, kriging is the best unbiased predictor whether or not your data is normally distributed. However, if the data is normally distributed, kriging is the best predictor among all unbiased predictors, not only those that are weighted averages. Kriging also relies on the assumption that all of the random errors are second-order stationarity, which is an assumption that the random errors have zero mean and the covariance between any two random errors depends only on the distance and direction that separates them, not their exact locations. Transformations and trend removal can help justify assumptions of normality and stationarity. Prediction, using ordinary, simple, and universal kriging for general Box–Cox transformations and arcsine transformations, is called Transgaussian kriging. The log transformation is a special case of a Box–Cox transformation, but it has special prediction properties and is known as Lognormal kriging. Here, the transformation and trend options that are available for each kriging method are shown. The tables below also show whether the transformation or the trend removal is performed first when both are selected. Further details on transformation and trend are given in Chapter 7, 'Using analytical tools when generating surfaces'.

Transformation and trend for primary variable:

Kriging type	BAL	NST	Trend
OK	yes (1st if TR)	no	TR (2nd if BAL)
SK	yes	yes	no
UK	yes (1st if T)	no	T (2nd if BAL)
IK	no	no	no
PK*	no	no	no
DK	yes (1st if TR)	yes (2nd if TR)	TR (1st if NST, 2nd if BAL)

Transformation and trend for secondary variable (cokriging):

Kriging type	BAL	NST	Trend
OK	yes (1st if TR)	no	TR (2nd if BAL)
SK	yes	yes	no
UK	yes (1st if T)	no	T (2nd if BAL)
IK	no	no	no
PK	yes (1st if TR)	no	TR (2nd if BAL)
DK	yes (1st if TR)	yes (2nd if TR)	TR (1st if NST, 2nd if BAL)

Definitions

Trend: fixed effects composed of spatial coordinates used in linear model

Primary Variable: variable to be predicted when using kriging or cokriging

Secondary Variables: covariables (not predicted) when using cokriging

Abbreviations

BAL—Box–Cox, arcsine, and log transformations

NST—normal score transformation

TR—trend removal, that is, external trend

T—trend, that is, internal trend

SV—secondary variable, that is, covariates for cokriging

*Note: For PK, the primary variable is composed of indicators of the original variable—this original variable is then considered a secondary variable for cokriging.

Understanding ordinary kriging

Ordinary kriging assumes the model,

$$Z(\mathbf{s}) = \mu + \varepsilon(\mathbf{s}),$$

where μ is an unknown constant. One of the main issues concerning ordinary kriging is whether the assumption of a constant mean is reasonable. Sometimes there are good scientific reasons to reject this assumption. However, as a simple prediction method, it has remarkable flexibility. The following figure is an example in one spatial dimension.

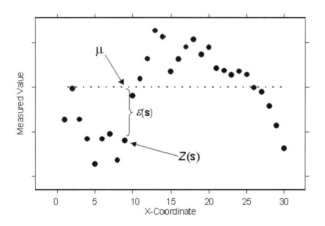

It looks like the data is elevation values collected from a line transect through a valley and over a mountain. It also looks like the data is more variable on the left and becomes smoother on the right. In fact, this data was simulated from the ordinary kriging model with a constant mean μ. The true but unknown mean is given by the dashed line. Thus, ordinary kriging can be used for data that seems to have a trend. There is no way to decide, based on the data alone, whether the observed pattern is the result of

autocorrelation alone (among the errors $\varepsilon(\mathbf{s})$ with μ constant) or trend (with $\mu(\mathbf{s})$ changing with $\mathbf{s}$). This is often a decision based on the scientific problem.

Ordinary kriging can use either semivariograms or covariances (which are the mathematical forms you use to express autocorrelation), it can use transformations and remove trends, and it can allow for measurement error; see Chapter 7, 'Using analytical tools when generating surfaces', for more details.

Creating a map using ordinary kriging

Use ordinary kriging to produce prediction, quantile, probability, or standard error maps. It will assume an unknown constant mean. The data points need to be sampled from a phenomenon that is continuous in space.

Tip

Important parameters

An appropriate transformation, a possible detrending surface, covariance/semivariogram models, and search neighborhoods.

Tip

Using a database file instead of a point layer

On the Choose Input Data and Method dialog box, a database file can be used in place of an ArcMap layer by clicking the Browse button and navigating to the desired database file.

See Also

For additional information on transformations, detrending, setting the parameters for the Semivariogram/Covariance Modeling and Searching Neighborhood dialog boxes, and understanding the Cross Validation dialog box, see Chapter 7, 'Using analytical tools when generating surfaces'.

Creating a prediction map

1. Click the point layer on which you wish to perform Ordinary Kriging in the ArcMap table of contents.

2. Start the Geostatistical Analyst.

3. Click the Attribute dropdown list, and click the attribute on which you wish to perform ordinary kriging.

4. Click the Kriging method.

5. Click Next.

6. Click Prediction under Ordinary Kriging.

7. Click Next.

8. Specify the desired parameters in the Semivariogram/Covariance Modeling dialog box and click Next.

9. Specify the desired parameters in the Searching Neighborhood dialog box and click Next.

10. Examine the results on the Cross Validation dialog box and click Finish.

11. On the Output Layer Information dialog box, click OK.

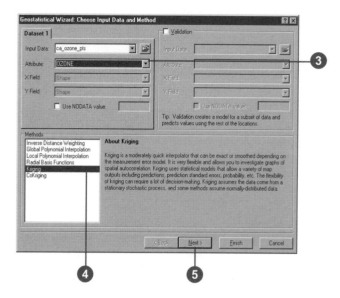

Creating a prediction standard error map

1. Right-click on the prediction surface in the ArcMap table of contents that was created using Ordinary Kriging and click Create Prediction Standard Error Map.

Creating a prediction map using validation

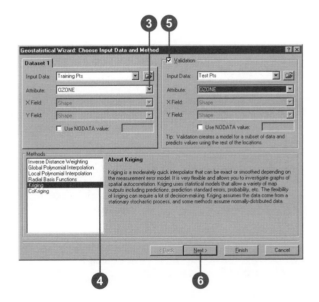

1. Click the point layer on which you wish to perform ordinary kriging in the ArcMap table of contents.

2. Start Geostatistical Analyst.

3. Click the Attribute dropdown list and specify the field on which you wish to perform ordinary kriging.

4. Click the Kriging method.

5. Check Validation and specify the validation dataset and attribute.

6. Click Next.

7. Follow steps 6 through 10 in 'Creating a prediction map' on the previous page and examine the results on the Validation dialog box and then click Finish.

Creating a prediction map while applying a transformation

1. Click the point layer on which you wish to perform ordinary kriging in the ArcMap table of contents.

2. Start the Geostatistical Analyst.

3. Click the Attribute field on which you wish to perform ordinary kriging.

4. Click the Kriging method.

5. Click Next.

6. Expand the list under Ordinary Kriging and click Prediction.

7. Click the desired transformation from the Transformation dropdown menu.

8. Click Next.

9. Follow steps 9 through 12 in 'Creating a prediction map using detrending' on the following page.

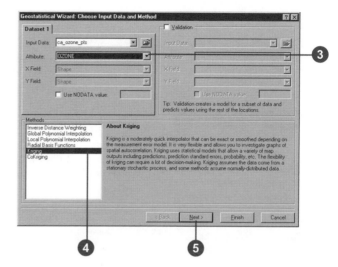

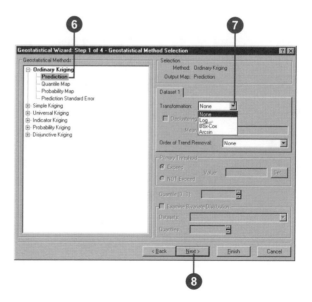

Tip

Detrending

Once a trend is removed from the input data points, ordinary kriging is performed on the residuals.

See Also

For additional information on transformations, detrending, setting the parameters for the Semivariogram/Covariance Modeling and Searching Neighborhood dialog boxes, and understanding the Cross Validation dialog box, see Chapter 7, 'Using analytical tools when generating surfaces'.

Creating a prediction map using detrending

1. Click the point layer on which you wish to perform ordinary kriging in the ArcMap table of contents.

2. Start Geostatistical Analyst.

3. Click the Attribute dropdown list and select the attribute on which you wish to perform ordinary kriging.

4. Click the Kriging method.

5. Click Next.

6. Click Prediction under Ordinary Kriging.

7. Click the Order of Trend Removal dropdown menu and choose an option.

8. Click Next.

9. Specify the desired parameters in the Detrending dialog box and click Next.

10. Specify the desired parameters in the Semivariogram/ Covariance Modeling dialog box and click Next.

11. Specify the desired parameters in the Searching Neighborhood dialog box and click Next.

12. Examine the results on the Cross Validation dialog box and click Finish.

13. On the Output Layer Information dialog box, click OK.

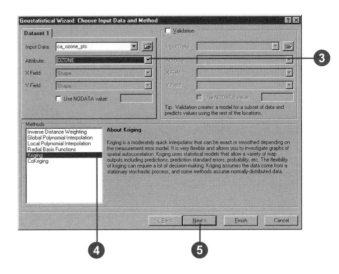

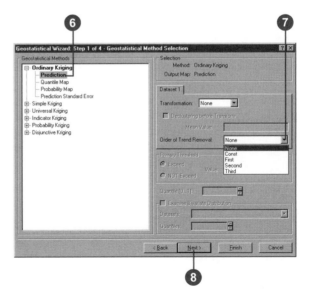

Understanding simple kriging

Simple kriging assumes the model,

$$Z(\mathbf{s}) = \mu + \varepsilon(\mathbf{s})$$

where μ is a known constant. For example, in the following figure, which uses the same data used for ordinary kriging and universal kriging concepts,

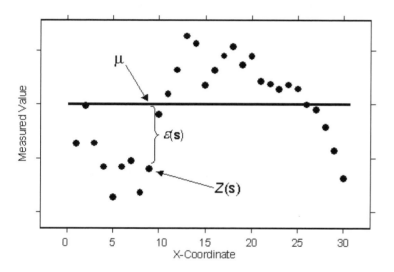

the observed data is given by the solid circles. The known constant—the solid line—is μ. This can be compared to ordinary kriging. For simple kriging, because you assume that you know μ exactly, then at the data locations you also know $\varepsilon(\mathbf{s})$ exactly. For ordinary kriging, you estimated μ, so you also estimated $\varepsilon(\mathbf{s})$. If you know $\varepsilon(\mathbf{s})$, then you can do a better job of estimating the autocorrelation than if you are estimating $\varepsilon(\mathbf{s})$. The assumption of exactly knowing the mean μ is often unrealistic. However, sometimes it makes sense to assume a physically based model gives a known trend. Then you can take the difference between that model and the observations, called residuals, and use simple kriging on the residuals, assuming the trend in the residuals is known to be zero.

Simple kriging can use either semivariograms or covariances (which are the mathematical forms you use to express autocorrelation), it can use transformations, and it can allow for measurement error; see Chapter 7, 'Using analytical tools when generating surfaces', for more details.

Creating a map using simple kriging

Use simple kriging to produce prediction, quantile, probability, or standard error maps. Simple Kriging assumes a known constant mean. The data points need to be sampled from a phenomenon that is continuous in space.

See Also

For additional information on transformations, setting the parameters for the Semivariogram/ Covariance Modeling and Searching Neighborhood dialog boxes, and understanding the Cross Validation dialog box, see Chapter 7, 'Using analytical tools when generating surfaces'.

Creating a prediction map

1. Click the point layer on which you wish to perform simple kriging in the ArcMap table of contents.

2. Start the Geostatistical Analyst.

3. Click the Attribute field on which you wish to perform simple kriging.

4. Click the Kriging method.

5. Click Next.

6. Expand the list under Simple Kriging and click Prediction.

7. Specify the Mean Value.

8. Click Next.

9. Specify the desired parameters in the Semivariogram/ Covariance Modeling dialog box and click Next.

10. Specify the desired parameters in the Searching Neighborhood dialog box and click Next.

11. Examine the results on the Cross Validation dialog box and click Finish.

12. On the Output Layer Information dialog box, click OK.

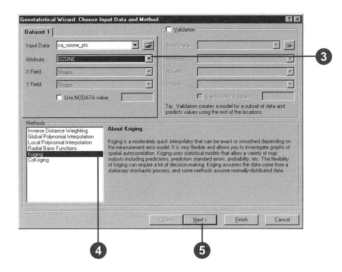

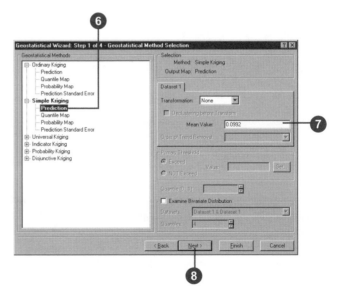

Creating a quantile map

1. Follow the steps in 'Creating a prediction map' on the previous page, except click Quantile Map in step 6, rather than Prediction.

2. Click the Quantile up and down arrow buttons to specify the quantile level.

3. Follow steps 7 through 12 in 'Creating a prediction map' on the previous page.

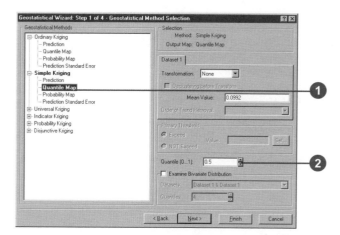

Creating a probability map

1. Follow the steps in 'Creating a prediction map' on the previous page, except click Probability Map in step 6, rather than Prediction.

2. Type a value in the Threshold input or click the Set... button and set the threshold on the Primary Threshold selection dialog box.

3. Click either the Exceed or NOT Exceed radio buttons.

4. Click Next.

5. Follow steps 7 through 12 in 'Creating a prediction map' on the previous page.

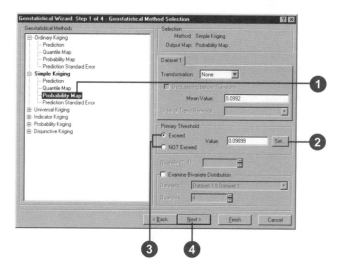

Creating training and test datasets

When performing validation, two datasets are used: a training dataset and a test dataset. The training dataset contains the measured locations on which the interpolation will be performed. The test dataset will be used to validate the predictions. The training dataset is entered as Dataset 1 and the test dataset as the Validation dataset. See 'Performing validation on a geostatistical layer created from a subset' in Chapter 9 to obtain additional information on creating subsets.

Using validation

Make sure that there are enough data samples in the training set to portray an accurate representation of the surface. If the training set is too small, abnormal data values can skew the model parameters and the output results.

Creating a prediction standard error map

1. Right-click on the prediction surface in the ArcMap table of contents that was created using simple kriging and click Create Prediction Standard Error Map.

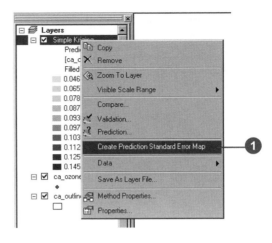

Tip

Exploratory Spatial Data Analysis tools

Use exploratory spatial data analysis to help make decisions on transformations and the effect of unusual observations on covariance/variogram models and confirm your decisions using validation and cross-validation.

See Also

For additional information on transformations, setting the parameters for the Semivariogram/ Covariance Modeling and Searching Neighborhood dialog boxes, and understanding the Cross Validation dialog box, see Chapter 7, 'Using analytical tools when generating surfaces'.

Creating a prediction map while applying a transformation

1. Click the point layer on which you wish to perform simple kriging in the ArcMap table of contents.

2. Start the Geostatistical Analyst.

3. Click the Attribute field on which you wish to perform simple kriging.

4. Click the Kriging method.

5. Click Next.

6. Expand the list under simple kriging and click Prediction.

7. Click the desired transformation from the Transformation dropdown menu.

8. Click Next.

9. Follow steps 9 through 12 in 'Creating a prediction map', earlier in the chapter.

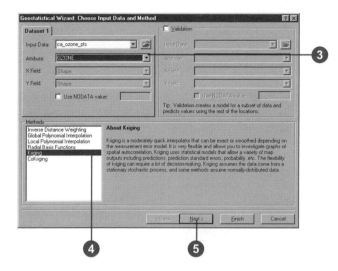

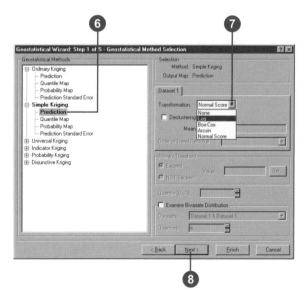

Using declustering

If you use the normal score transform, and your data has been preferentially sampled with higher densities of points in some areas, try declustering the data. See Chapter 7, 'Using analytical tools when generating surfaces'.

See Also

For additional information on transformations, setting the parameters for the Semivariogram/ Covariance Modeling and the Searching Neighborhood dialog boxes, and understanding the Cross Validation dialog box, see Chapter 7, 'Using analytical tools when generating surfaces'.

Creating a prediction map while applying a transformation with declustering

1. Click the point layer on which you wish to perform simple kriging in the ArcMap table of contents.

2. Start the Geostatistical Analyst.

3. Click the Attribute field on which you wish to perform simple kriging.

4. Click the Kriging method.

5. Click Next.

6. Expand the list under Simple Kriging and click Prediction.

7. Click Normal Score under the Transformation dropdown menu.

8. Check Declustering before Transform.

9. Click Next.

10. Specify the desired parameters in the Declustering dialog box and click Next.

11. Specify the desired parameters in the Normal Score Transformation dialog box and click Next.

12. Follow steps 9 through 12 in 'Creating a prediction map', earlier in the chapter.

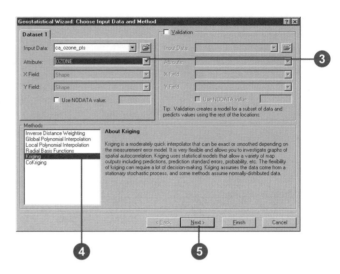

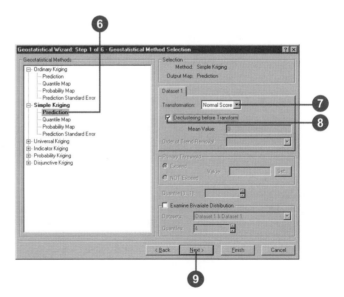

Tip

Bivariate distribution

Try checking your data for bivariate normality. See Chapter 7, 'Using analytical tools when generating surfaces'.

See Also

For additional information on setting the parameters for the Detrending, Semivariogram/ Covariance Modeling and Searching Neighborhood dialog boxes and understanding the Cross Validation dialog box, see Chapter 7, 'Using analytical tools when generating surfaces'.

Examining the bivariate distribution when creating a prediction map

1. Click the point layer on which you wish to perform simple kriging in the ArcMap table of contents.

2. Start Geostatistical Analyst.

3. Click the Attribute field on which you wish to perform simple kriging.

4. Click the Kriging method.

5. Click Next.

6. Expand the list under Simple Kriging and click Prediction.

7. Check Examine Bivariate Distribution.

8. Specify Mean Value and the number of Quantiles to check.

9. Click Next.

10. Specify the desired parameters in the Semivariogram/ Covariance Modeling dialog box and click Next.

11. Explore the Semivariogram/ Covariance Modeling (Examine Bivariate Distribution) dialog box and click Next.

12. Follow steps 10 through 12 in 'Creating a prediction map', earlier in the chapter.

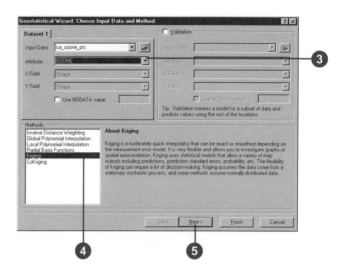

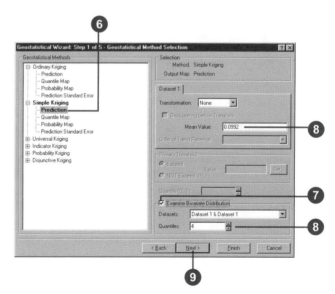

Understanding universal kriging

Universal kriging assumes the model,

$$Z(\mathbf{s}) = \mu(\mathbf{s}) + \varepsilon(\mathbf{s}),$$

where $\mu(\mathbf{s})$ is some deterministic function. For example, in the following figure, which has the same data that was used for ordinary kriging concepts, the observed data is given by the solid circles.

Universal kriging can use either semivariograms or covariances (which are the mathematical forms you use to express autocorrelation); it can use transformations, in which trends should be removed; and it can allow for measurement error. See Chapter 7, 'Using analytical tools when generating surfaces', for more details.

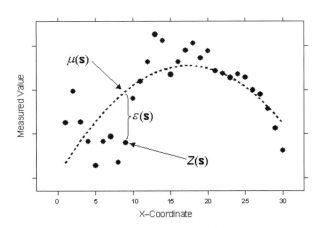

A second-order polynomial is the trend—the long dashed line—and it is $\mu(\mathbf{s})$. If you subtract the second-order polynomial from the original data, you obtain the errors, $\varepsilon(\mathbf{s})$, which are assumed to be random. The mean of all $\varepsilon(\mathbf{s})$ is 0. Conceptually, the autocorrelation is now modeled from the random errors $\varepsilon(\mathbf{s})$. The figure above looks just like a polynomial regression from any basic statistics course. In fact, that is what universal kriging is. You are doing regression with the spatial coordinates as the explanatory variables. However, instead of assuming the errors $\varepsilon(\mathbf{s})$ are independent, you model them to be autocorrelated. Again, the advice from ordinary kriging: there is no way to decide on the proper decomposition, based on the data alone.

Creating a map using universal kriging

Use universal kriging to produce prediction, quantile, probability, or standard error maps. It will assume a trending mean. The data points need to be sampled from a phenomenon that is continuous in space.

See Also

For additional information on transformations, detrending, setting the parameters for the Semivariogram/Covariance Modeling and Searching Neighborhood dialog boxes, and understanding the Cross Validation dialog box, see Chapter 7, 'Using analytical tools when generating surfaces'.

Creating a prediction map

1. Click the point layer on which you wish to perform universal kriging in the ArcMap table of contents.

2. Start Geostatistical Analyst.

3. Click the Attribute field on which you wish to perform universal kriging.

4. Click the Kriging method and click Next.

5. Under Universal Kriging, expand the list and click Prediction.

6. Click the Order of Trend dropdown menu and click the desired order.

7. Click Next.

8. Specify the desired parameters in the Detrending dialog box and click Next.

9. Specify the desired parameters in the Semivariogram/ Covariance Modeling dialog box and click Next.

10. Specify the desired parameters in the Searching Neighborhood dialog box and click Next.

11. Examine the results on the Cross Validation dialog box and click Finish.

12. On the Output Layer Information dialog box, click OK.

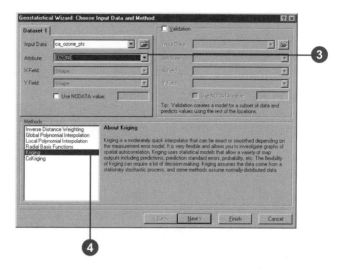

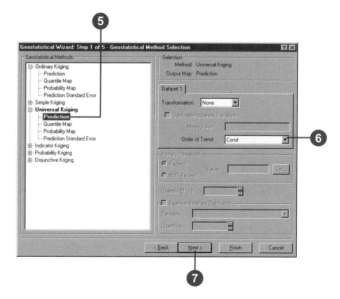

Utilizing ESDA for determining transformations

Use Exploratory Spatial Data Analysis to help make decisions on transformations, detrending, and the effect of unusual observations on covariance/variogram models. Confirm your decisions using validation and cross-validation.

Creating a prediction standard error map

1. Right-click on the prediction surface in the ArcMap table of contents that was created using universal kriging and click Create Prediction Standard Error Map.

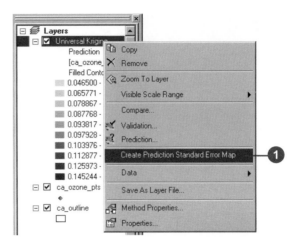

Understanding thresholds

A variable that is continuous may be made into a binary (0 or 1) variable by choosing some threshold. In the Geostatistical Analyst, if values are above the threshold, they become a 1, and if they are below the threshold, they become a 0.

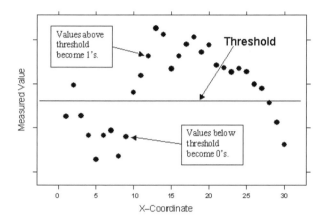

Understanding indicator kriging

Indicator kriging assumes the model,

$$I(\mathbf{s}) = \mu + \varepsilon(\mathbf{s}),$$

where m is an unknown constant and $I(\mathbf{s})$ is a binary variable. The creation of binary data may be through the use of a threshold for continuous data, or it may also be the case that the observed data is 0 or 1. For example, you may have a sample that consists of information on whether or not a point is forest or nonforest habitat, where the binary variable indicates class membership. Using binary variables, indicator kriging proceeds exactly as for ordinary kriging. For example, in the following figure, which has the same data that was used for ordinary kriging, universal kriging, and simple kriging concepts, the data has been converted to binary values using the threshold shown in the 'Understanding thresholds' concepts on the previous page.

will be between 0 and 1 and predictions from indicator kriging can be interpreted as probabilities of the variable being a 1 or of being in the class that is indicated by a 1. If a threshold was used to create the indicator variable, then the resulting interpolation map shows the probabilities of exceeding (or being below) the threshold.

It is also possible to create several indicator variables for the same dataset by choosing multiple thresholds. In this case, one threshold creates the primary indicator variable, and the other indicator variables are used as secondary variables in cokriging.

Indicator kriging can use either semivariograms or covariances (which are the mathematical forms you use to express autocorrelation); see Chapter 7, 'Using analytical tools when generating surfaces', for more details.

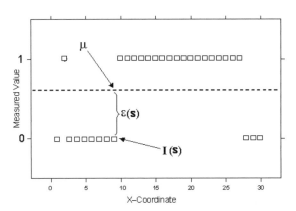

The observed binary data is given by the open squares. The unknown mean for all indicator variables is shown by the dashed line, and it is μ. This can be compared to ordinary kriging. As for ordinary kriging, you assume that $\varepsilon(\mathbf{s})$ is autocorrelated. Notice that because the indicator variables are 0 or 1, the interpolations

Creating a map using indicator kriging

Use indicator kriging to produce a probability or standard error of indicators map. Indicator kriging assumes an unknown constant mean. The data points need to be sampled from a phenomenon that is continuous in space.

Tip

Important parameters

The specified threshold (which determines which predictions will receive a "0" and which will receive a "1"), covariance/ semivariogram models, and search neighborhoods

Tip

Selecting a threshold

Estimation of semivariogram/ covariance becomes difficult when the indicator variables are primarily all zeros or ones. Choose a threshold that gives a mix of zeros and ones.

See Also

For additional information on transformations, setting the parameters for the Semivariogram/ Covariance Modeling and Searching Neighborhood dialog boxes, and understanding the Cross Validation dialog box, see Chapter 7, 'Using analytical tools when generating surfaces'.

Creating a probability map

1. Click the point layer on which you wish to perform indicator kriging in the ArcMap table of contents. Start the Geostatistical Analyst.

2. Click the Attribute field on which you wish to perform indicator kriging.

3. Click the Kriging method.

4. Click Next.

5. Expand the list under Indicator Kriging and click Probability Map.

6. Type the Threshold value or click the Set... button and set the threshold on the Primary Threshold selection dialog box.

7. Click either the Exceed or NOT Exceed radio buttons.

8. Click Next.

9. Set additional cutoffs on the Additional Cutoffs selection dialog box.

10. Specify the desired parameters in the Semivariogram/ Covariance Modeling and Searching Neighborhood dialog boxes and click Next in each dialog box.

11. Examine the results on the Cross Validation dialog box and click Finish.

12. On the Output Layer Information dialog box, click OK.

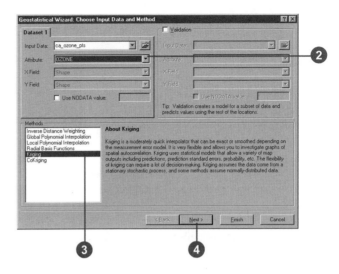

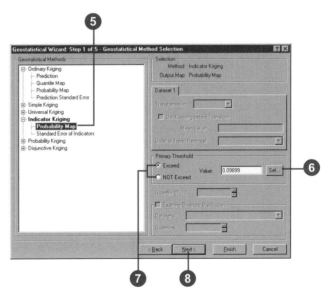

Understanding probability kriging

Probability kriging assumes the model,

$$I(\mathbf{s}) = I(Z(\mathbf{s}) > c_t) = \mu_1 + \varepsilon_1(\mathbf{s})$$

$$Z(\mathbf{s}) = \mu_2 + \varepsilon_2(\mathbf{s}),$$

where μ_1 and μ_2 are unknown constants and $I(\mathbf{s})$ is a binary variable created by using a threshold indicator $I(Z(\mathbf{s}) > c_t)$. Notice that now there are two types of random errors, $\varepsilon_1(\mathbf{s})$ and $\varepsilon_2(\mathbf{s})$, so there is autocorrelation for each of them and cross-correlation between them. Probability kriging strives to do the same thing as indicator kriging, but it uses cokriging in an attempt to do a better job. For example, in the following figure, which uses the same data used for ordinary kriging, universal kriging, simple kriging, and indicator kriging concepts, notice the datum labeled $Z(\mathbf{u}=9)$, which has an indicator variable of $I(\mathbf{u}) = 0$, and $Z(\mathbf{s}=10)$, which has an indicator variable of $I(\mathbf{s}) = 1$.

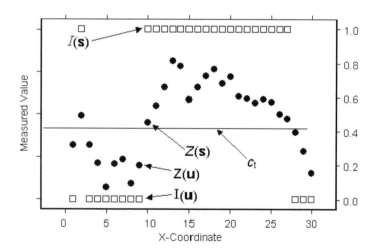

If you wanted to predict a value halfway between them, at x-coordinate 9.5, then using indicator kriging alone would give a

prediction near 0.5. However, you can see that $Z(\mathbf{s})$ is just barely above the threshold, but $Z(\mathbf{u})$ is well below the threshold. Therefore, you have some reason to believe that an indicator prediction at location 9.5 should be less than 0.5. Probability kriging tries to exploit the extra information in the original data in addition to the binary variable. However, it comes with a price. You have to do much more estimation, which includes estimating the autocorrelation for each variable as well as their cross-correlation. Each time you estimate unknown autocorrelation parameters, you introduce more uncertainty, so probability kriging may not be worth the extra effort.

Probability kriging can use either semivariograms or covariances (which are the mathematical forms you use to express autocorrelation) and cross-covariances (which are the mathematical forms you use to express cross-correlation); see Chapter 7, 'Using analytical tools when generating surfaces', for more details.

Creating a map using probability kriging

Use probability kriging to produce a probability or standard error of indicators map. The data points need to be sampled from a phenomenon that is continuous in space.

Tip

Important parameters

The specified threshold (which determines which predictions will receive a "0" and which will receive a "1"), covariance/variogram models, and search neighborhoods establishing the model.

Tip

Selecting a threshold

Estimation of semivariogram/covariance becomes difficult when the indicator variables are primarily all zeros or ones. If possible, choose a threshold that gives a mix of zeros and ones.

See Also

For additional information on transformations, detrending, setting the parameters for the Semivariogram/Covariance Modeling and Searching Neighborhood dialog boxes, and understanding the Cross Validation dialog box, see Chapter 7, 'Using analytical tools when generating surfaces'.

Creating a probability map

1. Click the point layer on which you wish to perform probability kriging in the ArcMap table of contents.

2. Start the Geostatistical Analyst.

3. Click the Attribute field on which you wish to perform probability kriging.

4. Click the Kriging method.

5. Click Next.

6. Expand the list under Probability Kriging and click Probability Map.

7. Type in the Threshold value or click the Set... button and set the threshold on the Primary Threshold selection dialog box.

8. Click either the Exceed or NOT Exceed radio buttons.

9. Click Next.

10. Specify the desired parameters in the Semivariogram/Covariance Modeling and Searching Neighborhood dialog boxes and click Next in each dialog box. ▶

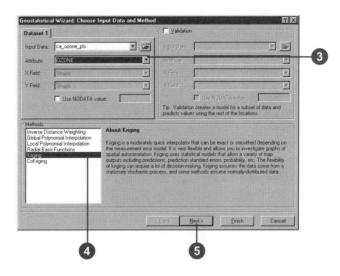

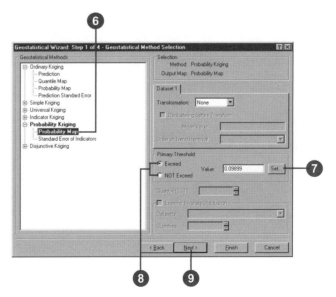

11. Examine the results on the Cross Validation dialog box and click Finish.

12. On the Output Layer Information dialog box, click OK.

Understanding disjunctive kriging

Disjunctive kriging assumes the model,

$$f(Z(s)) = \mu_1 + \varepsilon(s)$$

where μ_1 is an unknown constant and $f(Z(s))$ is some arbitrary function of $Z(s)$. Notice that you can write $f(Z(s)) = I(Z(s) > c_t)$, so indicator kriging is a special case of disjunctive kriging. In the Geostatistical Analyst, you can predict either the value itself or an indicator with disjunctive kriging.

By way of comparison, ordinary kriging uses linear combinations of the data so that the final predictor is,

$$\hat{Z}(s_0) = \sum_{i=1}^{n} \lambda_i Z(s_i),$$

where $\hat{Z}(s_0)$ is the predicted value, $\{Z(s_i)\}$ is the data, and $\{\lambda_i\}$ is the kriging weights. Ordinary kriging tries to find the optimal weights, $\{\lambda_i\}$. Indicator kriging forms the predictor,

$$\hat{I}(Z(s_0) > c_t) = \sum_{i=1}^{n} \lambda_i I(Z(s_i) > c_t),$$

and tries to find the optimal weights, $\{\lambda_i\}$. However, you might be able to find more general functions of the data that will help you predict some function of the variable at the prediction location.

Disjunctive kriging generalizes indicator kriging to form the predictor,

$$\hat{g}(Z(s_0)) = \sum_{i=1}^{n} f_i(Z(s_i)),$$

In the Geostatistical Analyst, the functions $g(Z(s_0))$ available are simply $Z(s_0)$ itself and $I(Z(s_0) > c_t)$. In general, disjunctive kriging tries to do more than ordinary kriging. While the rewards may be greater, so are the costs. Disjunctive kriging requires the bivariate normality assumption (see Chapter 7, 'Using analytical tools when generating surfaces') and approximations to the functions $f_i(Z(s_i))$; the assumptions are difficult to verify, and the solutions are mathematically and computationally complicated.

Disjunctive kriging can use either semivariograms or covariances (which are the mathematical forms you use to express autocorrelation), and it can use transformations and remove trends; see Chapter 7, 'Using analytical tools when generating surfaces', for more details.

Creating a map using disjunctive kriging

Use disjunctive kriging to produce a prediction, probability, standard error of indicators, or standard errors map.

The data points need to be sampled from a phenomenon that is continuous in space and have a bivariate normal distribution.

Tip

Important parameters

An appropriate transformation and detrending, covariance/semivariogram models, and search neighborhoods.

Tip

Using a database file instead of a point layer

On the Choose Input Data and Method dialog box, a database file can be used in place of an ArcMap input layer by clicking the Browse button and navigating to the desired database file.

See Also

For additional information on transformations, detrending, setting the parameters for the Semivariogram/Covariance Modeling and Searching Neighborhood dialog boxes, and understanding the Cross Validation dialog box, see Chapter 7, 'Using analytical tools when generating surfaces'.

Creating a prediction map

1. Click the point layer on which you wish to perform disjunctive kriging in the ArcMap table of contents.

2. Start Geostatistical Analyst.

3. Click the Attribute field on which you wish to perform disjunctive kriging.

4. Click the Kriging method.

5. Click Next.

6. Expand the list under Disjunctive Kriging and click Prediction. Specify Mean Value. Optionally, specify Normal Score Transformation (NST) and click Next.

7. If an NST was indicated, specify the desired parameters in the NST dialog box and click Next.

8. Specify the desired parameters in the Semivariogram/Covariance Modeling dialog box and click Next.

9. Specify the desired parameters in the Searching Neighborhood dialog box and click Next.

10. Examine the results on the Cross Validation dialog box and click Finish.

11. On the Output Layer Information dialog box, click OK.

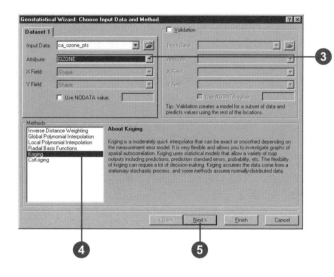

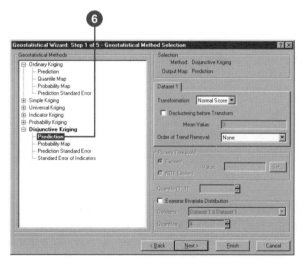

Creating a probability map

1. Follow the steps in 'Creating a prediction map' on the previous page, except click on Probability Map in step 6 rather than Prediction.

2. Type in the Threshold value or click the Set... button and set the threshold on the Primary Threshold selection dialog box.

3. Click either the Exceed or NOT Exceed radio buttons.

4. Specify Mean Value and Normal Score Transformation. Click Next.

5. Follow steps 7 through 11 in 'Creating a prediction map' earlier in the chapter.

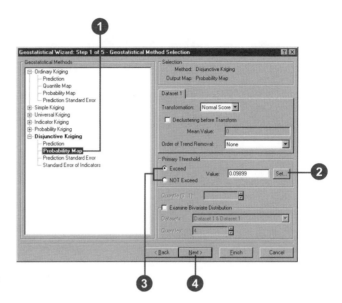

Creating a prediction standard error map

1. Right-click on the prediction surface in the ArcMap table of contents that was created using disjunctive kriging and click Create Prediction Standard Error Map.

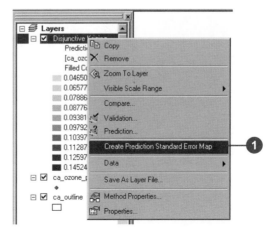

Creating a standard error of indicators map

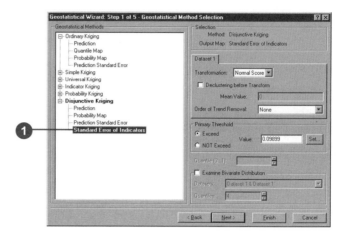

1. Follow the steps for 'Creating a probability map' previously in this chapter, except click Standard Error of Indicators in step 6 rather than Prediction.

Creating a prediction map with declustering

1. Click the point layer on which you wish to perform disjunctive kriging in the ArcMap table of contents.

2. Start the Geostatistical Analyst.

3. Click the Attribute field on which you wish to perform disjunctive kriging.

4. Click the Kriging method.

5. Click Next.

6. Expand the list under Disjunctive Kriging and click Prediction.

7. Click Normal Score under the Transformation dropdown menu.

8. Check Declustering before Transform.

9. Click Next.

10. Specify the desired parameters in the Declustering dialog box and click Next.

11. Specify the desired parameters in the Normal Score Transformation dialog box and click Next.

12. Follow steps 8 through 11 in 'Creating a prediction map', previously in this chapter.

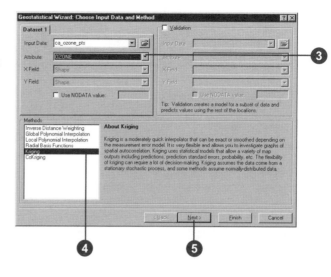

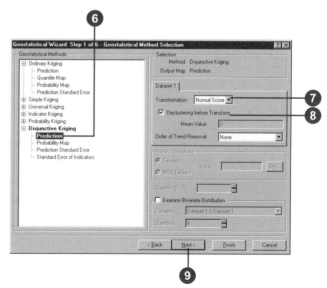

Examining the bivariate distribution when creating a prediction map

1. Click the point layer on which you wish to perform disjunctive kriging in the ArcMap table of contents.

2. Click the Geostatistical Analyst toolbar and click Geostatistical Wizard.

3. Click the Attribute field on which you wish to perform disjunctive kriging.

4. Click the Kriging method. Click Next.

5. Expand the list under Disjunctive Kriging and click Prediction.

6. Check Examine Bivariate Distribution and specify Mean Value or NST.

7. Specify the desired parameters in the Semivariogram/ Covariance Modeling dialog box and click Next.

8. Explore the Semivariogram/ Covariance Modeling dialog box (Examine Bivariate Distribution) and click Next.

9. Follow steps 9 through 11 in 'Creating a prediction map', previously in this chapter.

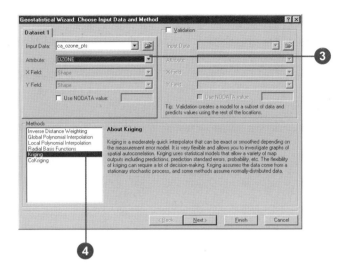

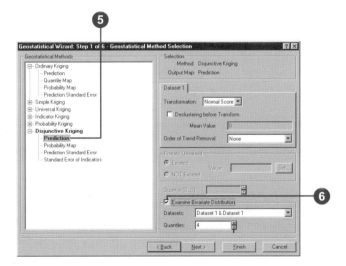

Understanding cokriging

Cokriging uses information on several variable types. The main variable of interest is Z_1, and both autocorrelation for Z_1 and cross-correlations between Z_1 and all other variable types are used to make better predictions. It is appealing to use information from other variables to help make predictions, but it comes at a price. Cokriging requires much more estimation, which includes estimating the autocorrelation for each variable as well as all cross-correlations. Theoretically, you can do no worse than kriging because, if there is no cross-correlation, you can fall back on just autocorrelation for Z_1. However, each time you estimate unknown autocorrelation parameters, you introduce more variability, so the gains in precision of the predictions may not be worth the extra effort.

Ordinary cokriging assumes the models,

$$Z_1(\mathbf{s}) = \mu_1 + \varepsilon_1(\mathbf{s})$$

$$Z_2(\mathbf{s}) = \mu_2 + \varepsilon_2(\mathbf{s}),$$

where μ_1 and μ_2 are unknown constants. Notice that now you have two types of random errors, $\varepsilon_1(\mathbf{s})$ and $\varepsilon_2(\mathbf{s})$, so there is autocorrelation for each of them and cross-correlation between them. Ordinary cokriging attempts to predict $Z_1(\mathbf{s}_0)$, just like ordinary kriging, but it uses information in the covariate $\{Z_2(\mathbf{s})\}$ in an attempt to do a better job. For example, the following figure has the same data that was used for ordinary kriging, only here a second variable is added.

Notice that the data Z_1 and Z_2 appears autocorrelated. Also notice that when Z_1 is below its mean μ_1, then Z_2 is often above its mean μ_2, and vice versa. Thus, Z_1 and Z_2 appear to have negative cross-correlation. In this example, each location $\mathbf{s}$ had both $Z_1(\mathbf{s})$ and $Z_2(\mathbf{s})$; however, this is not necessary, and each variable type can have its own unique set of locations. The main variable of interest is Z_1, and both autocorrelation and cross-correlation are used to make better predictions.

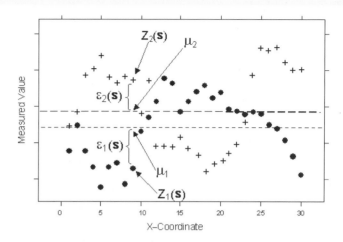

The other cokriging methods, including universal cokriging, simple cokriging, indicator cokriging, probability cokriging, and disjunctive cokriging, are all generalizations of the foregoing methods to the case where you have multiple datasets. For example, indicator cokriging can be implemented by using several thresholds for your data, then using the binary data on each threshold to predict the threshold of primary interest. In this way, it is similar to probability kriging but can be more robust to outliers and other erratic data.

Cokriging can use either semivariograms or covariances (which are the mathematical forms you use to express autocorrelation) and cross-covariance (which is the mathematical form you use to express cross-correlation), it can use transformations and remove trends, and it can allow for measurement error in the same situations as for the various kriging methods (ordinary kriging, simple kriging, and universal kriging); see Chapter 7, 'Using analytical tools when generating surfaces', for more details.

Creating a map using cokriging

Use cokriging to produce prediction, probability, quantile, standard error of indicators, and standard error maps under the same conditions as for each kriging method discussed earlier throughout this chapter.

See Also

For additional information on transformations, detrending, setting the parameters for the Semivariogram/Covariance Modeling and Searching Neigh-borhood dialog boxes, and understanding the Cross Valida-tion dialog box, see Chapter 7, 'Using analytical tools when generating surfaces'.

Creating a prediction map

1. Click the point layers on which you wish to perform cokriging in the ArcMap table of contents.

2. Click the Geostatistical Analyst toolbar and click Geostatistical Wizard.

3. Click the CoKriging method.

4. Click the Attribute field on which you wish to perform cokriging for all datasets (switch between dataset tabs to specify the parameters).

5. Click Next.

6. Click the desired cokriging method and output layer type in the Geostatistical Methods list. Click Next.

7. Specify the parameters in the Detrending dialog box if the Order of Trend Removal was specified for all datasets. Click Next.

8. Specify the parameters in the Semivariogram/Covariance Modeling dialog box for all datasets. Click Next.

9. Specify the desired param-eters in the Searching Neighborhood dialog box for all datasests and click Next.

10. Examine the results on the Cross Validation dialog box and click Finish.

11. On the Output Layer Informa-tion dialog box, click OK.

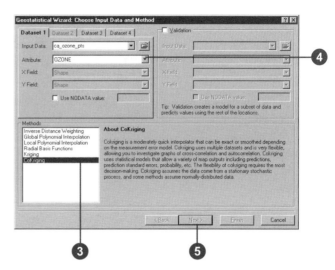

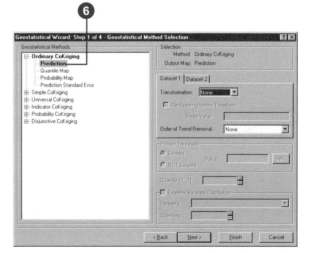

Using analytical tools when generating surfaces 7

IN THIS CHAPTER

• **Investigating spatial structure: variography**

• **Determining the neighborhood search size**

• **Performing cross-validation to assess parameter selections**

• **Assessing decision protocol using validation**

• **Comparing one model with another**

• **Modeling distributions and determining transformations**

• **Checking for the bivariate normal distribution**

• **Implementing declustering to adjust for preferential sampling**

• **Removing trends from the data**

There are many steps that you go through when creating a surface. In each of these steps, you specify a number of parameters. Geostatistical Analyst provides a series of dialog boxes containing analytical tools to assist you in determining the values for the parameters. Some of these dialog boxes and tools are applicable to almost all interpolation methods such as specifying the search neighborhood, cross-validation, and validation. Others are specific to the geostatistical methods (kriging and cokriging), such as modeling semivariograms, transformations, detrending, declustering, and checking for bivariate normal distributions.

Within each dialog box, there are a series of tasks that can be accomplished using the tools. In this chapter, the concepts for the most frequently performed tasks are discussed and the steps identified. Depending on your data, none, some, or all of the tasks and their parameters might be explored. As with all parameters, Geostatistical Analyst provides reliable defaults, some of which have been calculated specifically for your data. However, you may have additional insight into your data from prior knowledge of the phenomena under study or that you gained through the exploratory tools provided with Geostatistical Analyst, which you can use to refine the parameters to create an even more accurate surface.

Investigating spatial structure: variography

Semivariograms and covariance functions

The semivariogram and covariance functions quantify the assumption—that things nearby tend to be more similar than things that are farther apart. They both measure the strength of statistical correlation as a function of distance. The semivariogram is defined as,

$$\gamma(\mathbf{s}_i, \mathbf{s}_j) = \tfrac{1}{2} \operatorname{var}(Z(\mathbf{s}_i) - Z(\mathbf{s}_j)),$$

where *var* is the variance.

If two locations $\mathbf{s}_i$ and $\mathbf{s}_j$ are close to each other in terms of the distance measure of $d(\mathbf{s}_i, \mathbf{s}_j)$, then they are expected to be similar, and so the difference in their values, $Z(\mathbf{s}_i) - Z(\mathbf{s}_j)$, will be small. As $\mathbf{s}_i$ and $\mathbf{s}_j$ get farther apart, they become less similar, and so the difference in their values, $Z(\mathbf{s}_i) - Z(\mathbf{s}_j)$, will become larger. This can be seen in the following figure, which shows the anatomy of a typical semivariogram.

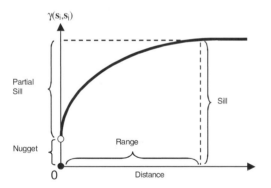

Notice that the variance of the difference increases with distance, so the semivariogram can be thought of as a dissimilarity function. There are several terms that are often associated with this function, and they are also used in the Geostatistical Analyst.

The height that the semivariogram reaches when it levels off is called the sill. It is often composed of two parts: a discontinuity at the origin, called the nugget effect, and the partial sill, which added together give the sill. The nugget effect can be further divided into measurement error and microscale variation and since either component can be zero, the nugget effect can be comprised wholly of one or the other. The distance at which the semivariogram levels off to the sill is called the range.

The covariance function is defined to be,

$$C(\mathbf{s}_i, \mathbf{s}_j) = \operatorname{cov}(Z(\mathbf{s}_i), Z(\mathbf{s}_j)),$$

where cov is the covariance.

Covariance is just a scaled version of correlation. So, when two locations, $\mathbf{s}_i$ and $\mathbf{s}_j$, are close to each other, then they are expected to be similar, and so their covariance (correlation) will be large. As $\mathbf{s}_i$ and $\mathbf{s}_j$ get farther apart, they become less similar and so their covariance becomes zero. This can be seen in the following figure, which shows the anatomy of a typical covariance function.

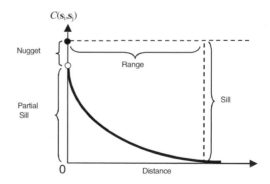

Notice that the covariance function decreases with distance, so it can be thought of as a similarity function.

There is a relationship between the semivariogram and the covariance function, which is,

$$\gamma(\mathbf{s}_i, \mathbf{s}_j) = \text{sill} - C(\mathbf{s}_i, \mathbf{s}_j),$$

and this relationship can be seen from the figures. Because of this equivalence, you can do prediction in the Geostatistical Analyst using either function. (Recall that all semivariograms in the Geostatistical Analyst have sills.)

Semivariograms and covariances cannot be just any function. In order for the predictions to have nonnegative kriging standard errors, only some functions may be used as semivariograms and covariances. The Geostatistical Analyst offers several choices that are acceptable, and you can try different ones for your data. You can also have models that are made by adding several models together—this construction provides valid models, and you can add up to four of them in the Geostatistical Analyst. There are some instances when semivariograms exist, but covariance functions do not. For example, there is a linear variogram, but it does not have a sill, and there is no correspond-ing covariance function. Only models with sills are used in the Geostatistical Analyst. There are no hard-and-fast rules on choosing the "best" variogram model. You can look at your empirical semivariogram or covariance function and pick a model that looks appropriate. You can also use validation and cross-validation as a guide.

Understanding measurement error

Three of the kriging methods—ordinary, simple, and universal—allow the use of measurement error models. Measurement error occurs when it is possible to have several observations at the same location, and they differ. For example, you might extract a sample from the ground or air and then divide that sample into several subsamples to be measured. You may want to do this if the instrument that measures the samples has some variation. As another example, you may send subsamples of a soil sample to different laboratories for analysis. There may be other times when the variation in instrument accuracy is documented. In this case, you may want to simply input the known measurement variation into your model. The measurement error model is,

$$Z(\mathbf{s}) = \mu(\mathbf{s}) + \varepsilon(\mathbf{s}) + \delta(\mathbf{s}),$$

where $\delta(\mathbf{s})$ is measurement error and $\mu(\mathbf{s})$ and $\varepsilon(\mathbf{s})$ are the same as for the kriging models in Chapter 6. In this model, the nugget effect is composed of the variance of $\varepsilon(\mathbf{s})$ (called microscale variation) plus the variance of $\delta(\mathbf{s})$ (called measurement error). In the Geostatistical Analyst, you can specify a proportion of the estimated nugget effect as microscale variation and measurement variation, or you can have Geostatistical Analyst estimate measurement error for you if you have multiple measurements per location, or you can input a value for measurement variation. The default is absent of (zero) measurement variation. When there is no measurement error, kriging is an exact interpolator, meaning that if a prediction is made at a location where data has been collected, then the predicted value is the same as the measured value. However, when measurement errors exist, consider predicting the filtered value, $\mu(\mathbf{s}_o) + \varepsilon(\mathbf{s}_o)$, which does not have the measurement error term. At locations where data has been collected, the filtered value is not the same as the measured value. The effect of choosing measurement error models is that your final map can be smoother and have smaller standard errors than the exact kriging version. This is illustrated with an example in the figures below; exact one-dimensional kriging and smooth kriging are shown when there are only two data locations (at 1 and 2) with values -1 and 1 for a model without measurement variation and one where the nugget effect is all measurement variation.

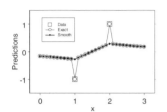 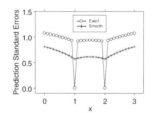

Anisotropy: Directional semivariograms and covariances functions

Because you are working in two-dimensional space, you might expect that the semivariogram and covariance functions change not only with distance but also with direction. This is called anisotropy. Consider two points, s_i and s_j, and the vector that separates them, which we denote as $s_i - s_j$. This vector will have a distance on the x-coordinate as well as the y-coordinate. Alternatively, you can think of the vector as having a distance and an angle in polar coordinates. Here anisotropy is described for the semivariogram; similar ideas for the covariance function should be obvious. The semivariogram, when plotted on the two-dimensional coordinate axes, looks like the following diagram:

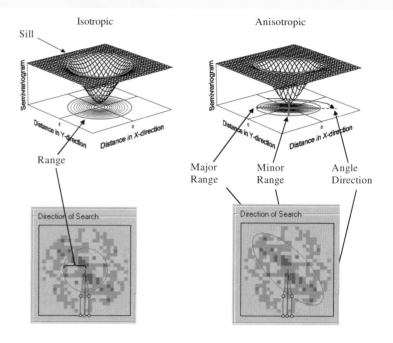

The isotropic model is the same in all directions, whereas the anisotropic model reaches the sill more rapidly in some directions than others. The length of the longer axis to reach the sill is called the major range, and the length of the shorter axis to reach the sill is called the minor range, and you also have the angle of rotation of the line that forms the major range. In the Geostatistical Analyst, an outline of the range is given in blue, over the empirical semivariogram surface.

Empirical semivariograms and covariance functions

The semivariogram and covariance functions are theoretical quantities that you cannot observe, so you estimate them from your data, using what is called the empirical semivariogram and empirical covariance functions. Often, you can gain insight into the quantities by looking at the way they are estimated. Look at the empirical semivariogram first. Suppose that you take all pairs of data that are a similar distance and direction from each other such as those connected by the green lines in the following figure.

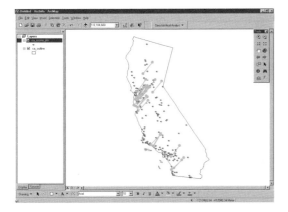

For all of the pairs of locations $\mathbf{s}_i$ and $\mathbf{s}_j$ that are joined by lines, compute

$$\text{average}[(z(\mathbf{s}_i) - z(\mathbf{s}_j))^2],$$

where $z(\mathbf{s}_i)$ is the measured value at location $\mathbf{s}_i$. If all of the pairs of locations $\mathbf{s}_i$ and $\mathbf{s}_j$ are close to each other, it is expected that $z(\mathbf{s}_i)$ and $z(\mathbf{s}_j)$ will be similar in value so that when you take the differences and square them, the average should be small. As $\mathbf{s}_i$ and $\mathbf{s}_j$ get farther apart, it is expected that their values will become more dissimilar so that when you take their differences and square them, the average will get larger.

Look at the covariance function. For all of the pairs of locations $\mathbf{s}_i$ and $\mathbf{s}_j$ that are joined by lines, you compute,

$$\text{average}[(z(\mathbf{s}_i) - \bar{z})(z(\mathbf{s}_j) - \bar{z})],$$

where $z(\mathbf{s}_i)$ is the measured value at location $\mathbf{s}_i$ and $\bar{z}$ is the mean of all of the data. If all of the pairs $\mathbf{s}_i$ and $\mathbf{s}_j$ are close to each other, it is expected that either both $z(\mathbf{s}_i)$ and $z(\mathbf{s}_j)$ will be above the mean $\bar{z}$ or that they will both be below the mean. Either way, their product is positive so that when you average all of the products, you expect a positive value. If $\mathbf{s}_i$ and $\mathbf{s}_j$ are far apart, then it is expected that about half the time the products will be negative and half the time they will be positive, so it is expected their average will be near zero.

In the Geostatistical Analyst, the average values calculated above, for all pairs that have a similar distance and angle, are plotted on a semivariogram or covariance surface. For example, here is an empirical semivariogram surface.

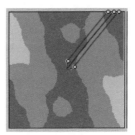

The size of the cells is called lag size, and the number of cells is called number of lags, and they can be set in the Geostatistical Analyst. The number of lags in this example is 12, counted as the number of adjacent cells in a straight horizontal or straight vertical line from the center to the edge of the figure.

Using the empirical data to estimate theoretical models

Now you need to use the empirical semivariogram and covariance functions to estimate the theoretical models, which are what are actually used to develop the kriging predictors and standard errors. In the following figure, the estimated theoretical model is shown, along with the empirical values.

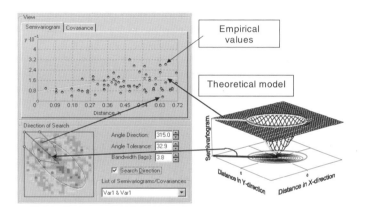

Cross-Covariance models

When you have multiple datasets and you want to use cokriging, then you need to develop models for cross-covariance. Because you have multiple datasets, you keep track of the variables with subscripts, with $Z_k(\mathbf{s}_i)$ indicating a random variable for the kth data type at location $\mathbf{s}_i$. Then the cross-covariance function between the kth data type and the mth data type is defined to be,

$$C_{km}(\mathbf{s}_i, \mathbf{s}_j) = \text{cov}(Z_k(\mathbf{s}_i), Z_m(\mathbf{s}_j)).$$

Now here is a subtle and often confusing fact: $C_{km}(\mathbf{s}_i, \mathbf{s}_j)$ can be asymmetric. In general, $C_{km}(\mathbf{s}_i, \mathbf{s}_j) \neq C_{mk}(\mathbf{s}_i, \mathbf{s}_j)$ (notice the switch in the subscripts). To see why, let us look at the following example.

Suppose that you have data arranged in one dimension, along a line, and it is

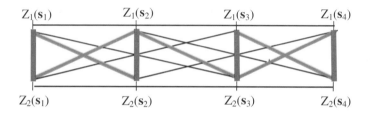

In the example above, the variables for type 1 and 2 are regularly spaced along the line, with the thick red line indicating highest cross-covariance, the green line indicating less cross-covariance, and the thin blue line the least cross-covariance, with no line indicating 0 cross-covariance. This figure shows that $Z_1(\mathbf{s}_i)$ and $Z_2(\mathbf{s}_j)$ have the highest cross-covariance when $\mathbf{s}_i = \mathbf{s}_j$, and the cross-covariance decreases as $\mathbf{s}_i$ and $\mathbf{s}_j$ get farther apart. In this example, $C_{km}(\mathbf{s}_i, \mathbf{s}_j) = C_{mk}(\mathbf{s}_i, \mathbf{s}_j)$. However, the cross-covariance can be "shifted":

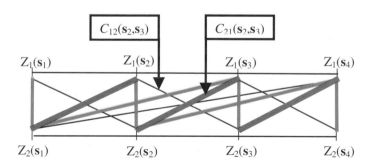

Now notice that, for example, $C_{12}(\mathbf{s}_2, \mathbf{s}_3)$ has the minimum cross-covariance (thin blue line) while $C_{21}(\mathbf{s}_2, \mathbf{s}_3)$ has the maximum cross-covariance (thick red line), so here $C_{km}(\mathbf{s}_i, \mathbf{s}_j) \neq C_{mk}(\mathbf{s}_i, \mathbf{s}_j)$. Relative to Z_1, the cross-covariances of Z_2 have been shifted -1 unit. In two dimensions, the Geostatistical Analyst will estimate any shift in the cross-covariance between the two datasets if you click on the shift parameters.

The empirical cross-covariances are computed as,

$$\text{average}[\,(z_1(\mathbf{s}_i) - \bar{z}_1)(z_2(\mathbf{s}_j) - \bar{z}_2)\,],$$

where $Z_k(\mathbf{s}_i)$ is the measured value for the kth dataset at location $\mathbf{s}_i$, $\bar{z}_k$ is the mean for the kth dataset, and the average is taken for all $\mathbf{s}_i$ and $\mathbf{s}_j$ separated by a certain distance and angle. As for the semivariograms, the Geostatistical Analyst shows both the empirical and fitted models for cross-covariance.

Choosing different covariance models, using compound covariance models, and choosing anisotropy will all cause the theoretical model to change, and you can make a preliminary choice of model by seeing how well it fits the empirical values. Changing the lag size and the number of lags and adding shifts will change the empirical covariance surface, which will cause a corresponding change in the theoretical model. The Geostatistical Analyst computes default values, but you should feel free to try different values and use validation, cross-validation, and scientific judgment to choose the best model.

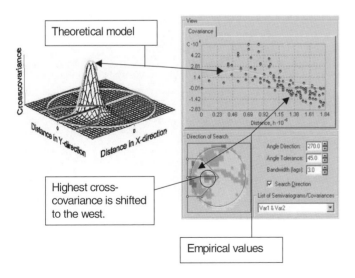

Theoretical model

Highest cross-covariance is shifted to the west.

Empirical values

The Semivariogram/Covariance Modeling dialog box

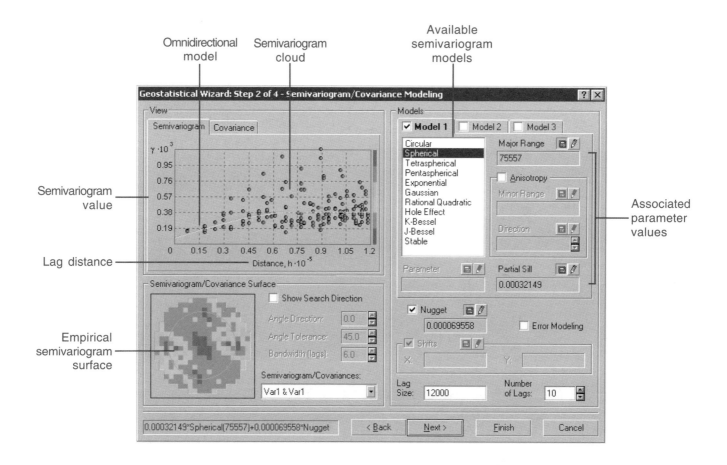

Omnidirectional model
Semivariogram cloud
Available semivariogram models

Semivariogram value
Lag distance
Empirical semivariogram surface

Associated parameter values

Modeling semivariograms and covariance functions

Modeling semivariograms and covariance functions fit a semivariogram or covariance to your data. The goal is to fit the best model (yellow line) to the semivariogram. The model will then be used in your predictions.

Explore for directional autocorrelation in your data. The sill, range, and nugget are the important characteristics of the model. If there is measurement error in your data, use measurement error models.

Tip

Selecting the model

Choose a semivariogram model that looks like it fits the empirical semivariogram cloud. Use validation and cross-validation to help choose from among similar models.

See Also

Chapter 3, 'The principles of geostatistical analysis', has a general discussion on spatial autocorrelation and modeling semivariograms and covariances. You may also want to look at Appendix A for the formulas.

Selecting a model

1. On the Semivariogram/ Covariance Modeling dialog box, click on the desired semivariogram model.

   You will notice that the yellow line modeling in the Semivariogram dialog box will change to reflect the model that is selected.

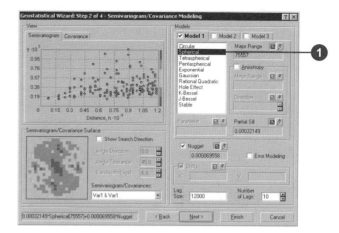

Exploring for directional autocorrelation

1. Check Show Search Direction.

2. Click the up or down arrows of the Angle Direction to explore for the desired directional angle.

   Alternatively, in the semivariogram map, click and hold the middle blue line and drag to the desired direction.

3. Click the up or down arrows of the Angle Tolerance to adjust the angle of tolerance.

   Alternatively, in the semivariogram map, click and hold either of the red directional indicator lines and drag to the desired angle.

4. Click the up or down arrows of the Bandwidth.

   Alternatively, in the semivariogram map, click and hold either of the purple lines located on the bounding square. Drag to the desired width.

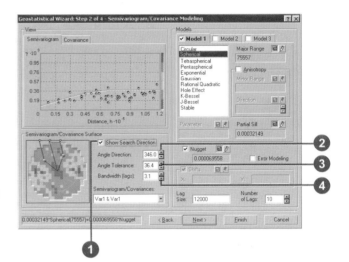

Checking the anisotropy check box

Notice the single yellow line becomes many lines when anisotropy is checked. The yellow lines show the semivariogram model for many different directions. The models (the yellow lines) are a theoretical "best fit" semivariogram model to the empirical semivariogram. The Geostatistical Analyst automatically calculates the optimum parameters (e.g., the Major Range, Minor Range, and Angle of Direction) to account for the anisotropic influence.

Checking the semivariogram after anisotropy is checked

Check Show Search Direction after checking Anisotropy. If the model fits well, the yellow line should change to fit the changing scatter of empirical semivariogram values when the angle of search direction is changed.

Calculating the optimal parameters

The pencil icon above the major and minor range and direction input boxes allows you to edit the input values. By clicking the calculator icon to the left of the pencil, the optimal values will be calculated and set for the input parameters.

Modeling anisotropy

1. Check Anisotropy on the Semivariogram/Covariance Modeling dialog box.

   Notice the single yellow line becomes many lines when anisotropy is checked.

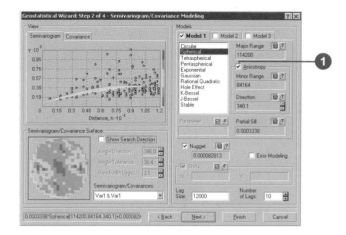

Altering the anisotropy parameters

1. Check Anisotropy on the Semivariogram/Covariance Modeling dialog box.

   Note: The Minor Range and Direction check boxes become active.

2. To change the major range, click the pencil icon above the Major Range input (which makes the input box active) and type in the desired range.

3. To change the minor range, click the pencil icon above the Minor Range input (which makes the input box active) and type in the desired range. ▶

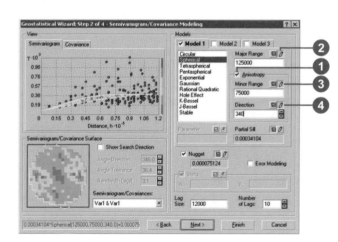

4. To change the angle direction, click the pencil icon above the Direction input (which makes the input box active) and type in the desired angle.

Changing the lag size and number of lags

1. On the Semivariogram/ Covariance Modeling dialog box, type the desired Lag Size.

2. Click the up or down arrows or type in the desired value in order to change the Number of Lags.

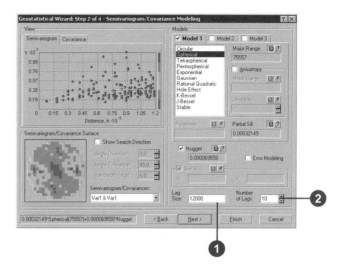

Changing the partial sill and nugget

1. On the Semivariogram/ Covariance Modeling dialog box, click on the pencil above the Partial Sill input (which makes the input box active) and type in the desired value.

2. Check the Nugget check box, click on the pencil icon above the Nugget input (which makes the input box active), and type in the desired value.

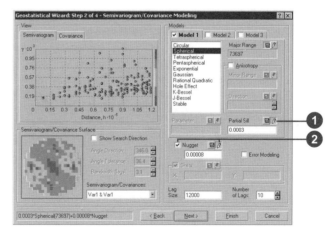

Handling measurement error

1. Check the Error Modeling check box.

2. Move the scroll bar to determine the percentages of MicroStructure and Measurement Error for the nugget.

   Alternatively, type the percentages or values into the input boxes.

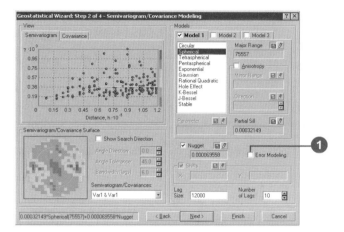

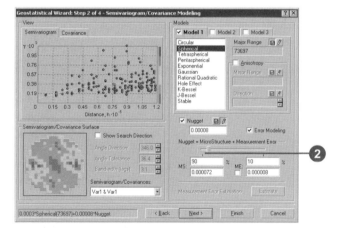

Determining the neighborhood search size

Things that are closer to one another are more alike—as the data locations become farther away from a location where the value is unknown, they may not be as useful when predicting the value at an unmeasured location. At some distance, the points will have no correlation with the prediction location, and it is possible that they may even be located in an area much different than the unknown location. Therefore, it is common practice to specify a search neighborhood that limits the number and the configuration of the points that will be used in the predictions. There are two controlling mechanisms to limit the points used, namely specifying the shape of the neighborhood and establishing constraints on the points within the shape.

The shape of the search neighborhood will be dictated by the input data. For instance, if your data is evenly sampled and has no directional autocorrelation (isotropy), you will want to include points evenly in all directions from the unknown location. To do so, you will probably want to specify your neighborhood shape to be a circle. However, if you know that there is directional autocorrelation (anisotropy), such as is caused by wind pollutants, you may wish to use an elliptical search neighborhood scheme with the major axis parallel to the wind when interpolating a surface. You will do so because you know that points upwind and downwind from the prediction location are more like the prediction location's value at longer distances than those perpendicular to the wind's direction.

The search neighborhood shape should be based on an understanding of the spatial locations and the spatial autocorrelation of the dataset. Understanding the spatial locations and autocorrelations is done through the ESDA tools and with the tools within the Geostatistical Analyst Wizard. For instance, in the dialog box below, you can see that a directional autocorrelation (i.e., anisotropy) is influencing the shape of the semivariogram. The semivariogram curve increases slowly in the NNW

direction (approximately 340°) and reaches its range at approximately 114 km (the lowest yellow line in the variogram). In the WSW direction, the semivariogram curve increases more rapidly (the uppermost yellow line). The range in this direction is approximately 84 km. Since points separated by a distance greater than the range are not correlated, the information can be used to define the search strategy.

Semivariogram envelope

Check Anisotropy to show semivariogram envelope (i.e., semivariogram curves for all directions).

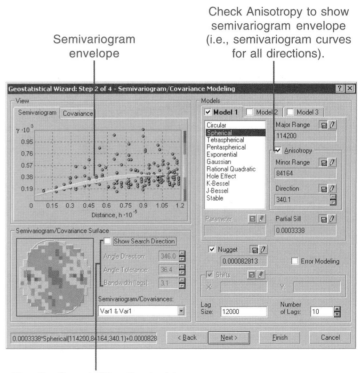

Use the Search Direction tool to determine the location of the range in a particular direction.

The search neighborhood in this example can be defined as an ellipse with semimajor and semiminor axes of 128 km and 74 km, respectively, and with a rotation angle of 340°.

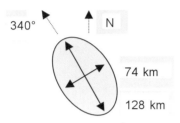

The Searching Neighborhood dialog box allows you to define the length of the semimajor and semiminor axes and the direction of the semimajor axis. A circle will have equal lengths for semimajor and semiminor axes.

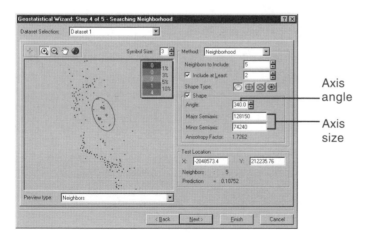

Once the shape is defined, the second mechanism for controlling the neighborhood involves establishing constraints within the shape. First, the number of points to be used within the neighborhood for the predictions must be defined. The Geostatistical Analyst allows you to select the desirable and minimum number of points to use. Second, to avoid bias in a particular direction, the circle or ellipse can be divided into sectors from which an equal number of points are selected.

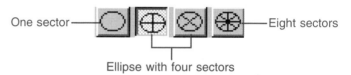

One sector — Eight sectors

Ellipse with four sectors

This is particularly useful when the sample points have been collected on transects or a grid. The diagram below demonstrates a case in which the points closest to the unknown location are those on a single transect. The constraints of the circle neighborhood below are that it should contain five neighbors in each prediction. The unknown location is identified in green, and the five closest neighbors are in yellow. Other points within the circle are not included because they are farther away.

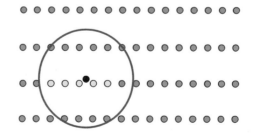

A better prediction might be made if points from the other transects are included in the prediction. The diagram below shows a four-sector neighborhood that should include at least three points in each sector but no more than five. A total of 16 points will be used in predicting the unknown point below (in green). The points that will be used from each sector are colored by sector.

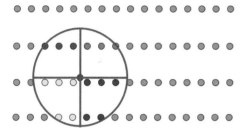

The number of points and sectors used should be defined objectively and based on the spatial locations of the sample data. You need enough points to provide a meaningful prediction at any given location; however, you do not want to include points that are too far away from the prediction location. For example, if you selected a maximum of five points and a minimum of two points (i.e., the least amount to be included) and four sectors, the total number of points to be used would be 20. If the minimum required points are not available in any given sector, the software selects the nearest available point(s) outside that sector. However, the search outside the sector will be limited to the area that falls within the area defined by extending the sector lines indefinitely. If five points are not available in any given sector extension, the total number of points will be less than 20.

The points highlighted in the data view window give an indication of the absolute value of the weights that will be associated with each point in the calculation of the value at the prediction location (the center of the circle or ellipse). In the example below,

the prediction location is at the intersection of the sectors, and four points (red) will have weights of more than 10 percent. The larger the absolute value of the weight, the more impact the point will have on the calculation of the value at the prediction location.

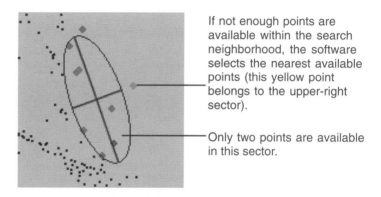

If not enough points are available within the search neighborhood, the software selects the nearest available points (this yellow point belongs to the upper-right sector).

Only two points are available in this sector.

Besides using the semivariogram, there are several other means for determining the search neighborhood shape and constraints. And the examination of the spatial locations of the samples in ArcMap can also assist in the neighborhood definition. For example, the samples may have been taken on transects, creating a grid with the points closer together in the east–west direction than in the north–south direction. In this situation, an appropriate search ellipse may have the semimajor axis in the north–south direction. The axes of the ellipse can be defined in such a way that a relatively equal number of points are within the bounds (or limits) of that ellipse in both directions.

The Searching Neighborhood dialog box

Number of points used to predict a value at a test location.

The minimum number of points to be used (they may lie outside the search ellipse).

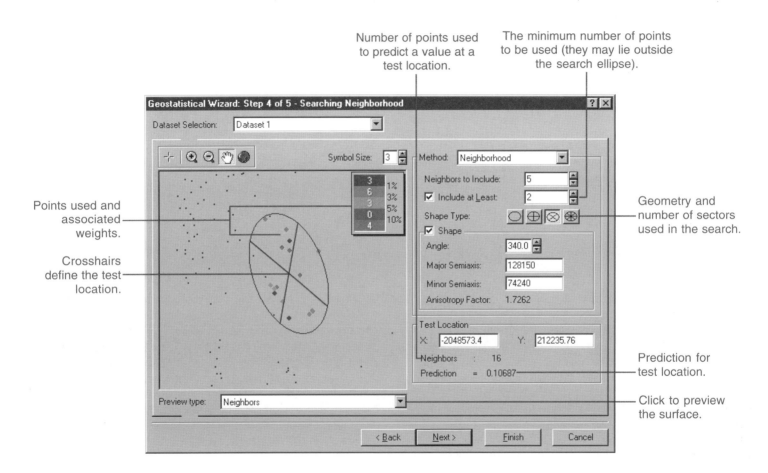

Points used and associated weights.

Crosshairs define the test location.

Geometry and number of sectors used in the search.

Prediction for test location.

Click to preview the surface.

Determining the neighborhood search size

The neighborhood search size defines the neighborhood shape and the constraints of the points within the neighborhood that will be used in the prediction of an unmeasured location.

You set the neighborhood parameters by looking for the locations of the points in the data view window and using prior knowledge gained in ESDA and semivariogram/covariance modeling.

Tip

Assessing a neighborhood

The impact of the search neighborhood can be assessed using the cross-validation and validation tools that are available in Geostatistical Analyst. If necessary, the search neighborhood can be redefined and another surface created.

Changing the number of points to include in a neighborhood

1. On the Searching Neighborhood dialog box, click the Neighbors to Include up and down arrows.

   Alternatively, type in the desired value.

2. To set a minimum of points to include in the neighborhood, check the Include at Least check box and click the up and down arrows until the desired value is reached.

   Alternatively, type the value in the input field.

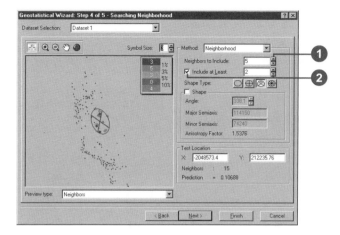

Tip

Weight values

Weights are displayed as absolute values, that is, -6 percent and 6 percent are therefore "equal".

Tip

It is possible for the Minor semiaxis value to be greater than the Major semiaxis.

Altering the shape of the neighborhood

1. On the Searching Neighborhood dialog box, click the desired ellipse icon to change the default neighborhood shape type.

2. Check the Shape check box.

   The controls in the shape frame will become active.

3. Click the Angle up or down arrows or type in the desired angle to alter the angle of the ellipse.

4. Type the desired value in the Major and Minor Semiaxis input fields to alter the shape of the ellipse.

   In the display window of the dialog box, the ellipse will reflect the changes.

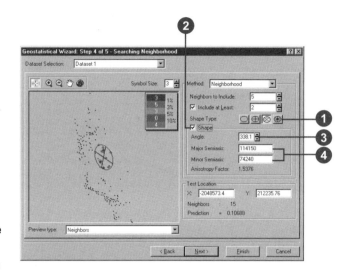

Tip

The predicted value

On the Searching Neighborhood dialog box go to the Test Location frame; there the values in the X and Y input fields represent the map coordinates for the prediction (which is also the center of the ellipse in the display window).

Determining the prediction for a specific location

1. The number of neighbors used for prediction and the prediction are displayed below the input fields (in the bottom right of the dialog box). To initiate a new prediction location, click the desired location in the display area of the dialog box.

2. Alternatively, enter the location in the X and Y input fields.

    The prediction and number of neighbors are updated immediately with the new location.

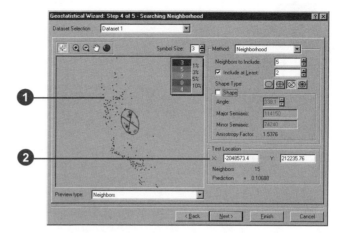

Altering the map view

1. On the Searching Neighborhood dialog box, to zoom in on the map display, click the Zoom In button, then drag a box around the area of the map on which the zoom will occur.

2. To zoom out on the map display, click the Zoom Out button.

3. To pan around in the map display, click the Pan button and move the mouse into the map display, hold down the left mouse button, and move the cursor.

   The map will move in coordination with the cursor.

4. To display the map using the full extent, click the Full Extent button.

5. To preview the output surface, click the Preview type dropdown menu and click Surface. To return to the previous view, click Neighbors.

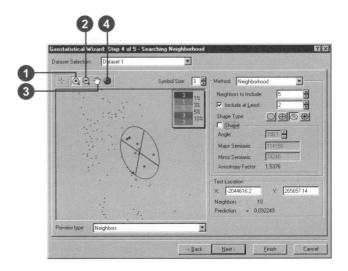

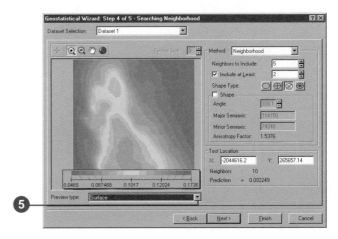

Performing cross-validation and validation

Before you produce the final surface, you should have some idea of how well the model predicts the values at unknown locations. Cross-validation and validation help you make an informed decision as to which model provides the best predictions. The calculated statistics serve as diagnostics that indicate whether the model and/or its associated parameter values are reasonable.

Cross validation and validation withhold one or more data samples and then make a prediction to the same data location. In this way, you can compare the predicted value to the observed value and from this get useful information about the kriging model (e.g., the semivariogram parameters and the searching neighborhood). The difference between cross-validation and validation will be discussed next.

Cross-validation uses all of the data to estimate the autocorrelation model. Then it removes each data location, one at a time, and predicts the associated data value. For example, the diagram below shows 10 randomly distributed data points. Cross-validation omits a point (red point) and calculates the value of this location using the remaining nine points (blue points). The predicted and actual values at the location of the omitted point are compared. This procedure is repeated for a second point, and so on. For all points, cross-validation compares the measured and predicted values. In a sense, cross-validation "cheats" a little by using all of the data to estimate the autocorrelation model. After completing cross-validation, some data locations may be set aside as unusual, requiring the autocorrelation model to be refit.

Validation first removes part of the data—call it the test dataset—and then uses the rest of the data—call it the training dataset—to develop the trend and autocorrelation models to be used for prediction. In the Geostatistical Analyst, you create the test and training datasets using the Create Subset tools. Other than that, the types of graphs and summary statistics used to compare predictions to true values are similar for both validation and cross-validation. Validation creates a model for only a subset of the data, so it does not directly check your final model, which should include all available data. Rather, validation checks whether a "protocol" of decisions is valid, for example, choice of semivariogram model, choice of lag size, choice of search neighborhood, and so on. If the decision protocol works for the validation dataset, you can feel comfortable that it also works for the whole dataset.

Geostatistical Analyst gives several graphs and summaries of the measurement values versus the predicted values. Starting with the plots, a scatter plot of predicted versus measurement values is given. One might expect that these should scatter around the 1:1 line (the black dashed line below). However, the slope is usually less than one. It is a property of kriging that tends to underpredict large values and overpredict small values, as shown in the following figure.

 And so on for all points

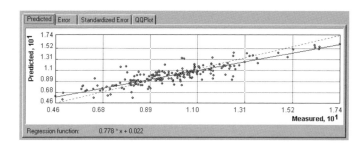

The fitted line through the scatter of points is given in blue with the equation given just below the plot. The error plot is the same as the prediction plot, except here the true values are subtracted from the predicted values. For the standardized error plot, the measurement values are subtracted from the predicted values and then divided by the estimated kriging standard errors. All three of these plots help to show how well kriging is predicting. If all the data was independent (no autocorrelation), all predictions will be the same (every prediction would be the mean of the measured data), so the blue line would be horizontal. With autocorrelation and a good kriging model, the blue line should be closer to the 1:1 (black dashed) line. You can also see the scatter about the line (a few are given in the figure above as green lines). The tighter the scatter about the 1:1 line, the better.

The final plot is a QQPlot. This shows the quantiles of the difference between the predicted and measurement values divided by the estimated kriging standard errors and the corresponding quantiles from a standard normal distribution. If the errors of the predictions from their true values are normally distributed, the points should lie roughly along the dashed line. If the errors are normally distributed, you can be confident of using methods that rely on normality (e.g., quantile maps in ordinary kriging).

See Chapter 4, 'Exploratory Spatial Data Analysis', for more on QQPlots.

Finally, some summary statistics on the kriging prediction errors are given in the lower left. You use these as diagnostics for three basic ideas:

1. You would like your predictions to be unbiased (centered on the measurement values). If the prediction errors are unbiased, the mean prediction error should be near zero. However, this value depends on the scale of the data, so to standardize these the standardized prediction errors give the prediction errors divided by their prediction standard errors. The mean of these should also be near zero.

2. You would like your predictions to be as close to the measurment values as possible. The root-mean-square prediction errors are computed as the square root of the average of the squared distances of the green lines in the prediction plot above. The shorter the green lines, the closer the predictions are to their true values, and the smaller the root-mean-square prediction errors. This summary can be used to compare different models by seeing how closely they predict the measurement values. The smaller the root-mean-square prediction error, the better.

3. You would like your assessment of uncertainty, the prediction standard errors, to be valid. Each of the kriging methods gives the estimated prediction kriging standard errors. Besides making predictions, we estimate the variability of the predictions from the measurement values. It is important to get the correct variability. For example, in ordinary kriging (assuming the residuals are normally distributed) the quantile and probability maps depend on the kriging standard errors as much as the predictions themselves. If the average standard errors are close to the root-mean-square prediction errors, then you are correctly assessing the variability in prediction.

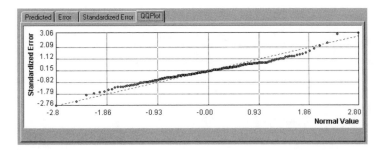

If the average standard errors are greater than the root-mean-square prediction errors, then you are overestimating the variability of your predictions; if the average standard errors are less than the root-mean-square prediction errors, then you are underestimating the variability in your predictions. Another way to look at this is to divide each prediction error by its estimated prediction standard error. They should be similar, on average, and so the root-mean-square standardized errors should be close to one if the prediction standard errors are valid. If the root-mean-square standardized errors are greater than 1, you are underestimating the variability in our predictions; if the root-mean-square standardized errors are less than 1, you are overestimating the variability in your predictions.

The Cross Validation and Validation dialog box

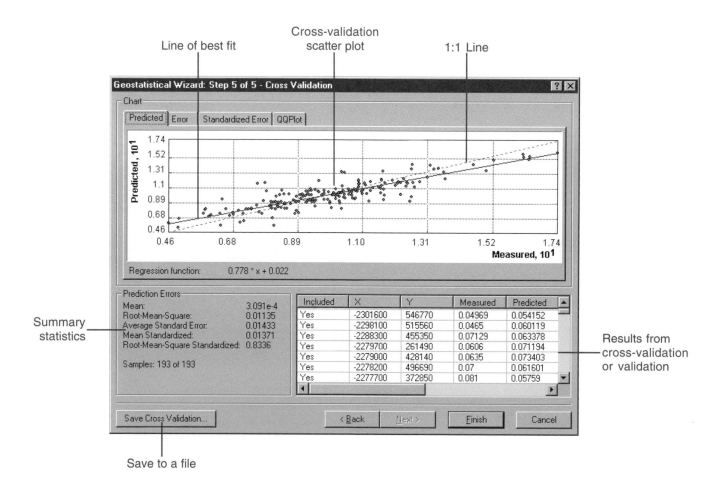

Line of best fit

Cross-validation scatter plot

1:1 Line

Geostatistical Wizard: Step 5 of 5 - Cross Validation

Chart

| Predicted | Error | Standardized Error | QQPlot |

Regression function: 0.778 * x + 0.022

Prediction Errors

Mean: 3.091e-4
Root-Mean-Square: 0.01135
Average Standard Error: 0.01433
Mean Standardized: 0.01371
Root-Mean-Square Standardized: 0.8336

Samples: 193 of 193

Included	X	Y	Measured	Predicted
Yes	-2301600	546770	0.04969	0.054152
Yes	-2298100	515560	0.0465	0.060119
Yes	-2288300	455350	0.07129	0.063378
Yes	-2279700	261490	0.0606	0.071194
Yes	-2279000	428140	0.0635	0.073403
Yes	-2278200	496690	0.07	0.061601
Yes	-2277700	372850	0.081	0.05759

Summary statistics

Results from cross-validation or validation

Save Cross Validation...   < Back   Next >   Finish   Cancel

Save to a file

Performing cross-validation to assess parameter selections

Cross-validation allows you to determine "how good" your model is. Your goal should be to have standardized mean prediction errors near 0, small root-mean-square prediction errors, average standard error near root-mean-square prediction errors, and standardized root-mean-square prediction errors near 1.

The spread of the points should be as close as possible around the dashed gray line. Look for points that deviate greatly from the line.

Examining the predicted fit

1. On the Cross Validation dialog box, select either the Predicted, Error, Standardized Error, or QQPlot tab according to the desired method in which you want to view the results.

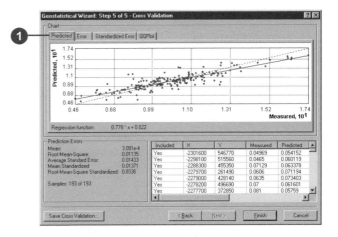

Selecting a particular point

1. On the Cross Validation dialog box, in the table at the bottom right, click on the row representing the point of interest.

   When a row is selected, the point is highlighted in the chart above.

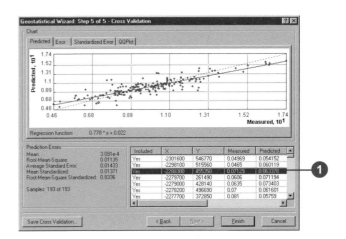

Tip

Viewing a saved table

To view the saved table, click Add on the Standard toolbar, navigate to the database, double-click it, then add the tables. Right-click on them in the ArcMap table of contents and click Open.

Saving the cross-validation statistics to a file

1. Click Save Cross Validation.

2. Navigate to the location to save the dataset.

3. Type the name of the dataset.

4. Click the type of dataset.

5. Click Save.

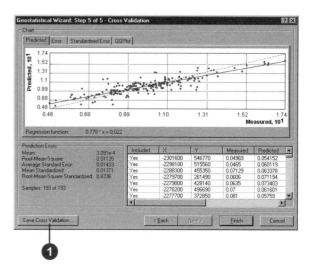

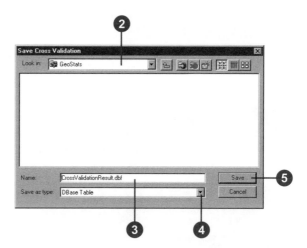

Assessing decision protocol using validation

Validation allows you to evaluate your predictions.

Your goal should be to have standardized mean prediction errors near 0, small root-mean-square prediction errors, average standard errors near root-mean-square prediction errors, and standardized root-mean-square prediction errors near 1.

The spread of the points should be as close as possible around the dashed gray line. Look for points that deviate greatly from the line.

Tip

Dividing the training and test data

Keep the slider in the center to split the data in half equally between training and test data.

See Also

See 'Performing cross-validation or validation to see how well the parameters fit' (prior to these tasks) for a comparison of cross-validation and validation.

Creating the subsets to use for validation

1. Add the dataset that you wish to subset to ArcMap.

2. Click Create Subsets.

3. Click the dropdown arrow and click on the dataset that you wish to subset.

4. Click Next.

5. Optionally, change the location and/or name for the output geodatabase file.

6. Optionally, change the default subset names.

7. Click and drag the slider to the required position.

8. Click Finish.

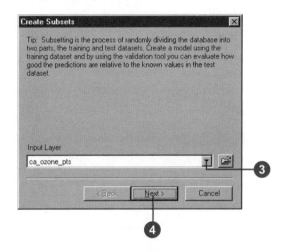

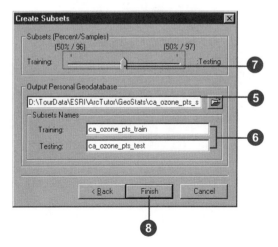

Viewing all rows and columns

Use the scroll bars to view all rows and columns in the table.

Tip

Highlighting values

When a row is selected, the point is highlighted in the chart above. Click a column to sort by. This can help find specific points in the graph.

Tip

Opening a saved table

To view a saved table, click Add on the Standard toolbar of ArcMap, navigate to the database, double-click it, then add the tables. Right-click on them in the ArcMap table of contents and click Open.

Performing validation

1. Click the Add Data button and navigate to the test and training datasets (created following the steps on the previous page). Click Add.

2. Start the Geostatistical Analyst Wizard.

3. Click the Input Data dropdown arrow and click the training layer (created by subsetting the original dataset on the previous page).

4. Click the Attribute dropdown arrow and click the attribute you want to use in the interpolation.

5. Check the Validation check box.

6. Click the Input Data dropdown arrow and click the test dataset (created by subsetting the original dataset on the previous page).

7. Click the Attribute dropdown arrow and click the same attribute you chose for the training dataset.

8. Click the Method you wish to use.

9. Click Next on this and all subsequent dialog boxes until you reach the Validation dialog box.

10. Optionally, click to save the validation table to a data-base.

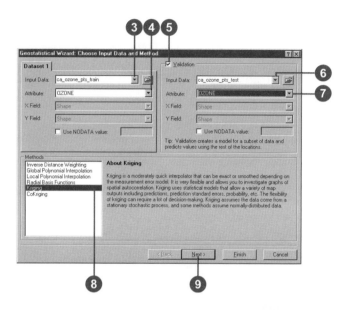

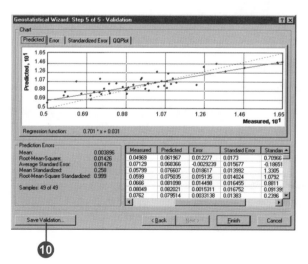

Comparing one model with another

Comparison helps you determine how good the model that created a geostatistical layer is relative to another model. The two geostatistical layers that you are comparing could have been created by two different models (e.g., IDW and ordinary kriging), or they could have been created with the same model but with different parameters. In the first case, you are comparing which method is best for your data and, in the second, you are examining the effects of different input parameters on a model when creating the output surface.

The Comparison dialog box uses the cross-validation statistics as discussed in the previous section. However, it allows you to examine the statistics and the plots side by side. Generally, the best model is the one that has the standardized mean nearest to zero, the smallest root-mean-square prediction error, the average standard error nearest the root-mean-square prediction error, and the standardized root-mean-square prediction error nearest to one.

It is common practice to create many surfaces before one is identified as "best" and will be final in itself or will be passed into a larger model (e.g., a suitability model for siting houses) to solve an existing problem. You can systematically compare each surface with another, eliminating the "worst" of the two being compared, until the two "best" surfaces remain and are compared with one another. You can conclude that for this particular analysis the best of the final two surfaces is the "best" surface possible.

Concerns when comparing methods and models

There are two issues when comparing the results from different methods and/or models: one is optimality, and the other is validity.

For example, the root-mean-square prediction error may be smaller for a particular model. Therefore, you might conclude that this is the "optimal" model. However, when comparing to another model, the root-mean-square prediction error may be closer to the average estimated prediction standard error. This is a more valid model because when you predict at a point without data, you only have the estimated standard errors to assess your uncertainty of that prediction. When the average estimated prediction standard errors are close to the root-mean-square prediction errors from cross-validation, then you are confident that the prediction standard errors are appropriate.

As well as the statistics provided in the Comparison dialog box, you should also use prior information that you have on the dataset and that you derived in ESDA when evaluating which model is "best". Refer to the previous section on cross-validation and validation for a complete discussion on how the statistics have been derived and how they should be used.

The Cross Validation Comparison dialog box

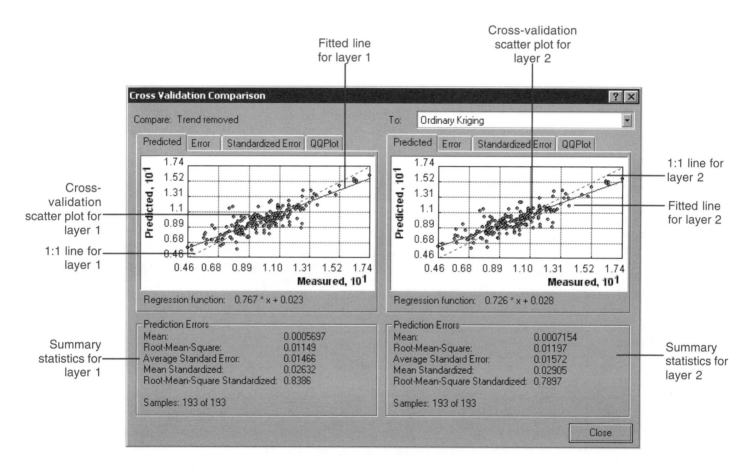

Fitted line
for layer 1

Cross-validation
scatter plot for
layer 2

Cross Validation Comparison

Compare: Trend removed   To: Ordinary Kriging

| Predicted | Error | Standardized Error | QQPlot |

Cross-
validation
scatter plot for
layer 1

1:1 line for
layer 1

1:1 line for
layer 2

Fitted line
for layer 2

Regression function: 0.767 * x + 0.023

Regression function: 0.726 * x + 0.028

Summary
statistics for
layer 1

Prediction Errors
Mean: 0.0005697
Root-Mean-Square: 0.01149
Average Standard Error: 0.01466
Mean Standardized: 0.02632
Root-Mean-Square Standardized: 0.8386

Samples: 193 of 193

Prediction Errors
Mean: 0.0007154
Root-Mean-Square: 0.01197
Average Standard Error: 0.01572
Mean Standardized: 0.02905
Root-Mean-Square Standardized: 0.7897

Samples: 193 of 193

Summary
statistics for
layer 2

Close

Comparing one model with another

When comparing models you should look for one with the standardized mean nearest to zero, the smallest root-mean-square prediction error, the average prediction standard error nearest the root-mean-square prediction error, and the standardized root-mean-square prediction error nearest to one.

To compare models you must have two geostatistical layers for comparison (created using the Geostatistical Analyst). These two layers may have been created using different interpolation methods (e.g., IDW and ordinary kriging) or that were created using the same method with different parameters.

See Also

See 'Performing cross-validation or validation to see how well the parameters fit' (prior to these tasks) for a comparison of cross-validation and validation.

Performing comparison

1. Right-click one of the layers in the ArcMap table of contents you wish to compare and click on Compare.

2. Click the second layer in the comparison in the To dropdown menu.

3. Click the various tabs to see the different results of the comparison.

4. Click Close to close the Cross Validation Comparison dialog box.

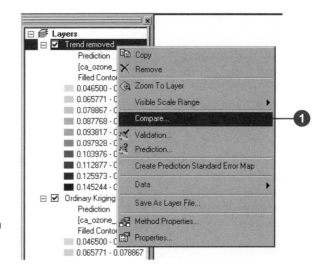

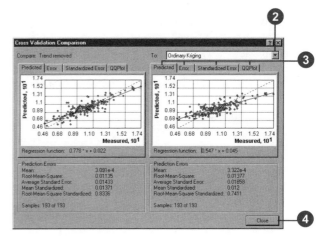

Modeling distributions and determining transformations

Box–Cox, arcsine, and log transformations

The Geostatistical Analyst allows the use of several transformations including the Box–Cox (also known as power transformations), logarithmic, and arcsine. Suppose you observe data $Z(\mathbf{s})$, and there is some transformation $Y(\mathbf{s}) = t(Z(\mathbf{s}))$. Usually, you want to find the transformation so that $Y(\mathbf{s})$ is normally distributed. Now, what often happens is that the transformation also yields data that has constant variance through the study area. Now examine each transformation.

The Box–Cox transformation is

$$Y(\mathbf{s}) = (Z(\mathbf{s})^\lambda - 1)/\lambda$$

for $\lambda \neq 0$. For example, suppose that your data is composed of counts of some phenomenon. For these types of data, the variance is often related to the mean. That is, if you have small counts in part of your study area, the variability in that local region will be smaller than the variability in another region where the counts are larger. In this case, the square root transformation will help to make the variances more constant throughout the study area and often makes the data appear normally distributed as well. The square root transformation is a special case of the Box–Cox transformation when $\lambda = \frac{1}{2}$.

The log transformation is actually also a special case of the Box–Cox transformations when $\lambda = 0$; the transformation is

$$Y(\mathbf{s}) = \ln(Z(\mathbf{s}))$$

for $Z(\mathbf{s}) > 0$, and ln is the natural logarithm. A consequence of the log transformation is the prediction method known as lognormal kriging, whereas for all other values of λ, the associated prediction method is known as transgaussian kriging. The log transformation is often used where the data has a skewed distribution and there are few very large values. These large values may be localized in your study area, and the log transformation will help to make the variances more constant and normalize your data.

The arcsine transformation is

$$Y(\mathbf{s}) = \sin^{-1}(Z(\mathbf{s}))$$

for $Z(\mathbf{s})$ between 0 and 1. The arcsine transformation can be used for data that is proportions or percentages. Often, when data is proportions, the variance is smallest near 0 and 1 and largest near 0.5. Then the arcsine transformation often yields data that has constant variance throughout the study area and often makes the data appear normally distributed as well.

Normal score transformation

The normal score transformation ranks your dataset, from lowest to highest values, and matches these ranks to equivalent ranks from a normal distribution; then the transformation is defined by taking values from the normal distribution at that rank. This can be seen from the following figures. In the first, see a histogram of the data, which is commonly plotted when doing exploratory data analysis. However, an equivalent expression of the data is to use the cumulative distribution, given on the right.

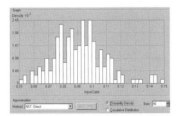 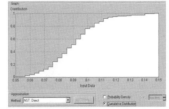

Work with the cumulative distribution to obtain the normal score transformation. Take the observed cumulative distribution and match it with a cumulative distribution of a standard normal distribution. This can best be seen via the graphic procedure given below.

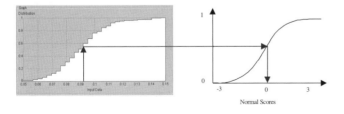

In this example, a value near 0.09 in the original data is transformed to a value just above zero as a normal-score transformation. In the Geostatistical Analyst, there are three approximation methods: direct, linear, and Gaussian kernels. The direct method uses the observed cumulative distribution; the linear method fits lines between each "step" of the cumulative distribution; and the Gaussian kernels method approximates the probability distribution by fitting a linear combination of density cumulative distributions. After making predictions on the transformed scale, it is necessary to back-transform to get the predictions back to the original scale. For example, if you use direct approximation of normal distribution, the back transformation will look like this:

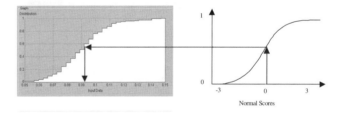

The choice of approximation method depends on the assumptions you are willing to make and the smoothness of the approximation. The direct method is the least smooth and has the fewest assumptions; the linear method is in between; and the Gaussian kernels method has the smoothest back transformation, but it also has the strongest assumptions (that the data distribution can be approximated by a finite mixture of normal distributions).

The Normal Score Transformation distribution dialog box

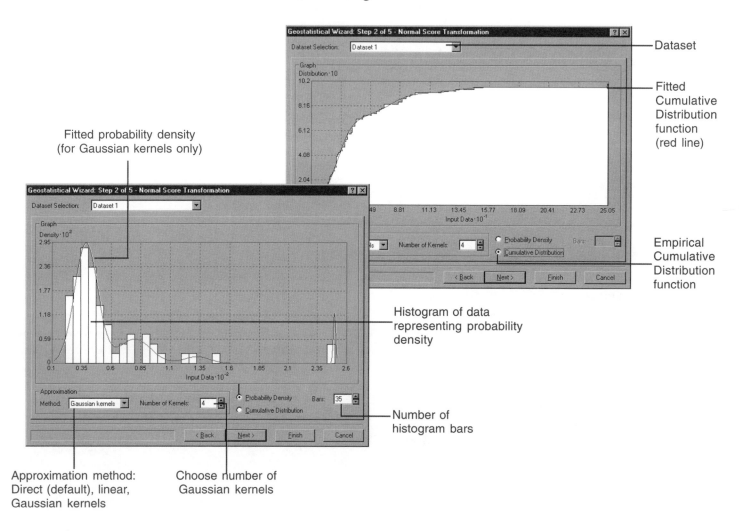

Fitted probability density
(for Gaussian kernels only)

Dataset

Fitted
Cumulative
Distribution
function
(red line)

Empirical
Cumulative
Distribution
function

Histogram of data
representing probability
density

Number of
histogram bars

Approximation method:
Direct (default), linear,
Gaussian kernels

Choose number of
Gaussian kernels

Comparing normal score transformation to other transformations

The normal score transformation (NST) can be compared to the Box–Cox, arcsine, and log (BAL) transformations. The most fundamental difference is that the NST transformation function changes with each particular dataset, whereas BAL does not (e.g., the log transformation function is always the natural logarithm). However, the goal of the NST is to make all random errors for the whole population (not only the sample) normally distributed. Thus, it is important that the cumulative distribution from the sample reflects the true cumulative distribution of the whole population. From the point of view of classical statistics, the NST transformation when applied to nonspatial data could be viewed as a rank-based method. However, NST can be useful for geostatistics because when the data is dependent it may be easier to detect and model autocorrelation using the NST. For this reason, the NST must occur after detrending since covariance and variograms are calculated on residuals after trend correction. Contrast this with BAL transformation, where any relationship between the variance and the trend is removed. Hence, after the BAL transformation the trend and model autocorrelation is removed (optionally). It is often a consequence that residuals that are approximately normally distributed appear, but it is not a specific goal of BAL transformation like it is for the NST transformation.

Using transformations (log, Box–Cox, and arcsine)

Using transformations makes variances constant throughout your study area and makes the data more normally distributed.

Use the histogram and normal QQPlots in ESDA to try different transformations to attain a normal distribution.

Some geostatistical methods are critically dependent on the data coming from a normal distribution—for example, disjunctive kriging and quantile and probability maps for ordinary, simple, and universal kriging. So, transformatting the data can make the data more normal.

Tip

When you can transform
The transformation option can be accessed using either the kriging or the cokriging methods on the Choose Input Data and Method dialog box.

Using transformations

1. On the Geostatistical Method Selection dialog box, click the desired transformation in the Transformation dropdown menu.

2. Click Next.

3. Follow the dialog boxes to create a surface.

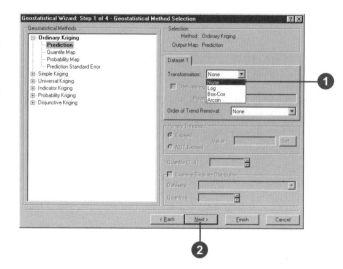

Using the normal score transformation

The normal score transformation transforms your data to univariate normality for use with simple and disjunctive kriging.

It is a good idea to compare the fitted model to the empirical cumulative distribution function for each of the three NST approximation methods.

Modeling distributions

1. Click the Simple or Disjunctive Kriging interpolation method to use for the distribution.

2. On the Geostatistical Method Selection dialog box, click Normal Score in the Transformation dropdown list.

3. Click Next.

4. Alternatively, click Cumulative Distribution to switch the display of the graph.

5. Alternatively, type the number of bars you wish to display in the chart.

6. Click the Dataset Selection dropdown arrow to switch between datasets (only for cokriging where you have two or more datasets).

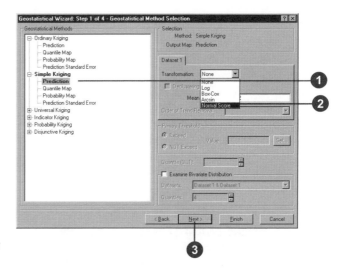

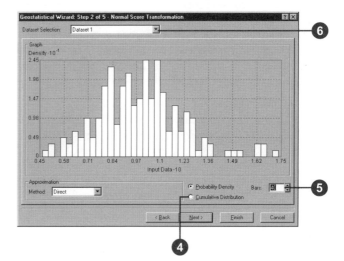

Checking for the bivariate normal distribution

Disjunctive kriging requires that the data has a bivariate normal distribution. Also, to develop probability and quantile maps, assume that the data comes from a full multivariate normal distribution. To check for a univariate normal distribution, you can use normal QQPlots. Now check for bivariate normality. (Neither of these checks guarantees that the data comes from a full multivariate normal distribution, but it is often reasonable to assume so based on these diagnostic tools.) Consider the following probability statement:

$$f(p,\mathbf{h}) = Prob[Z(\mathbf{s}) \leq z_p, Z(\mathbf{s}+\mathbf{h}) \leq z_p]$$

where z_p is the standard normal quantile for some probability p. For example, a familiar standard normal quantile occurs when $p = 0.975$, then $z_p = 1.96$; when $p = 0.5$, then $z_p = 0$; and when $p = 0.025$, then $z_p = -1.96$. The probability statement above takes a variable Z at location $\mathbf{s}$, and another variable Z at some other location $\mathbf{s}+\mathbf{h}$, and gives the probability that they are *both* less than z_p. This probability statement is a function $f(p,\mathbf{h})$, depending on p (and consequently z_p) and $\mathbf{h}$. The function will also depend on the amount of autocorrelation between $Z(\mathbf{s})$ and $Z(\mathbf{s}+\mathbf{h})$.

Now assume that $Z(\mathbf{s})$ and $Z(\mathbf{s}+\mathbf{h})$ have a bivariate normal distribution. If the autocorrelation is known, then there are formulas for $f(p,\mathbf{h})$. First, suppose $\mathbf{h}$ is constant, and only p changes. Then, we would expect the function to look like this:

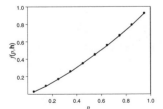 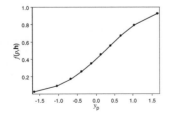

The right panel looks like a cumulative probability distribution. Now, suppose that p is fixed, and $f(p,\mathbf{h})$ changes with $\mathbf{h}$.

First, suppose that $\mathbf{h}$ is very small. In that case, $Prob[Z(\mathbf{s}) \leq z_p, Z(\mathbf{s}+\mathbf{h}) \leq z_p]$ is very nearly the same as $Prob[Z(\mathbf{s}) \leq z_p] = p$. Next, suppose that $\mathbf{h}$ is very large. In that case, $Prob[Z(\mathbf{s}) \leq z_p, Z(\mathbf{s}+\mathbf{h}) \leq z_p]$ is very nearly the same as $Prob[Z(\mathbf{s}) \leq z_p] \times Prob[Z(\mathbf{s}+\mathbf{h}) \leq z_p] = p^2$ (because $Z(\mathbf{s})$ and $Z(\mathbf{s}+\mathbf{h})$ are very nearly independent). Thus, for fixed p, it is expected that $f(p,\mathbf{h})$ varies between p and p^2. Now, considering $f(p,\mathbf{h})$ as a function of both p and the length of $\mathbf{h}$, you might observe something like the following figure.

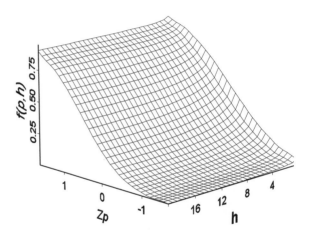

This function can be converted to semivariograms and covariance functions for indicators. If $Prob[Z(\mathbf{s}) \leq z_p, Z(\mathbf{s}+\mathbf{h}) \leq z_p] = E[I(Z(\mathbf{s}) \leq z_p) \times I(Z(\mathbf{s}+\mathbf{h}) \leq z_p)]$, where I(*statement*) is the indicator function that is 1 if *statement* is true, otherwise it is 0, then the covariance function for the indicators for fixed p is

$$C_I(\mathbf{h};p) = f(p,\mathbf{h}) - p^2$$

and the variogram for indicators for fixed p is,

$$\gamma_I(\mathbf{h};p) = p - f(p,\mathbf{h})$$

Therefore, you can estimate the variogram and covariance function on the indicators of the original data and use these to obtain the expected variograms and covariance functions of indicators for various values of p. For example, they will look like this:

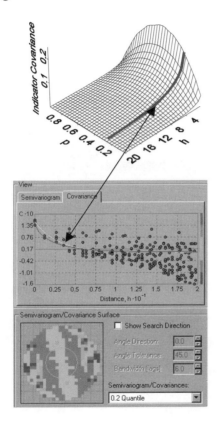

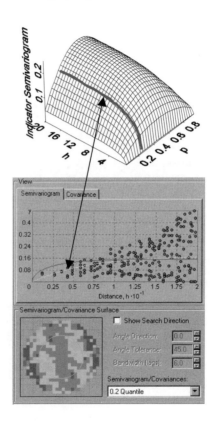

The red dots in the figure above (from the Semivariogram/Covariance Modeling dialog) are the values for the empirical covariance and semivariogram on the indicator variables. The green line is the theoretical curve of an indicator semivariogram or indicator covariance, assuming the data comes from a bivariate normal distribution, and the yellow line is fitted to the observed indicator data. Thus, the green line and the yellow line should be similar if the data has a bivariate normal distribution.

The Examine Bivariate Distribution dialog box

Empirical covariance on indicators

Theoretical curve of indicator covariance, assuming data comes from bivariate normal distribution (green line)

Fitted covariance function to empirical covariance on indicators (yellow line)

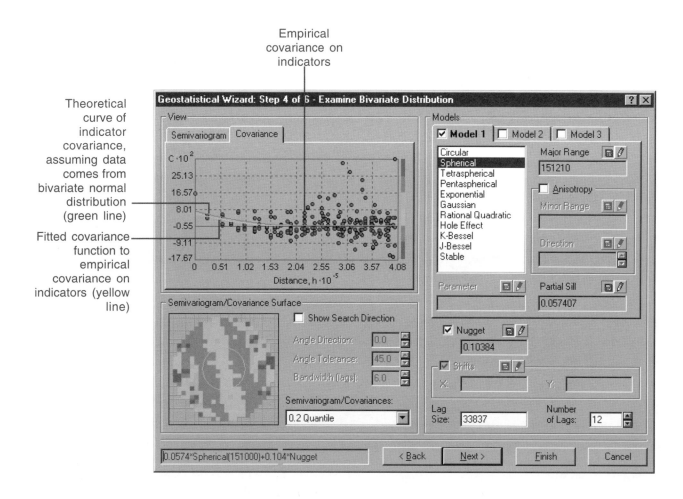

Checking for bivariate distribution

This is a means to determine if the data comes from a bivariate normal distribution. The yellow and green lines should be close to each other if the data comes from a bivariate normal distribution.

Disjunctive kriging requires the data to come from a bivariate normal distribution. Probability and quantile maps in simple kriging require that the data comes from a multivariate normal distribution, and the bivariate check can help justify the multivariate assumption.

Tip

Methods that enable the bivariate distribution to be checked

Use either kriging or cokriging and then either a simple kriging/cokriging method or a disjunctive kriging/cokriging method in the Geostatistical Method Selection dialog box.

Checking for bivariate distribution

1. Click the Add Data button on the ArcMap toolbar and add the layer you wish to check for bivariate distribution.

2. Start the Geostatistical Wizard.

3. Click either Kriging or Cokriging.

4. Click Next on the Choose Input Data and Method dialog box.

5. Click the Simple or Disjunctive Kriging/Cokriging method to use.

6. Check Examine Bivariate Distribution and select Normal Score Transformation.

7. Choose the Dataset combination you wish to use (cokriging only).

8. Type the number of quantiles to check.

9. Click Next.

10. Click the Approximation Method in the dropdown menu, set the parameters, and click either Probability Density or Cumulative Distribution radio buttons on the Normal Score Transformation dialog box. Click Next. ▶

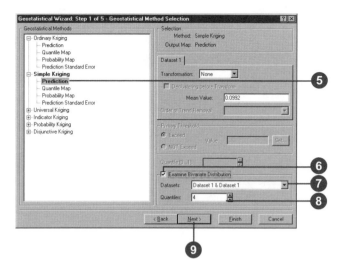

11. Specify the desired parameters in the Semivariogram/ Covariance Modeling dialog box and click Next.

12. Explore the bivariate distribution on the Examine Bivariate Distribution dialog box. Click Next.

Implementing declustering to adjust for preferential sampling

Very often the spatial locations of your data are not randomly or regularly spaced. For various reasons, the data may have been sampled preferentially, with a higher density of sample points in some places than in others. As you saw in the previous section, it is important that for proper implementation of the normal score transformation, the histogram (and so also the cumulative distribution) of the sample properly reflect the histogram of whole population. If data is preferentially sampled when it is spatially autocorrelated, the resulting histogram from the sample may not reflect the histogram of the population. The following figures give an example.

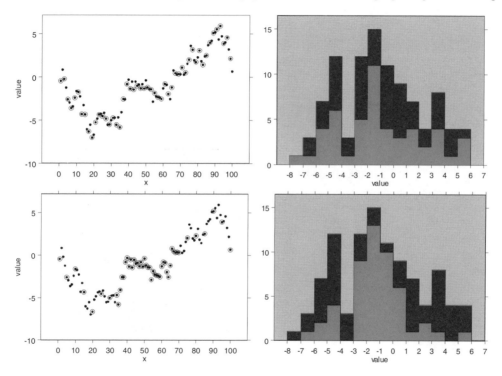

In the upper-left figure, the whole population of values at 100 locations along a line are given as solid circles. These were simulated from a spatially autocorrelated process with a constant mean and strong positive autocorrelation. The sampled data is every other point, beginning with the first one, and is shown with circles. To the right, the histogram of the population is given in blue, and the histogram of the sample is given in violet.

Because the sample is half of the whole population, the sample histogram bars should be about half as high as for the population, with some variation, and this appears to be the case. In the lower left, the data is preferentially sampled, with samples occurring at every fifth location up to location 34, then it is every location up to location 70, and then every fifth location again to the end. The end result is, again, that half of the whole population is sampled. The preferential sampling toward the middle of the spatial locations causes a higher proportion of the middle data values to occur in the sample, and hence the histogram bars are nearly equal to the population bars for values ranging from -3 to 1. In conjunction with this, the lower and higher values are underrepresented in the sample histogram.

One solution to preferential sampling is to weight the data, with data in densely sampled areas receiving less weight (which would shrink the sample histogram bars for the values between -3 and 1 in the preferentially sampled example above) and data in sparsely sampled areas receiving greater weight (which would expand the sample histogram bars at the lower and higher data values). Geostatistical Analyst allows for two methods. The default method is cell declustering. Here, rectangular cells are arranged over the data locations in a grid, and the weight attached to each data location is inversely proportional to the number of data points in its cell. An example is given in the following figure.

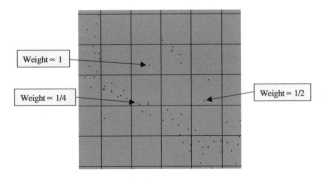

Choosing the grid size is all that remains. Several schemes can be adopted, and you can consult the literature to choose one. One tool Geostatistical Analyst provides is a graph that shows the weighted mean value among all the data for various cell sizes. It has been suggested to choose the cell size corresponding to the minimum weighted mean if the data has been preferentially sampled in areas of high values and, conversely, pick the cell size corresponding to the maximum weighted mean if the data has been preferentially sampled in areas of low values.

Another scheme uses a polygonal method that defines a polygon around each spatial data location such that all locations within that polygon are closer to the data location than any other data location, as shown in the following figure.

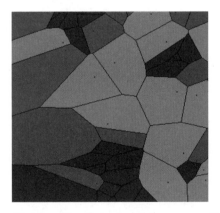

The data locations are shown as small dots, and the polygons are drawn around them, with color shading indicating the size of the polygons. The idea is to weight each data location in proportion to the area that it "represents". The problem with this method is that it is difficult to define weights toward the edge. The edge points can often receive large weights unless a border encloses the data. In Geostatistical Analyst, the border is a rectangle, which often gives too much weight to edge locations.

The Declustering dialog box

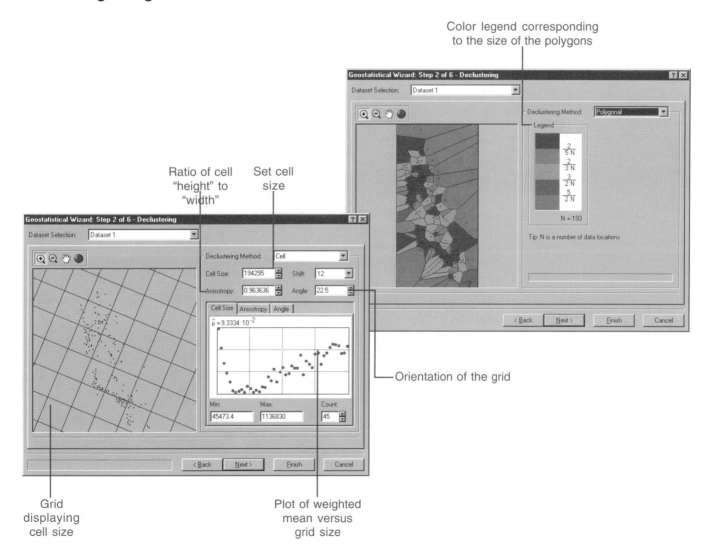

Color legend corresponding to the size of the polygons

Ratio of cell "height" to "width"

Set cell size

Orientation of the grid

Grid displaying cell size

Plot of weighted mean versus grid size

Declustering to adjust for preferential sampling

There are two ways to decluster your data: by the cell method and by Voronoi polygons.

Samples should be taken so they are representative of the entire surface. However, many times the samples are taken where the concentration is most severe, thus skewing the view of the surface. Declustering accounts for skewed representation of the samples by weighting them appropriately so that a more accurate surface can be created.

Tip

Tip

Using declustering

Declustering is only used when you choose normal score transformation as the transformation method.

Use probability, simple, or disjunctive kriging/cokriging to access the normal score transformation method.

Performing cell declustering

1. Click Kriging or Cokriging on the Choose Input Data and Method dialog box.

2. Click either Probability, Disjunctive, or Simple Kriging or Cokriging methods.

3. Click the Normal Score transformation in the Transformation dropdown menu.

4. Check Declustering before Transform.

5. Click Next.

6. Click the Dataset Selection dropdown arrow and click the dataset you wish to display (cokriging only).

7. Specify the desired parameters.

8. Click the tabs to switch between the Cell Size, Anisotropy, and Angle charts.

9. Change cell size, anisotropy, shift, and angle to find the extremum in the graph.

10. Alternatively, click the Declustering Method dropdown arrow and click Polgonal to switch to a polygon declustering display.

11. Click Next. ▶

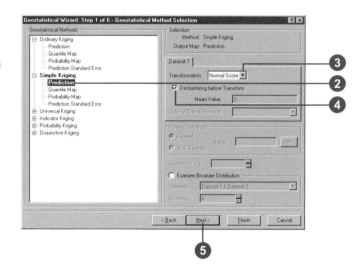

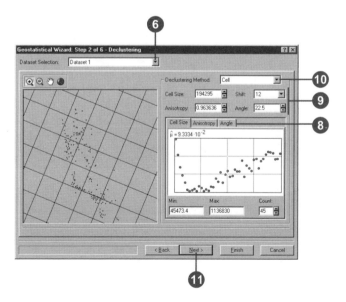

12. Click the Approximation Method in the dropdown menu, set the parameters, and click either Probability Density or Cumulative distribution radio buttons on the Normal Score Transformation dialog box. Click Next.

13. Specify the desired parameters in the Semivariogram/ Covariance Modeling dialog box and click Next.

14. Specify the desired parameters in the Searching Neighborhood dialog box and click Next.

15. Examine the results on the Cross Validation dialog box and click Finish.

16. On the Output Layer Information dialog box, click OK.

Removing trends from the data

Sometimes you may want to remove a surface trend from your data and use kriging or cokriging on the detrended (called residual) data. Consider the additive model,

$$Z(\mathbf{s}) = \mu(\mathbf{s}) + \varepsilon(\mathbf{s})$$

where $\mu(\mathbf{s})$ is some deterministic surface (called the trend) and $\varepsilon(\mathbf{s})$ is spatially autocorrelated error. Conceptually, the trend is fixed, which means that if you simulate data again and again, then the trend never changes. However, you do see fluctuations in the simulated surfaces due to the autocorrelated random errors. Usually, the trend changes gradually through space, while the random errors change more quickly. A meteorological example of a trend might be where you observe (and know theoretically) a temperature gradient with latitude. However, observations on any given day show local variations due to weather fronts, ground cover, cloud patterns, and so on, that are not so predictable, so the local variations are modeled as being autocorrelated.

Unfortunately, there is no magical way to decompose data uniquely into a trend and random errors. The following is offered to serve as a useful guide. In the following figure, data was simulated from two models. One was from the ordinary kriging model, where $Z(\mathbf{s}) = \mu + \varepsilon(\mathbf{s})$ and the errors $\varepsilon(\mathbf{s})$ were autocorrelated. The process had a mean $\mu = 0$ with an exponential semivariogram. Another dataset was simulated from a universal kriging model with $\mu(\mathbf{s}) = \beta_0 + \beta_1 x(\mathbf{s}) + \beta_2 x^2(\mathbf{s})$, shown by the solid line, but the errors were independent, with mean 0 and variance 1.

As you can see, it is difficult to tell which is which (the blue circles are from the ordinary kriging model, and the red circles are from the universal kriging model with independent errors). Spatial autocorrelation can allow flexible prediction surfaces, and this example shows that it can be difficult to decide among the models based on the data alone. In general, you should stick to ordinary kriging unless you have strong reasons to remove a trend surface. The reason is that it is best to keep your models as

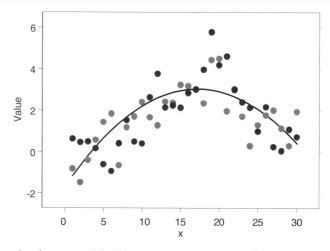

simple as possible. If you remove a trend surface, then there are more parameters to estimate. A two-dimensional quadratic surface adds five parameters beyond the intercept parameter that need to be estimated. The more parameters that are estimated, the less precise the models become. However, there may be times when the spatial coordinates serve as a proxy to some known trend in the data. For example, crop production may change with latitude—not because of the coordinates themselves but because temperature, humidity, rainfall, and so on, change with latitude. In these cases, it may make sense to remove trend surfaces. Again, keep the surfaces as simple as possible such as first- or second-order polynomials. The Geostatistical Analyst also allows local polynomial smoothing as an option to remove a trend. There is a very real danger of overfitting data when using trends and leaving too little variation in the residuals to properly account for the uncertainty in prediction. Always be sure to check your models with cross-validation, and especially validation, when you use trend models.

The Detrending dialog box (Standard option)

The dataset being detrended

The neighborhood search size

The power of the polynomial

Searching Neighborhood settings

Controls for the trend display

The estimated trend display

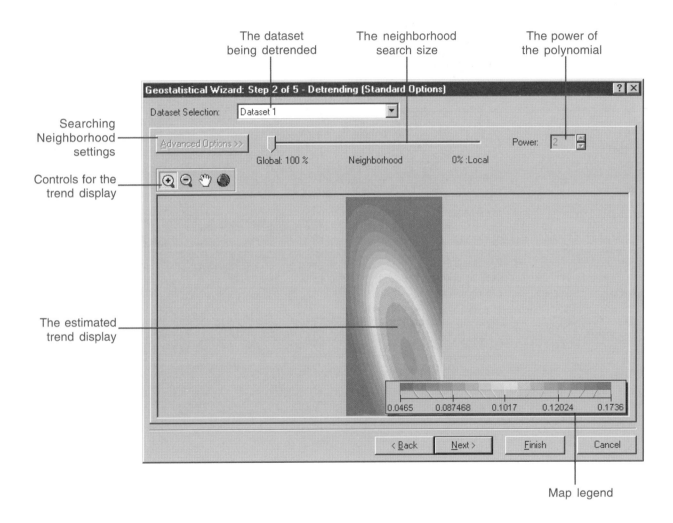

Map legend

Removing global and local trends from the data: detrending

Use the ESDA Trend Analysis tool (see Chapter 4, 'Exploratory Spatial Data Analysis') to examine if there is a global trend in the data.

Basically, you are decomposing your data into a deterministic trend component and an autocorrelated random component. Once the trend is removed, you will carry out kriging on the residuals. Before the final predictions are actually calculated, the trend is added back to the output surface.

Using the slider to estimate the trend

1. On the Geostatistical Method Selection dialog box, click either Ordinary Kriging, Universal Kriging, or Disjunctive Kriging and the desired output surface type in the Geostatistical Method tree view.

2. Click the dropdown arrow on the Order of Trend Removal and click the order for the trend.

3. Click Next.

   Note: If the order of trend is anything but None, then the Detrending dialog box will follow when clicking Next.

4. On the Detrending dialog box, by moving the slider between the two extremes, you define the window size for fitting the polynomial from Global to Local.

   Alternatively, to set the neighborhood parameters click Advanced Options>>.

5. Click Next.

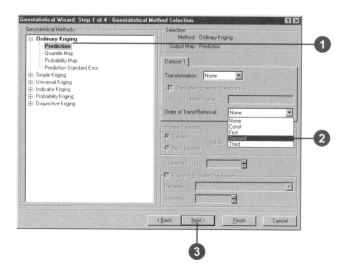

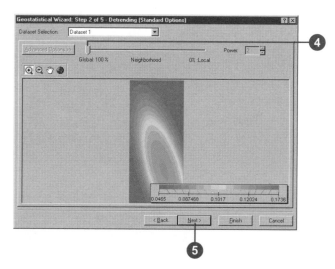

Displaying and managing geostatistical layers

8

IN THIS CHAPTER

- **What is a geostatistical layer?**

- **Adding layers**

- **Working with layers in a map**

- **Managing layers**

- **Viewing geostatistical layers in ArcCatalog**

- **Representing a geostatistical layer**

- **Changing the symbology of a geostatistical layer**

- **Data classification**

- **Setting the scales at which a geostatistical layer will be displayed**

- **Predicting values for locations outside the area of interest**

- **Saving and exporting geostatistical layers**

ArcMap and Geostatistical Analyst provide a wide variety of tools with which to display and manage your data. With the display tools, you can create fine cartographic output and explore or analyze your data to gain greater insights in order to make more effective decisions. Exploration is particularly important when using Geostatistical Analyst because through these insights you are able to build better models and create more accurate surfaces.

Even though the management tools may not directly aid in the creation of surfaces with Geostatistical Analyst, these tools are indispensable for organizing and ordering the map session as well as your own thinking.

Many of the display and management tools that are applicable to any ArcMap layer are also applicable to a geostatistical layer. In this chapter, we will only discuss the general layer tools that are most often used when working with Geostatistical Analyst and the tools that are specific to a geostatistical layer. Please refer to *Using ArcMap* for additional tools that can be applied to all layer types, including geostatistical layers.

What is a geostatistical layer?

In ArcMap, geographic data is represented in layers. There are different layer types to represent different data. An ArcMap feature layer may contain polygons representing soil types, points identifying biomass measured at specific locations, or lines presenting a network of trails. A raster layer can represent an aerial photograph or a grid of distances from roads. Other layer types include a TIN layer for three-dimensional surfaces, a CAD layer to store CAD map sheets, and a geostatistical layer to store the results of analysis from the Geostatistical Analyst.

A geostatistical layer's functionality is similar to all ArcMap layers. You can add it to ArcMap, remove it, display it, and alter the symbology in countless ways. However, a geostatistical layer differs from other layers because of the way it is created and stored. A geostatistical layer can only be created by the Geostatistical Analyst. Most ArcMap layer types store the reference to the data source, the symbology for displaying the layer, and other defining characteristics. A geostatistical layer stores the source of the data from which it was created (usually a point feature layer), the symbology, and other defining characteristics, but it also stores the model parameters from the interpolation. From the Properties dialog for a geostatistical layer, you can view both the original data source and the model parameters.

Not only can you identify the source of the input points and the model parameters, but you can also retrieve general information with the General tab, see and alter the layer's map extent with the Extent tab, change the symbology with the Symbology tab, and set the transparency and whether to show map tips with the Display tab.

A geostatistical layer can be viewed in four different formats: filled contours, contours, grid, or hillshade. You can also combine multiple formats in a single display of the layer to achieve various effects. A full range of symbology and controlling parameters exists for each format.

Filled contours

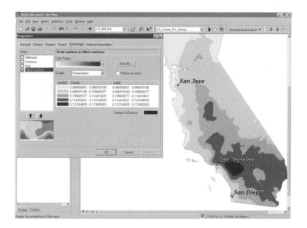

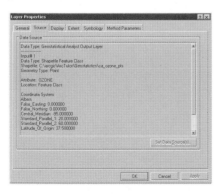

Contours

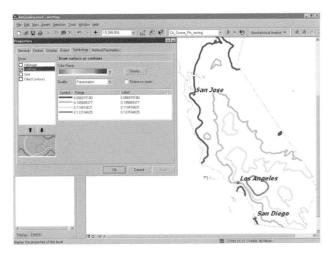

Hillshade

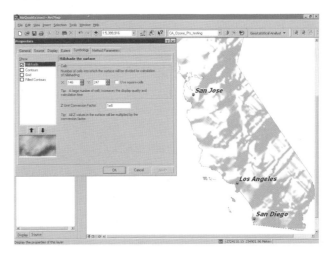

Grid

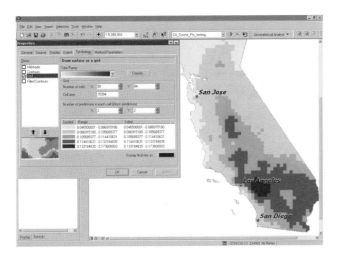

Combination of contours, filled contours, and hillshade

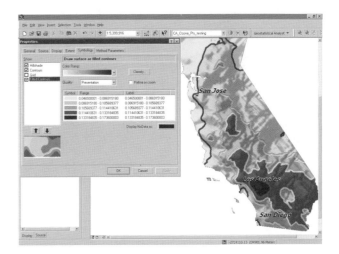

Adding layers

In ArcMap, geographic data is represented in layers. There are several different types of layers, but the ones of particular interest to the Geostatistical Analyst are point, polygon, and raster.

The feature layer can represent polygon features such as soil types or land use, linear features such as road networks, or point features such as incidents of crime or samples taken of a pollutant. A point feature layer is typically used as input into the Geostatistical Analyst. The geostatistical layer represents the surface created from analysis in the Geostatistical Analyst. A raster layer may represent a satellite scene, a scanned image, or the grid representation of forest-stand types. Many times, a geostatistical layer is converted into a raster layer for further analysis.

Tip

Revealing hidden layers

Layers that you add may be "hidden". To view a layer that you can't see, right-click the layer and click Zoom To Layer.

Adding layers

1. Click the Add Data button on the ArcMap Standard toolbar.

2. Click the Look in dropdown arrow and navigate to the folder that contains the layer.

3. Click the layer.

4. Click Add.

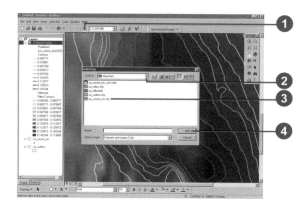

Adding a group layer

1. Right-click on Layers in the ArcMap table of contents and click New Group Layer.

2. Right-click the resulting New Group Layer in the table of contents and click Properties.

3. Click the General tab.

4. Optionally, name the group layer.

5. Optionally, check the Visible check box to make the Group Layer visible.

6. Optionally, set the Scale Range.

7. Click the Group tab.

8. Click Add and navigate to a dataset you wish to add.

9. Click Add.

10. Continue adding the desired datasets to the group by repeating steps 8 and 9.

11. Click OK.

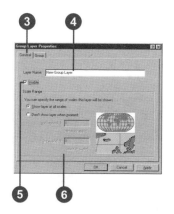

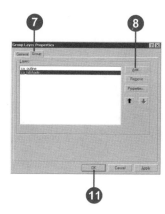

Working with layers in a map

There are many tools in ArcMap that allow you to work with layers in a map. Some of the more common ones that are particularly useful to the Geostatistical Analyst user are turning the display of the layer on or off, controlling the order of the display of the layers, and zooming and panning around in a layer. These tools can be used for analysis or for the creation of fine cartographic output.

When using these tools for analysis, you can explore the input point layer to be interpolated, as well as investigate the resulting geostatistical layer.

Once a desirable presentation of the results is achieved, the output can then be saved in the map session.

See Also

See also Using ArcMap *for additional tools that manipulate the display of a layer in a map.*

Turning the display of a layer on or off

1. Check the check box to the left of the layer name to turn the layer on or off.

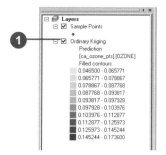

Moving a layer to change its drawing order

1. In the table of contents, click and drag the layer up or down to the desired position.

   A black line indicates where the layer will be placed.

2. Release the mouse pointer to drop the layer into the new position.

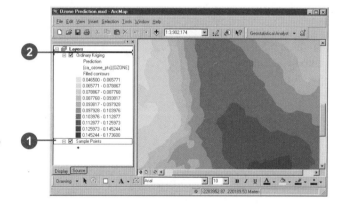

Zooming and panning a layer

1. Click View in the ArcMap menu bar, click Toolbars, and check Tools.

2. Various tools, accessed through icons on the Tools toolbar, can be used to explore the map.

Zoom In		Zoom Out
Fixed Zoom In		Fixed Zoom Out
Pan		Full Extent
Go Back to Previous Extent		Go to Next Extent
Select Features		Select Graphics
Identify Features		Find
Measure		Hyperlink

Managing layers

ArcMap provides a suite of tools to manage layers. Although these tools do not aid in exploration or analysis, they order your map session. Some of the most relevant tools to the Geostatistical Analyst are saving, renaming, copying, and removing geostatistical layers.

You may wish to rename a geostatistical layer, because, by default, a geostatistical layer is named according to the method that was used to create it, followed by a number (e.g., Ordinary Kriging_2). This will become confusing when you are creating several surfaces using the same method but with different parameters or when you are using the same method on different datasets.

Copying a geostatistical layer is particularly useful when you wish to create another output surface type with the same model parameters.

Removing a geostatistical layer is useful so that you can delete layers that were used when exploring parameters.

Changing the name of a layer

1. Click the layer in the table of contents to select it.

2. Click again on the name.

   This will highlight the name and enable it to be changed.

3. Type the new name.

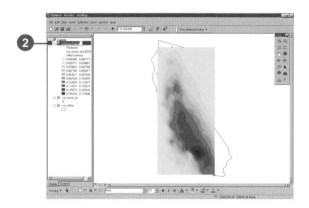

Copying a layer

1. Right-click the layer you want to copy and click Copy.

2. Right-click the Layers data frame.

3. Click Paste Layer(s).

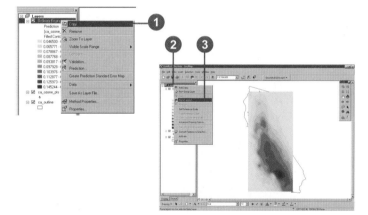

Removing a layer

1. Right-click the layer you want to remove and click Remove.

Viewing geostatistical layers in ArcCatalog

Geostatistical layers can be viewed and managed with ArcCatalog. ArcCatalog allows you to browse your data quickly and to establish links to databases and folders residing locally or on the network.

You can preview the map representation of the geostatistical layer, or you can view the metadata associated with it in ArcCatalog™.

Tip

Metadata

A comprehensive metadata strategy is essential to keep track of geographical or geostatistical data.

Tip

Accessing ArcCatalog

ArcCatalog can also be accessed from ArcMap by clicking on the ArcCatalog icon on the Standard toolbar.

Starting ArcCatalog and enabling Geostatistical Analyst

1. Click the Start button on the Windows taskbar.

2. Point to Programs.

3. Point to ArcGIS.

4. Point to ArcCatalog.

    The ArcCatalog window appears. Now, click the Tools menu, click Extensions, and check Geostatistical Analyst. Click Close.

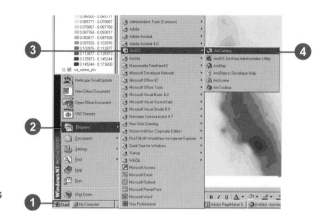

Previewing data

1. Start ArcCatalog.

2. Navigate to the desired geostatistical layer in the table of contents.

3. Click the Preview tab.

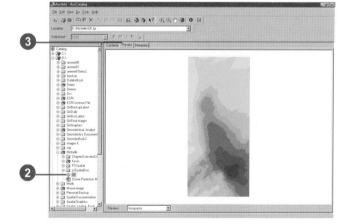

See Also

See Using ArcCatalog *for more information about metadata and how to create it.*

Viewing layer metadata

1. Start ArcCatalog.

2. Navigate to the desired geostatistical layer in the table of contents.

3. Click the Metadata tab.

4. Click the Description tab to retrieve a general description of the layer.

5. Click the Spatial tab to explore the spatial character- istics of the layer such as its bounding coordinates.

6. Click the Attributes tab to examine other information about the layer.

7. Input or change any meta- data information.

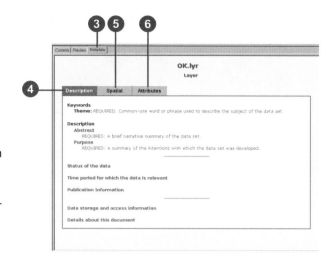

Representing a geostatistical layer

There are four ways a geostatistical layer can be represented.

Filled contours is the polygon representation of the geostatistical layer. It is assumed for the graphical display that the values for all locations inside the polygon are the same.

Grid is the raster representation of the geostatistical layer. It is assumed that the prediction is for the center of each cell or average for each cell (when prediction is used).

Contours is the isoline representation of the geostatistical layer. You can choose to display the lines in either draft or presentation quality.

Hillshade creates a shaded relief representation of the geostatistical layer.

Combinations of the four representations above can be used simultaneously.

Tip

Viewing multiple datasets

To view two datasets at the same time, represent one as contours and superimpose it over the other surface.

Displaying a geostatistical layer as filled contours

1. Right-click the desired geostatistical layer in the ArcMap table of contents and click Properties.

2. Click the Symbology tab.

3. Click Filled Contours in the Show list and check the accompanying check box.

4. Set the desired parameters.

5. Click OK.

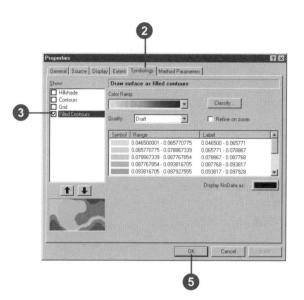

Displaying a geostatistical layer as a grid

1. Right-click the desired geostatistical layer in the ArcMap table of contents and click Properties.

2. Click the Symbology tab.

3. Click Grid in the Show list and check the accompanying check box.

4. Set the desired parameters.

5. Click OK.

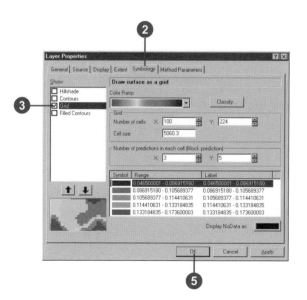

Displaying the geostatistical layer as a hillshade

1. Click the desired geostatistical layer in the ArcMap table of contents and click Properties.

2. Click the Symbology tab.

3. Click Hillshade in the Show list and check the accompanying check box.

4. Set the desired parameters.

5. Click OK.

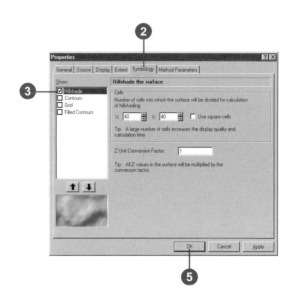

Displaying the geostatistical layer as contours

1. Click the desired geostatistical layer in the ArcMap table of contents and click Properties.

2. Click the Symbology tab.

3. Click Contours in the Show list and check the accompanying check box.

4. Set the desired parameters.

5. Click OK.

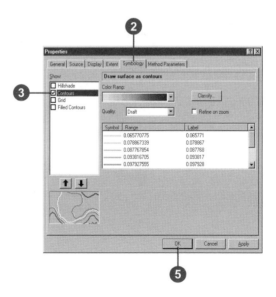

Changing the symbology of a geostatistical layer

ArcMap provides many tools to aid in the display of layers. Using these tools you can make attractive maps but, more importantly, the tools allow you to explore and analyze the data in the layer in a wide variety of ways.

ArcMap displays the layer using system-defined defaults. However, these defaults can be adjusted. An overall color scheme can be selected from a set of predefined color schemes, or the color scheme can be changed interactively.

Tip

Zooming

As you zoom in on the map, the graduated symbols of the input point feature layer will not increase in size. If you want them to get bigger, you need to set a reference scale. Right-click the data frame and click Set Reference Scale.

Changing the color scheme

1. Right-click the geostatistical layer and click Properties.

2. Click the Symbology tab.

3. Click on either Contours, Grid, or Filled Contours for the layer from the Show list.

4. Click the Color Ramp dropdown arrow and click a color scheme.

5. Click OK.

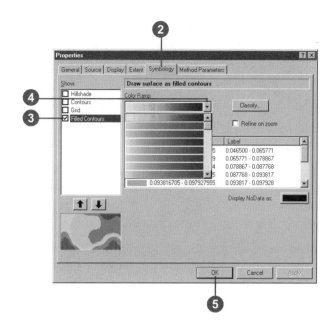

Changing the color interactively

1. Right-click a symbol from the legend of a geostatistical layer.

2. Click a color for the symbol.

   All values in the display represented with this symbol will be displayed in the chosen color.

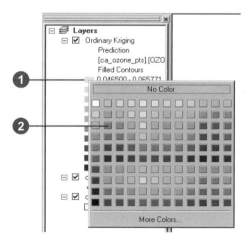

Data classification

When you perform a classification, you group similar features into classes by assigning the same symbol to each member of the class. Aggregating features into classes allows you to spot patterns in the data more easily. The definition of a class range determines which features fall into that class, which affects the appearance of the map. By altering the class breaks (the boundary between classes), you can create very different-looking maps. Classes can be created manually, or you can use a standard classification scheme.

Why set your class ranges manually?

Create classes manually if you are looking for features that meet a specific criterion or if you are comparing features to specific, meaningful values. To do this, you would manually specify the upper and lower limit for each class.

You may also manually classify data to emphasize a particular range of values such as those above or below a threshold value. For example, you may wish to emphasize areas below a certain elevation level that are susceptible to flooding.

Manual assignment of classes can also be a useful technique for isolating and highlighting ranges of data. For example, if your dataset had an overall range of 0.0465 to 0.1736 and you wish to isolate the higher values, to do so you might manually assign all values below 0.15 to one class and all values above to a second class.

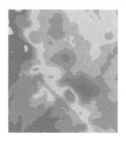

The diagram shows how selected ranges of data can be highlighted using a manual assignment of classes.

Using a standard classification scheme

How the class ranges and breaks are defined will determine the amount of data that falls into each class and the appearance of the map. There are two main components in a classification scheme: the number of classes into which the data is to be organized and the method by which classes are assigned. The number of classes is dependent on the objective of the analysis. The rules by which the data is assigned to a class, however, require a bit of explanation. For a geostatistical layer, there are three standard ways in which data can be assigned to classes:

- Equal interval
- Quantile
- Smart quantiles

These will be described on the following pages.

Equal interval

The range of possible values is divided into equal-sized intervals. Because there are usually fewer endpoints at the extremes, the numbers of values are less in the extreme classes. This option is useful to highlight changes in the extremes. It is probably best applied to familiar data ranges such as percentages or temperature. This option is most useful for Probability and Standard Error Map.

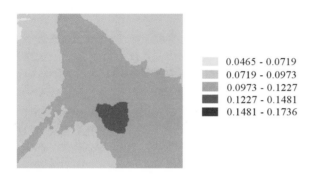

0.0465 - 0.0719
0.0719 - 0.0973
0.0973 - 0.1227
0.1227 - 0.1481
0.1481 - 0.1736

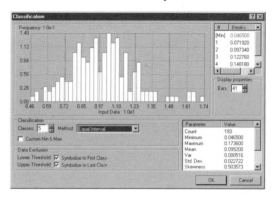

Quantile

The range of possible values is divided into unequal-sized intervals so that the number of values is the same in each class. Classes at the extremes and middle have the same number of values. Because the intervals are generally wider at the extremes, this option is useful to highlight changes in the middle values of the distribution.

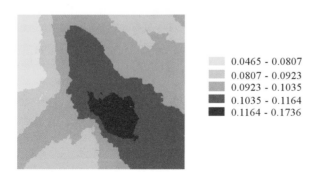

0.0465 - 0.0807
0.0807 - 0.0923
0.0923 - 0.1035
0.1035 - 0.1164
0.1164 - 0.1736

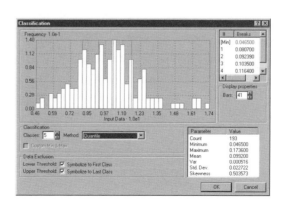

Smart quantiles

Smart quantiles are used to delineate classes based on natural groupings of data values. Break points are identified by looking for groupings and patterns inherent in the data. The features are divided into classes whose boundaries are set where there are relatively big jumps in the data values, so groups with similar values are placed in the same class. This is a compromise method between equal interval and quantile, with unequal-sized intervals such as quantile that generally get a bit wider at the extremes, but not so much as with the quantile method, so there is also a decreasing number of values in the extreme classes. This option tries to find a balance between highlighting changes in the middle values and the exteme values. It is useful for datasets such as rainfall, which may have more than 50 percent of the records equal to zero.

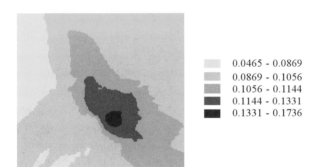

0.0465 - 0.0869
0.0869 - 0.1056
0.1056 - 0.1144
0.1144 - 0.1331
0.1331 - 0.1736

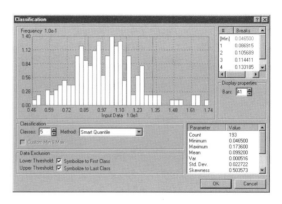

Classifying data

When you classify your data, you can use one of the standard classification schemes provided for geostatistical layers or create custom classes manually based on class ranges you specify.

If you choose one of the standard methods, simply choose the classification scheme and set the number of classes.

If you define your own classes, you can manually alter the class breaks or specify exact values for the class breaks that are suitable for your data.

Setting a predefined classification method

1. In the table of contents, right-click the geostatistical layer you want to classify and click Properties.

2. Click the Symbology tab.

3. Click Classify.

4. Click the Method dropdown arrow and click a classification method.

5. Click the up/down arrows on the Classes input box to set the desired number of classes.

6. Click OK on the Classification dialog box.

7. Click OK on the Layer Properties dialog box.

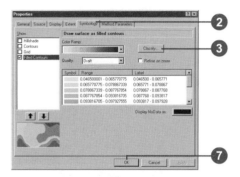

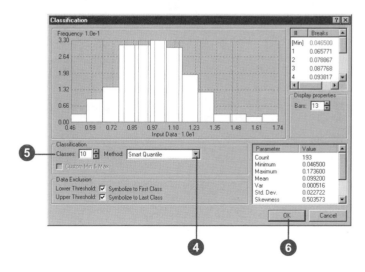

Manually altering the class breaks

1. In the table of contents, right-click the geostatistical layer you want to classify manually and click Properties.

2. Click the Symbology tab.

3. Click Classify.

4. Click the Method dropdown arrow and click Manual.

5. Click the up/down arrow of the Classes input box until the desired number of classes is reached.

6. Click and drag the class breaks to the desired position.

7. Alternatively, type in specific class breaks.

8. Alternatively, check the Custom Min & Max check box, then type specific minimum and maximum values to include in the classification.

9. Click OK on the Classification dialog box.

10. Click OK on the Symbology tab.

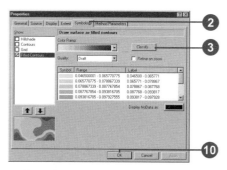

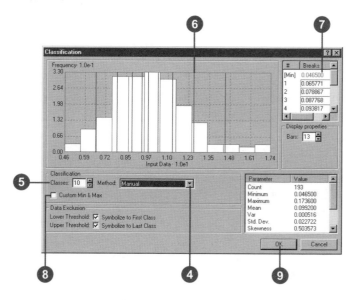

Setting the scales at which a geostatistical layer will be displayed

ArcMap will not usually display the landscape at the same size that it exists; thus, it must change the scale of the landscape to fit on the screen. A kilometer on the ground may be represented by a centimeter on the screen. The scale is the reduction (or enlargement) necessary to display the desired area.

As you zoom in and out of a map, the scale of the display changes. It may not be desirable for every layer to be viewed at every scale. For example, it would not be appropriate to display county boundaries when viewing a map of the world.

You can control what layers are displayed at what scales on the Properties dialog box for the layer.

Setting the scale range

1. Right-click the geostatistical layer and click Properties.

2. Click the General tab.

3. Click Don't show layer when zoomed.

4. Set the scale range by inputting the out beyond and in beyond entries.

5. Click OK.

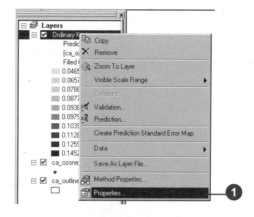

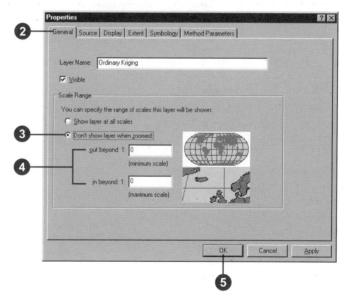

Predicting values for locations outside the area of interest

By default, the Geostatistical Analyst interpolates the values of the selected variable at all locations that lie within the minimum spatial bounding box. The minimum spatial bounding box is the smallest box that can be created to encompass all the input sample points. However, this bounding box may not produce a map to fully cover the area of interest. To create a prediction map that exceeds the bounding box is called extrapolation. The resulting geostatistical layer from an extrapolation will cover the area that you have identified.

Note that it is not recommended to extrapolate values for very distant locations. It is acceptable to extrapolate values close to actual sample points (for example, around the boundary of a geostatistical layer), but any further extrapolation may result in unreliable predictions.

Tip

To return to the default extent after specifying a new visible extent, click Default on the Extent tab.

Extrapolating values

1. Right-click the geostatistical layer that you want to extrapolate values for in the ArcMap table of contents and click Properties.

2. Click the Extent tab.

3. Click a custom extent entered below in the Set the extent to dropdown list.

4. Type the new values into the Visible Extent.

   Alternatively, use the extent of any other available layer.

5. Click OK.

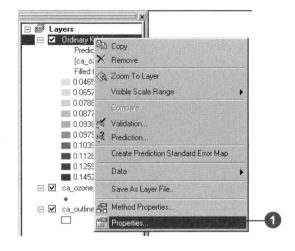

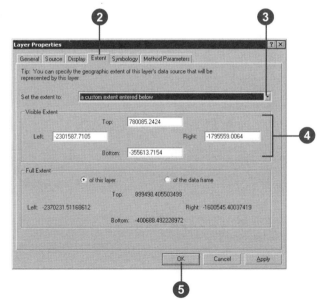

Saving and exporting geostatistical layers

An ArcMap geostatistical layer comprises a reference to the data stored on disk, the symbology used to display the layer, and a variety of other information relevant to the mode which may be used to creat a layer.

If the ArcMap session is saved, the layers in the table of contents and their accompanying definitions are stored in a file with an .mxd extension. However, if you want to add a layer to another ArcMap session while preserving the symbology, the layer can be saved to a file with an .lyr extension. The .lyr file does not make a copy of the source data but only references it.

To make a geostatistical layer persistent, a copy can be written to disk (excluding the layer definition) as either an ArcInfo™ grid or shapefile.

Tip

Distributing a geostatistical layer

If you plan to distribute your map to others, they will need access to both the map document and the data your layer references.

Saving a map composition

1. Click the File menu and click Save As.

2. Navigate to the directory in which you want to save the map.

3. Change the map name if desired.

4. Click Save.

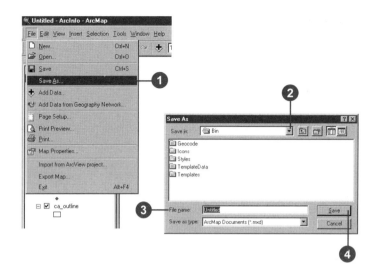

Saving individual layers

1. Right-click the geostatistical layer you wish to save in the ArcMap table of contents and click Save As Layer File.

2. Navigate to the directory in which you want to save the layer.

3. Change the layer name if desired.

4. Click Save.

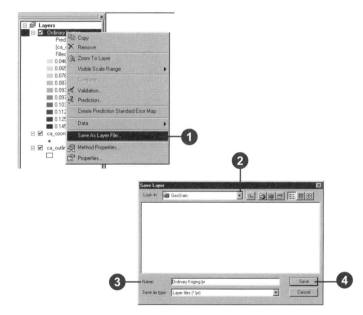

Exporting a geostatistical layer to a raster

1. Right-click the geostatistical layer in the ArcMap table of contents, click Data, and click Export to Raster.

2. Set the desired properties for the resulting raster such as the number of rows and columns, cell size, number of predictions in each cell (Block Interpolations), and the name and location for the raster.

3. Click OK.

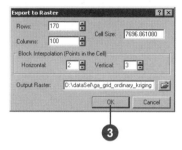

Exporting a geostatistical layer to a vector format

1. Right-click the geostatistical layer in the ArcMap table of contents, click Data, and click Export to Vector.

2. Specify the output format (e.g., shapefile, personal geodatabase, or SDE® database).

3. Select Contours or Filled Contours from the Export dropdown menu.

4. Click OK.

Additional geostatistical analysis tools   9

IN THIS CHAPTER

- **Changing the parameters of a geostatistical layer: method properties**

- **Predicting values for specified locations**

- **Performing validation on a geostatistical layer created from a subset**

- **Stratifying your data for better predictions**

There are many supporting tools in ArcMap and Geostatistical Analyst to assist in geostatistical analysis. You can change the parameters in a model, retrieve predictions for specific locations, perform validation from subsets, spatially divide your data, interpolate each division, and then combine the results. This chapter is not an exhaustive list of tools that will help with geostatistical analysis. Instead, it discusses some of the more commonly used tools that will aid in your analysis. But you should be aware that because Geostatistical Analyst is integrated into ArcMap, there are countless functions that you can and will use in your analysis. The more familiar you become with ArcMap and the supporting Geostatistical Analyst extensions, the more tools you will find that meet your specific need to create even more accurate surfaces.

Changing the parameters of a geostatistical layer: method properties

After creating a surface with the Geostatistical Analyst, you are able to view it in ArcMap. By using the multitude of display tools for a geostatistical layer, you may notice that certain areas of the newly created surface do not match with your knowledge of the area. Rather than produce a new surface, you may decide to improve the surface by changing the parameters that were used to create it. Through the method properties, you can return to the dialog boxes in the wizard environment and change any model parameter and examine the new output results.

Tip

Understanding method properties

The Method Properties dialog box will help you gain a better understanding of how the various available options affect the output surface.

Using method properties

1. Right-click the geostatistical layer in the ArcMap table of contents and click Method Properties.

   The options available depend on the technique used to create the original surface. Follow these steps when the prediction surface is created by a kriging method.

2. Click on the desired kriging method.

3. Click Next on the Geostatistical Method Selection dialog box.

4. Optionally, change any of the model parameters and click Next on the Semivariance/ Covariance Modeling dialog box.

5. Optionally, define a new search neighborhood and click Next on the Searching Neighborhood dialog.

6. Assess the cross-validation results. Has the output improved? If not, repeat steps 2 to 5. If yes, Click Finish on the Cross Validation dialog box.

7. Click OK on the Output Layer Information dialog box.

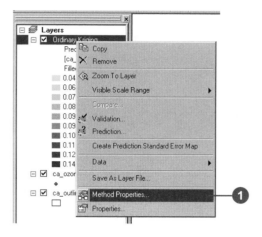

Predicting values for specified locations

Sometimes you are interested in predicting a value for a specific location or multiple locations and are not necessarily interested in the entire surface. For example, you may be concerned about the level of radiation at a particular house or the elevation at a proposed lookout tower.

If looking for prediction values for a few individual locations, the easiest way is to use map tips. However, if you wish to save the specific location predictions to an output layer for additional analysis, it is best to use the Prediction dialog box.

Tip

Selecting points using the attribute table

In addition to using the selection tool, points of interest can be selected using the attribute table (right-click the layer of interest and click Open Attribute Table).

Using map tips

1. Create a geostatistical layer using any of the methods discussed in Chapters 5 or 6.

2. Right-click the geostatistical layer and click Properties.

3. Click the Display tab.

4. Check Show MapTips.

5. Click OK.

6. Place the cursor over a point of interest on the layer.

   The value at that location is displayed.

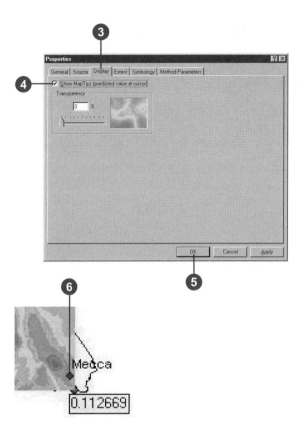

Predicting at specific locations from a point layer

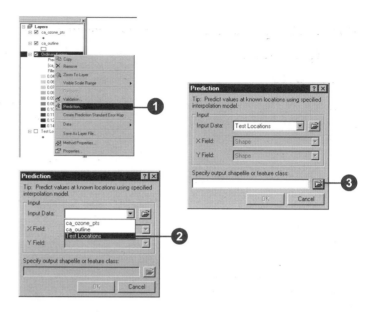

1. Right-click in the ArcMap table of contents the geostatistical layer that was created using observed data and click Prediction.

2. Click the Input Data dropdown arrow and click the layer containing the locations for which you want to obtain predictions.

3. Identify the directory to store the output dataset in by clicking the browse button next to Specify output shapefile or feature class.

4. Browse or type the directory and name for the output file.

5. Click Save and OK.

6. Add the prediction file to the ArcMap table of contents when prompted.

7. Right-click the prediction layer and click Open Attribute Table to display the results.

   The predicted values at the specified locations will be displayed in the table.

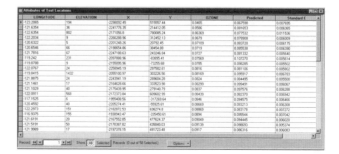

Performing validation on a geostatistical layer created from a subset

The most rigorous way to assess the quality of an output surface is to compare the predicted values for specified locations with those measured in the field. For some reason (time, money, and so on), it is often not possible to go back to the study area to collect an independent validation dataset. One solution is to divide the original dataset into two parts. One part can be used for modeling, that is, to create the output surface and the other for testing, that is, to validate the output surface.

Tip

Dividing the dataset

The relative percentages into which the dataset should be divided should be based on the number of available samples. You need enough sample points to create the output surface and to make the validation of that surface meaningful. Therefore, if the original sample number is small, it may be inappropriate to divide the dataset.

Creating subsets

1. Click the Geostatistical Analyst toolbar and click Create Subsets.

2. Click the Input Layer dropdown arrow and click the layer to be divided.

3. Click Next.

4. Click and drag the slider bar to an appropriate location to select the relative percentages of training and test data.

   By default, the output dataset is named according to the following convention: "input filedataset"+"_sets.mdb", for example, inputpoints_sets.mdb, where inputpoints is the name of the input dataset containing the points.

5. Click Finish.

   The training and test datasets form two tables in the personal geodatabase.

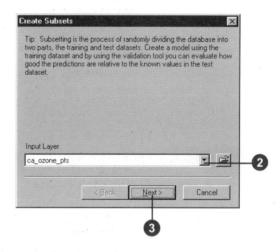

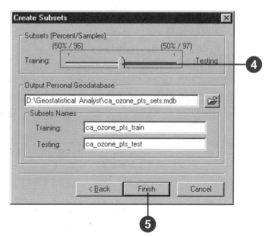

Performing validation using subsets

1. Click the Add Data icon on the Standard toolbar in ArcMap. Navigate to the folder in which the subset data was saved (if it is not in the ArcMap table of contents).

2. Click both the training and test layers (click one layer, then hold down the Shift key and click the other).

3. Click Add.

4. Click the Geostatistical Analyst toolbar and click Geostatistical Wizard.

5. Click the Input Data dropdown menu and click the training dataset.

6. Click an appropriate method.

7. Click Next and follow the dialog boxes to create a surface.

8. Right-click the newly created geostatistical layer and click Validation....

9. Click the test dataset in the Input Data dropdown menu.

10. Click the same attribute in the Attribute dropdown menu that the surface was created in.

11. Type a name and location for saving the output (validation) dataset.

12. Click OK. ▶

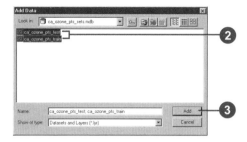

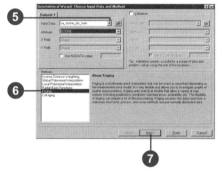

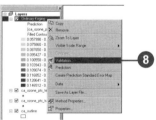

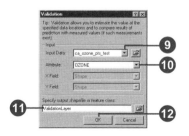

The resulting output files

Two files are created from the validation process: a shapefile containing the location of the test sample points and associated validation data and a table that provides a summary of the validation statistics, similar to those presented in the dialog box for cross-validation (see Chapter 7, 'Using analytical tools when generating surfaces').

13. When queried, add the validation layer to the ArcMap table of contents.

14. Right-click the new layer and click Open Attribute Table.

The results of the validation are displayed for assessment.

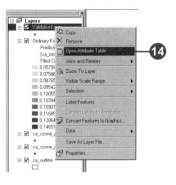

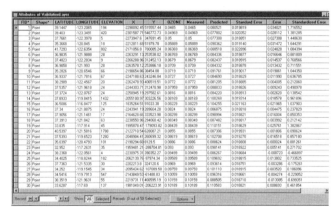

Appendix

A

IN THIS APPENDIX

- **Deterministic methods**

  - **Inverse distance weighted interpolation**

  - **Global polynomial interpolation**

  - **Local polynomial interpolation**

  - **Radial basis function interpolation**

- **Geostatistical methods**

  - **Declustering dialog box**

  - **Distribution modeling dialog box**

  - **Semivariogram/Covariance dialog box**

  - **Bivariate distribution dialog box**

  - **Kriging formulas**

  - **Cross Validation dialog box**

There are many formulas and unique implementation concepts underlying Geostatistical Analyst. The formulas and technical concepts are presented here in this appendix. It is assumed that you have some training in mathematics or geostatistics before reading this appendix.

Following the appendix are references from commonly used textbooks and journal articles for the mathematical details of the methods used in Geostatistical Analyst. In some cases, when the details are not easily found in textbooks, we give greater detail.

Deterministic methods

Inverse distance weighted interpolation

Inverse distance weighted interpolation is relatively simple and adequately described in Chapter 5, 'Deterministic methods for spatial interpolation'.

Global polynomial interpolation

Global polynomial interpolation simply uses multiple regression methods on all of the data. A response or trend surface is fitted to the x- and y-coordinates, which are the covariates. For a first-order trend, the model is,

$$Z(x_i, y_i) = \beta_0 + \beta_1 x_i + \beta_2 y_i + \varepsilon(x_i, y_i),$$

where $Z(x_i, y_i)$ is the datum at location (x_i, y_i), β_j are parameters, and $\varepsilon(x_i, y_i)$ is a random error. For the second-order trend, the model is

For the third-order trend, the model is

$$Z(x_i, y_i) = \beta_0 + \beta_1 x_i + \beta_2 y_i + \beta_3 x_i^2 + \beta_4 y_i^2 + \beta_5 x_i y_i + \varepsilon(x_i, y_i).$$

$$Z(x_i, y_i) = \beta_0 + \beta_1 x_i + \beta_2 y_i + \beta_3 x_i^2 + \beta_4 y_i^2 + \beta_5 x_i y_i + \beta_6 x_i^3 +$$
$$\beta_7 y_i^3 + \beta_8 x_i^2 y_i + \beta_9 x_i y_i^2 + \varepsilon(x_i, y_i),$$

and so on, up to a 10th order in the Geostatistical Analyst. Fitting regression models by estimating parameters $\{\beta_j\}$ uses ordinary least squares, which can be found in many statistical textbooks, for example, Snedecor and Cochran (1989).

Local polynomial interpolation

Local polynomial interpolation is similar to global polynomial interpolation, except that it uses data within localized "windows" rather than using all of the data, so it fits local trends and it uses weights. The window can be moved around, and the surface value at the center of the window, call it $\mu_0(x,y)$, is estimated at each point. Weighted least squares is used by minimizing,

$$\sum_{i=1}^{n} w_i (Z(x_i, y_i) - \mu_0(x_i, y_i))^2,$$

where n is the number of points within the window. Here, w_i is a weight,

$$w_i = \exp(-3d_{i0}/a),$$

where d_{i0} is the distance between the point and the center of the window and a is a parameter that controls how fast weights decay with distance. Finally, $\mu_0(x_i, y_i)$ is the value of the polynomial.

For first-order polynomial:

$$\mu_0(x_i, y_i) = \beta_0 + \beta_1 x_i + \beta_2 y_i,$$

For second-order polynomial:

$$\mu_0(x_i, y_i) = \beta_0 + \beta_1 x_i + \beta_2 y_i + \beta_3 x_i^2 + \beta_4 y_i^2 + \beta_5 x_i y_i,$$

and so on. The minimization occurs for the parameters $\{\beta_i\}$. The parameters are reestimated whenever the center point and, consequently, the window moves (Gandin, 1963).

Radial basis function interpolation

The Geostatistical Analyst uses a set of n basis functions, one for each data location. The predictor is a linear combination of the basis functions,

$$\hat{Z}(\mathbf{s}_0) = \sum_{i=1}^{n} \omega_i \phi(\|\mathbf{s}_i - \mathbf{s}_0\|) + \omega_{n+1}$$

where $\phi(r)$ is a radial basis function, $r = \|\mathbf{s}_i - \mathbf{s}_0\|$ is Euclidean distance between the prediction location $\mathbf{s}_0$ and each data location $\mathbf{s}_i$, and $\{\omega_i: i = 1, 2, \ldots, n + 1\}$ are weights to be estimated.

Let $\mathbf{w} = (\omega_1, \omega_2, \ldots, \omega_n)$, which are found by solving the system of equations,

$$\begin{pmatrix} \Phi & 1 \\ 1' & 0 \end{pmatrix}\begin{pmatrix} \mathbf{w} \\ \omega_{n+1} \end{pmatrix} = \begin{pmatrix} \mathbf{z} \\ 0 \end{pmatrix}$$

where Φ is a matrix with i,jth element $\phi(\|\mathbf{s}_i - \mathbf{s}_j\|)$ for the i,jth data pair, 1 is a column vector of all ones, and $\mathbf{z}$ is a column vector containing the data. If ϕ is the vector containing $\phi(\|\mathbf{s}_i - \mathbf{s}_0\|)$, then the predictor is,

$$\hat{Z}(\mathbf{s}_0) = \mathbf{w}'\phi + \omega_{n+1}.$$

Where ω_{n+1} is a bias parameter.

An equivalent predictor is to use,

$$\hat{Z}(\mathbf{s}_0) = \lambda'\mathbf{z},$$

where λ solves the equation,

$$\begin{pmatrix} \Phi & 1 \\ 1' & 0 \end{pmatrix}\begin{pmatrix} \lambda \\ m \end{pmatrix} = \begin{pmatrix} \varphi \\ 1 \end{pmatrix},$$

which has the advantage of showing the weights for each data. The weights are displayed in the Searching Neighborhood dialog box.

The radial basis functions used in the Geostatistical Analyst are:

1. Completely regularized spline function,

$$\phi(r) = -\sum_{n=1}^{\infty} \frac{(-1)^n(\sigma \cdot r)^{2n}}{n!n} = \ln(\sigma \cdot r/2)^2 + E_1\left(\sigma \cdot r/2\right) + C_E,$$

where ln is the natural logarithm, $E_1(x)$ is the exponential integral (Abramowitz and Stegun, 1965, p. 227) function, and C_E is the Euler constant (Abramowitz and Stegun, 1965, p. 255),

2. Spline with tension function,

$$\phi(r) = \ln(\sigma \cdot r/2) + K_0(\sigma \cdot r) + C_E,$$

where $K_0(x)$ is the modified Bessel function (Abramowitz and Stegun, 1965, p. 374),

3. Multiquadric function,

$$\phi(r) = \left(r^2 + \sigma^2\right)^{1/2},$$

4. Inverse multiquadric function,

$$\phi(r) = \left(r^2 + \sigma^2\right)^{-1/2},$$

5. Thin-plate spline function,

$$\phi(r) = \left(\sigma \cdot r\right)^2 \ln\left(\sigma \cdot r\right)$$

The optimal smoothing parameter σ is found by minimizing the root-mean-square prediction errors using cross-validation.

Radial basis functions are described in Bishop (1995, p. 164). Further descriptions of radial basis functions and their relationships to splines and kriging can be found in Cressie (1993, p. 180) and Chiles and Delfiner (1999, p. 272).

Geometric anisotropy

Geometric anisotropy is accounted for by a coordinate transformation:

$$\mathbf{s}^+ = \begin{pmatrix} \sqrt{r} & 0 \\ 0 & 1/\sqrt{r} \end{pmatrix} \begin{pmatrix} \cos(\theta) & \sin(\theta) \\ -\sin(\theta) & \cos(\theta) \end{pmatrix} \mathbf{s}$$

where θ is the rotation angle and r is the ratio of the major and minor axes of the resulting ellipse. Distance is then calculated as $\left\| \mathbf{s}_i^+ - \mathbf{s}_0^+ \right\|$.

Geostatistical methods

Declustering dialog box

Cell declustering

For various reasons, the data may have been sampled preferentially, with a higher density of sample points in some places than in others. For some transformation methods, such as the normal score transformation, it is important that the histogram of the sample properly reflect the histogram of the whole population. The solution to preferential sampling is to weight the data, with data in densely sampled areas receiving less weight. See explanations in Journel (1983), Isaaks and Srivastava (1989, p. 421), Cressie (1993, p. 352), and Goovaerts (1998, p. 76).

Default—Morisita's index

The default method in Geostatistical Analyst is to use a square grid of cells with a cell size that is determined from the maximum value of Morisita's index (Morisita, 1959; see also Cressie, 1993, p. 590), where Morisita's index is a function of cell size.

Polygonal method

An optional method is to allow the weights to depend on the size of polygons that surround each point. The polygons are constructed by finding all possible points that are closer to a sample point than any other sample point. Thus, each sample point has a polygon of influence. In mathematics, these are called Voronoi diagrams and Thiessen polygons. For explanations, see Isaaks and Srivastava (1989, p. 238), and Goovaerts (1998, p. 79). In Geostatistical Analyst, the outer boundary is a little larger than the smallest (unrotated) rectangle that contains all of the locations. The rectangle is formed by taking the largest x-coordinate and y-coordinate plus $1/2 * \sqrt{S/N}$, where S is the area of the rectangle and N is the number of datasets. The smallest x-coordinate and y-coordinate are likewise made a bit smaller. The outer boundary has considerable effect on the weights for edge points.

Distribution modeling dialog box

Normal-score transformation

For some of the kriging methods, it is important that the data be normally distributed. One way to force the data to be normally distributed is to use the normal score transformation. For explanations, see Journel and Huijbregts (1978, p. 478), Isaaks and Srivastava (1989, p. 469), Cressie (1993, p. 281), Rivoirard (1994, p. 46), Goovaerts (1998, p. 266), and Chiles and Delfiner (1999, p. 380). However, many of the figures given in these references are misleading by showing that the cumulative distribution function for the raw data is continuous. In reality, it is a step function. Let the order statistics for the data be $Z(\mathbf{s}_{(1)})$, $Z(\mathbf{s}_{(2)})$, … $Z(\mathbf{s}_{(n)})$, where $Z(\mathbf{s}_{(1)})$ is the lowest value and $Z(\mathbf{s}_{(n)})$ is the highest value. Suppose that there are only four values (n = 4); then the empirical cumulative distribution function will look something like the following:

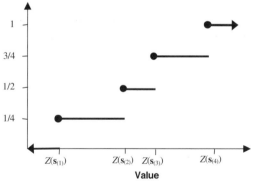

This function can be smoothed in various ways. Also note that the weights on the y-axis need not be increments of $(1/n)$ if cell declustering is used. The Geostatistical Analyst gives several methods to provide transformations.

Direct

From the empirical distribution function, it uses values that are halfway up the "step". Here is the correspondence between the original data and the transformed data.

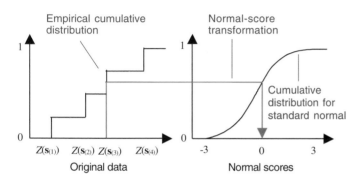

Linear

The linear method makes piece-wise linear interpolations from the original cumulative distribution function. It is easily grasped from a figure,

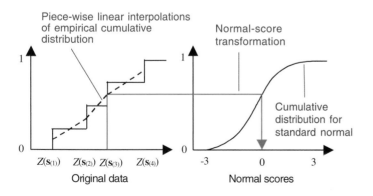

Gaussian mixture

A mixture of Gaussian distributions can be used to smooth the probability density function. We model the probability density function as

$$p(z) = \sum_{i=1}^{K} \alpha_i p_i(z; \mu_i, \sigma_i^2)$$

where

$$\sum_{i=1}^{K} \alpha_i = 1$$

and

$$p_i(z; \mu_i, \sigma_i^2) = \frac{1}{\sqrt{2\pi}\sigma_i} \exp\left[-\frac{(z - \mu_i)^2}{2\sigma_i^2} \right]$$

The parameters α_i, μ_i, and σ_i are estimated by maximum likelihood, assuming a mixture of normal distributions and independent data. The cumulative distribution is found through numerical integration,

$$P(z) = \int_{-\infty}^{z} p(x)dx$$

and a correspondence is set up with $P(z)$ and the cumulative distribution for a standard normal, just as was done for the direct and linear methods.

Semivariogram/Covariance dialog box

Variogram definitions

Definitions of the variogram and semivariogram are given in virtually all texts on geostatistics (e.g., Journel and Huijbregts, 1978, p. 31; Cressie, 1993, p. 58; Goovaerts, 1997, p. 68; Armstrong, 1998, p. 19; Chiles and Delfiner, 1999, p. 31; Stein, 1999, p. 39). Note that some authors define it as $2\gamma(\mathbf{h})$ and others as $\gamma(\mathbf{h})$. Here, the convention that $2\gamma(\mathbf{h})$ is the variogram and $\gamma(\mathbf{h})$ is the semivariogram, is maintained.

Covariance definitions

Definitions of the covariance function in a spatial setting are also given in virtually all texts on geostatistics (e.g., Journel and Huijbregts, 1978, p. 31; Isaaks and Srivistava, 1989, p. 221; Cressie, 1993, p. 53; Goovaerts, 1997, p. 68; Armstrong, 1998, p. 19; Chiles and Delfiner, 1999, p. 30; Stein, 1999, p. 15).

Estimating the variogram

The empirical semivariogram is an estimator for the theoretical quantity given by the definition of a semivariogram. The empirical semivariogram estimator is given in virtually all texts on geostatistics (e.g., Journel and Huijbregts, 1978, p. 194; Isaaks and Srivastava, 1989, p. 60; Cressie, 1993, p. 69; Goovaerts, 1997, p. 82; Armstrong, 1998, p. 47; Chiles and Delfiner, 1999, p. 36; Stein, 1999, p. 39).

Estimating the covariance

The empirical covariance is an estimator for the theoretical quantity given by the definition of the covariance function. The empirical covariance estimator is given in texts on geostatistics (e.g., Journel and Huijbregts, 1978, p. 192; Isaaks and Srivastava, 1989, p. 59; Cressie, 1993, p 70; Goovaerts, 1997, p. 86; Chiles and Delfiner, 1999, p. 31; Stein, 1999, p. 39).

Binning the variogram and covariance estimates into lag classes

The empirical variogram and covariance estimates are usually binned into lag classes based on the vector $\mathbf{h} = (h_x, h_y)^t$ that separates the pair of locations, and then the semivariogram or covariance values are averaged within each bin. Most often, binning is done in radial sectors; we will call this the sector method.

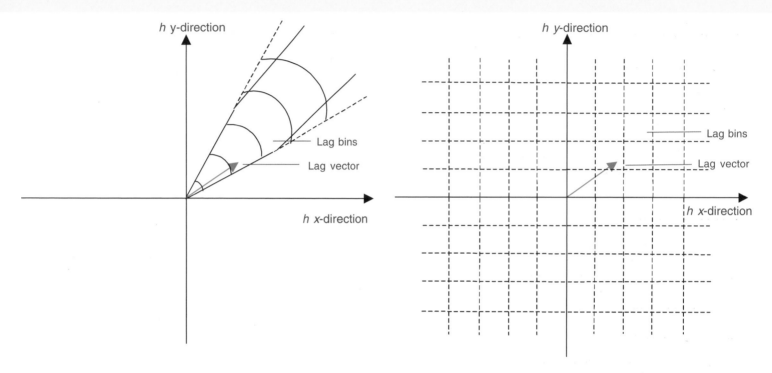

For example, this is the method that is used most commonly in software packages, including GSLIB (Deutsch and Journel, 1992, p. 45), Splus (*Splus Spatial Stats User Manual*), and SAS (Technical Report). Instead, the Geostatistical Analyst assigns lags to a regular grid; we will call this the grid method.

However, for regularly spaced data, the borders of the lag bins present problems. In order to get around this problem and make the empirical semivariogram smoother, the Geostatistical Analyst uses a kernel method to assign weighted semivariogram values for each cell, depending on how close it is to the center of the cell. The weights for the cell containing the dot can be taken as the product of the two marginal profiles, as seen in the following figure. All cells are computed in a similar fashion. Note that there will be four weights for any lag, and they will sum to one.

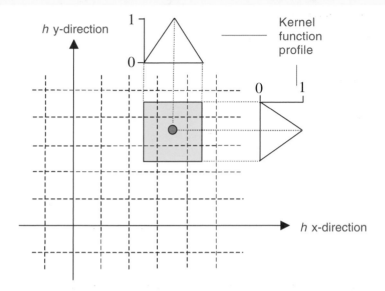

Here, any lag vector that falls within the area shaded in yellow contributes to the lag bin with the red dot in the center. The closer to the center of the lag bin, the higher the weight. This is done for all lag bins.

Semivariogram and covariance models

Relationship between semivariograms and covariance

In the following, the formulas for only the semivariograms will be presented. It is easy to get covariances from semivariograms, and vice versa, using the relationships between semivariogram and covariance models. For intrinsically stationary processes,

$$C(\mathbf{h};\theta) = \gamma(\infty;\theta) - \gamma(\mathbf{h};\theta),$$

and

$$\gamma(\mathbf{h};\theta) = C(\mathbf{0};\theta) - C(\mathbf{h};\theta),$$

where $\gamma(\infty;\theta)$ is the sill of the semivariogram and $C(\mathbf{0};\theta)$ is the origin of the covariance function. These relationships only hold for semivariograms that have sills, and all semivariogram models in Geostatistical Analyst have sills.

Geometric anisotropy

Geometric anisotropy can be created through the transformation

$$\gamma_a(\mathbf{h};\theta,\Theta) = \gamma(\|\Theta\mathbf{h}\|;\theta),$$

where Θ is a 2×2 matrix and $\gamma(\mathbf{h}; \theta)$ is one of the isotropic variogram models given below. Here, the vector $\mathbf{h} = (h_x, h_y)$ is rotated and scaled to a new coordinate system where the range of the variogram is an ellipse. In the Geostatistical Analyst, the major range is the long axis of the ellipse, and the minor range is the short axis of the ellipse. The major and minor range parameters are the values where the range equals the sill for models that attain sills or 95 percent of the sill for models that approach the sill asymptotically. For more details, see Journel and Huijbregts (1978, p. 175), Isaaks and Srivastava (1989, p. 377), Cressie (1993, p. 64), Goovaerts (1997, p. 90), or Armstrong (1998, p. 28), Chiles and Delfiner (1999, p 93).

Linear combinations of models

Here the basic semivariogram models are combined in linear combinations,

$$\gamma(\mathbf{h};\theta) = \gamma_1(\mathbf{h};\theta_1) + \gamma_2(\mathbf{h};\theta_2) + \dots$$

The Geostatistical Analyst allows up to three models as a linear combination in addition to the nugget-effect model.

Nugget effect

The semivariogram model is

$$\gamma(\mathbf{h};\boldsymbol{\theta}) = \begin{cases} 0 & \text{for} \quad \mathbf{h} = 0 \\ \theta_s & \text{for} \quad \mathbf{h} \neq 0 \end{cases}$$

where $\theta_s \geq 0$.

Circular

The semivariogram model is,

$$\gamma(\mathbf{h};\boldsymbol{\theta}) = \begin{cases} \dfrac{2\theta_s}{\pi}\left[\dfrac{\|\mathbf{h}\|}{\theta_r}\sqrt{1-\left(\dfrac{\|\mathbf{h}\|}{\theta_r}\right)^2} + \arcsin\dfrac{\|\mathbf{h}\|}{\theta_r}\right] & \text{for} \quad 0 \leq \|\mathbf{h}\| \leq \theta_r \\ \theta_s & \text{for} \quad \theta_r < \|\mathbf{h}\| \end{cases}$$

where $\theta_s \geq 0$ is the partial sill parameter and $\theta_r \geq 0$ is the range parameter.

Spherical

The semivariogram model is

$$\gamma(\mathbf{h};\boldsymbol{\theta}) = \begin{cases} \theta_s\left[\dfrac{3}{2}\dfrac{\|\mathbf{h}\|}{\theta_r} - \dfrac{1}{2}\left(\dfrac{\|\mathbf{h}\|}{\theta_r}\right)^3\right] & \text{for} \quad 0 \leq \|\mathbf{h}\| \leq \theta_r \\ \theta_s & \text{for} \quad \theta_r < \|\mathbf{h}\| \end{cases}$$

where $\theta_s \geq 0$ is the partial sill parameter and $\theta_r \geq 0$ is the range parameter.

Tetraspherical

The semivariogram model is

$$\gamma(\mathbf{h};\boldsymbol{\theta}) =$$

$$\begin{cases} \dfrac{2\theta_s}{\pi}\left(\arcsin\left(\dfrac{\|\mathbf{h}\|}{\theta_r}\right) + \dfrac{\|\mathbf{h}\|}{\theta_r}\sqrt{1-\left(\dfrac{\|\mathbf{h}\|}{\theta_r}\right)^2} + \dfrac{2}{3}\dfrac{\|\mathbf{h}\|}{\theta_r}\left(1-\left(\dfrac{\|\mathbf{h}\|}{\theta_r}\right)^2\right)^{\frac{3}{2}}\right) \\ \theta_s \end{cases}$$

$$\begin{array}{ll} \text{for} & 0 \leq \|\mathbf{h}\| \leq \theta_r \\ \text{for} & \theta_r < \|\mathbf{h}\| \end{array}$$

where $\theta_s \geq 0$ is the partial sill parameter and $\theta_r \geq 0$ is the range parameter.

Pentaspherical

The semivariogram model is

$$\gamma(\mathbf{h};\boldsymbol{\theta}) = \begin{cases} \theta_s\left[\dfrac{15}{8}\dfrac{\|\mathbf{h}\|}{\theta_r} - \dfrac{5}{4}\left(\dfrac{\|\mathbf{h}\|}{\theta_r}\right)^3 + \dfrac{3}{8}\left(\dfrac{\|\mathbf{h}\|}{\theta_r}\right)^5\right] & \text{for} \quad 0 \leq \|\mathbf{h}\| \leq \theta_r \\ \theta_s & \text{for} \quad \theta_r < \|\mathbf{h}\| \end{cases}$$

where $\theta_s \geq 0$ is the partial sill parameter and $\theta_r \geq 0$ is the range parameter.

Exponential

The semivariogram model is

$$\gamma(\mathbf{h};\boldsymbol{\theta}) = \theta_s \left[1 - \exp\left(- \frac{3\|\mathbf{h}\|}{\theta_r} \right) \right] \text{ for all } \mathbf{h},$$

where $\theta_s \geq 0$ is the partial sill parameter and $\theta_r \geq 0$ is the range parameter.

Gaussian

The semivariogram model is

$$\gamma(\mathbf{h};\boldsymbol{\theta}) = \theta_s \left[1 - \exp\left(-3 \left(\frac{\|\mathbf{h}\|}{\theta_r} \right)^2 \right) \right] \text{ for all } \mathbf{h},$$

where $\theta_s \geq 0$ is the partial sill parameter and $\theta_r \geq 0$ is the range parameter. Because this model has unstable behavior without nugget, by default the Geostatistical Analyst adds a small nugget to the model, equal to 1/1000 of the sample variance computed for the data.

Rational quadratic

The semivariogram model is

$$\gamma(\mathbf{h};\boldsymbol{\theta}) = \theta_s \frac{19 \left(\frac{\|\mathbf{h}\|}{\theta_r} \right)^2}{1 + 19 \left(\frac{\|\mathbf{h}\|}{\theta_r} \right)^2} \text{ for all } \mathbf{h},$$

where $\theta_s \geq 0$ is the partial sill parameter and $\theta_r \geq 0$ is the range parameter.

Hole effect

The semivariogram model is

$$\gamma(\mathbf{h};\boldsymbol{\theta}) = \begin{cases} 0 & \text{for } \mathbf{h} = \mathbf{0} \\ \theta_s \dfrac{1 - \sin\left(2\pi\|\mathbf{h}\|/\theta_r \right)}{\sin\left(2\pi\|\mathbf{h}\|/\theta_r \right)} & \text{for } \mathbf{h} \neq \mathbf{0} \end{cases}$$

where $\theta_s \geq 0$.

K-Bessel

The semivariogram model is

$$\gamma(\mathbf{h};\boldsymbol{\theta}) = \theta_s \left[1 - \frac{\left(\Omega_{\theta_k}\|\mathbf{h}\|/\theta_r \right)^{\theta_k}}{2^{\theta_k - 1}\Gamma(\theta_k)} K_{\theta_k}\left(\Omega_{\theta_k}\|\mathbf{h}\|/\theta_r \right) \right] \text{ for all } \mathbf{h},$$

where $\theta_s \geq 0$, $\theta_r \geq 0$, $\theta_k \geq 0$, Ω_{θ_k} is a value found numerically so that $\gamma(\theta_r) = 0.95\,\theta_s$ for any θ_k, $\Gamma(\theta_k)$ is the gamma function,

$$\Gamma(y) = \int_0^\infty x^{y-1}\exp(-x)dx$$

and $K_{\theta_k}(\bullet)$ is the modified Bessel function of the second kind of order θ_k (Abramowitz and Stegun, 1965, p. 374).

J-Bessel

The semivariogram model is

$$\gamma(\mathbf{h};\boldsymbol{\theta}) = \theta_s \left[1 - \frac{2^{\theta_d} \Gamma(\theta_d + 1)}{\left(\Omega_{\theta_d} \|\mathbf{h}\| / \theta_r \right)^{\theta_d}} J_{\theta_d} \left(\Omega_{\theta_d} \|\mathbf{h}\| / \theta_r \right) \right] \text{ for all } \mathbf{h}$$

where $\theta_s \geq 0$, $\theta_r \geq 0$, $\theta_d \geq 0$, Ω_{θ_d} must satisfy,

$$\min_{B>0, \gamma(B)=\theta_s, (\gamma')B \, <0} B = \theta_r$$

$\Gamma(\theta_k)$ is the gamma function,

$$\Gamma(y) = \int_0^\infty x^{y-1} \exp(-x) dx$$

and $J_{\theta_d}(\bullet)$ is the J-Bessel function (Abramowitz and Stegun, 1965, p. 358).

Stable

The semivariogram model is

$$\gamma(\mathbf{h};\boldsymbol{\theta}) = \theta_s \left[1 - \exp\left(-3 \left(\frac{\|\mathbf{h}\|}{\theta_r} \right)^{\theta_e} \right) \right] \text{ for all } \mathbf{h},$$

where $\theta_s \geq 0$ and $0 \leq \theta_e \leq 2$. Because this model has unstable behavior without nugget, by default the Geostatistical Analyst adds a small nugget to the model, equal to $1/1000$ of the sample variance computed from the data.

Crosscovariance models

Crosscovariance models in the Geostatistical Analyst use "coregionalization" models, which means that they are of the same families as the covariance forms of the semivariogram models listed above. Crossvariograms are not used in the Geostatistical Analyst. The traditional crossvariogram (Matheron, 1965) can only be used under certain conditions (Journel and Huijbregts, 1978, p. 236; Cressie, 1993, p. 67; Ver Hoef and Cressie, 1993), and it is not optimal otherwise. Crosscovariances allow models that can have spatial shifts (Journel and Huijbregts, 1978, p. 41; Ver Hoef and Cressie, 1993), and the empirical crosscovariance surface allows the user to visually inspect for such shifts.

Coregionalization models for crosscovariance (sometimes given as crossvariograms, but the ideas and models are readily adapted to crosscovariances) are described in Journel and Huijbregts (1978, p. 40), Isaaks and Srivastava (1989, p. 390), Goovaerts, (1997, p. 107), and Chiles and Delfiner (1999, p. 339). The Geostatistical Analyst adapts these models by allowing a spatial shift between any two variables (Ver Hoef and Cressie, 1993). This adds two parameters to the model to describe the shift in the x-coordinate and y-coordinate.

Fitting semivariogram and covariance models

The fitting algorithm begins by obtaining a preliminary estimate for the range of the data called stage 1. Use $Z_j^k(\mathbf{s}_i)$ to denote the jth measurement of variable type k at the ith spatial location $\mathbf{s}_i$.

Stage 1

Geostatistical Analyst first scales each dataset, $\widetilde{Z}_j^k(\mathbf{s}_i) = Z_j^k(\mathbf{s}_i)/s_k$ where s_k is the sample standard deviation. Stage 1 begins by assuming an isotropic model, and it computes the empirical semivariogram (or covariance) on the scaled data $\widetilde{Z}_j^k(\mathbf{s}_i)$ using the sector method (as defined earlier in the section 'Binning the variogram and covariance estimates into lag classes') over a large range of lag classes that progress in a geometric series. The lag classes are formed from intervals $\left| d^{k-1/2}, d^{k+1/2} \right|$, where $d = 1.25$ and k ranges from the smallest machine integer to the largest. The center of each lag class is taken to be $d^k \cosh(\frac{1}{2}\log d^k)$. Obviously, many lag classes are empty, and the Geostatistical Analyst only uses those that have data in them. Call this empirical (cross)covariance $\hat{C}_{ij}(h_k)$, where i indicates the ith variable type, j indicates the jth variable type, and k indicates the kth lag class. The first iteration of parameter estimates is obtained by minimizing,

$$\sum_{i=1}^{T}\sum_{j=1}^{T}\sum_{k=1}^{n_{ij}} w_{ij}(\mathbf{h}_k)\left(\widetilde{C}_{ij}\left(\mathbf{h}_k;\theta_{ij}\right) - \hat{C}_{ij}\left(\mathbf{h}_k\right)\right)^2 \qquad (1)$$

for θ, where θ_{ij} is the vector of parameters for the i,jth covariance function and θ contains all covariance parameters, where

$$w_{ij}(\mathbf{h}_k) = N_{ij}(\mathbf{h}_k)/\sum_{m=1}^{n_{ij}} N_{ij}(\mathbf{h}_m) \qquad (2)$$

and $N_{ij}(\mathbf{h}_k)$ is the number of pairs in the empirical (cross) covariance function for variables i and j in lag class k. Call this

estimate $\theta^{(1)}$. In the next iteration, the Geostatistical Analyst uses a Cressie's (1985) weighted least squares by minimizing (1) again, only this time let,

$$\varpi_{ij}(\mathbf{h}_k;\theta_{ij}^{(1)}) = \frac{N_{ij}(\mathbf{h}_k)}{\widetilde{C}_{ii}(\mathbf{0};\theta_{ii}^{(1)})\widetilde{C}_{jj}(\mathbf{0};\theta_{jj}^{(1)}) + \widetilde{C}_{ij}^2(\mathbf{h}_k;\theta_{ij}^{(1)})} \qquad (3)$$

and then these weights are normalized so that each (cross)covariance gets equal weight,

$$w_{ij}(\mathbf{h}_k) = \varpi_{ij}(\mathbf{h}_k;\theta_{ij}^{(1)})/\sum_{m=1}^{n_{ij}}\varpi_{ij}(\mathbf{h}_m;\theta_{ij}^{(1)}) \qquad (4)$$

Call this estimate $\theta^{(2)}$. Notice that if we use variograms rather than covariances $\theta_{ii}^{(2)}$ is,

$$\arg\min_{\theta_{ii}}\left[\sum_{k=1}^{n_{ij}} w_{ii}(\mathbf{h}_k)\left(\widetilde{\gamma}_{ii}\left(\mathbf{h}_k;\theta_{ii}\right) - \hat{\gamma}_{ii}\left(\mathbf{h}\right)\right)^2\right] \qquad (5)$$

where $w_{ii}(\mathbf{h}_k)$ is given by (2) and then $\theta_{ii}^{(2)}$ is obtained from (5) with weights as in (4) but now,

$$\varpi_{ij}(\mathbf{h}_k;\theta_{ii}^{(1)}) = \frac{N_{ij}(\mathbf{h}_k)}{\gamma_{ii}^2(\mathbf{h};\theta_{ii}^{(1)})}$$

The estimates $\theta^{(1)}$ and $\theta^{(2)}$ are two steps in an iteratively reweighted least-squares algorithm.

The estimate $\theta^{(2)}$ is only used to provide a range estimate for a default lag size for the grid method in estimating the empirical semivariogram or covariance. The default number of lags is 12, so the lag size for the grid method in the next section is taken to be 2*range/12.

Stage 2

Stage 2 essentially repeats stage 1, but on an empirical semivariogram or (cross)covariance on the scaled data $\widetilde{Z}_j^k(\mathbf{s}_i)$ that uses the grid method (as defined earlier in the section 'Binning the semivariogram and covariance estimate') where the default lag size is obtained from the range estimate in $\theta^{(2)}$ from Stage 1. It also allows for anisotropy and linear combinations of up to three (cross)covariance or semivariogram models in additions into lag classes to the nugget effect for each dataset,

$$\widetilde{C}_{ij}(\mathbf{h};\theta) = \sum_{u=1}^{S} B_u(i,j)\rho_u(\mathbf{h};\varphi_u).$$

Here, $B_u(i,j)$ is a partial sill parameter and is the i,jth component of $\mathbf{B}_u$, a $T \times T$ positive-definite matrix, where T is the number of *types* of variables, S is the number of different (cross)covariance models used in a linear combination, and the function $\rho_u(\mathbf{h};\varphi_u)$ is a normalized covariance model; $\rho_u(\mathbf{0};\varphi_u) = 1$, where φ_u are parameters that typically control the range (and/or shape) of the covariance model. As before, θ contains all of the parameters. The third iteration of parameter estimates, $\theta^{(3)}$ is obtained by minimizing (1) with weights (2) on the empirical covariance using the grid method, and then $\theta^{(4)}$ is obtained by minimizing (1) with weights from (4) and (3) on the empirical covariance using the grid method. These formulas are modified in an obvious way if we are using semivariograms, as was shown for stage 1. Now, change back to the original scale. The final (cross)covariance models are

$$C_{ij}(\mathbf{h}) = s_i\, s_j \widetilde{C}_{ij}(\mathbf{h};\theta_{ij}^{(4)}),$$

and for variograms they are

$$\gamma_{ii}(\mathbf{h}) = s_i^2 \widetilde{\gamma}_{ii}(\mathbf{h};\theta_{ii}^{(4)}).$$

If the user changes any parameters, such as lag size, then estimates are recalculated beginning at stage 2.

Bivariate distribution dialog box

Disjunctive kriging requires that all pairs of data have a bivariate normal distribution. This assumption is difficult to test in practice. The Geostatistical Analyst gives a visual tool to help assess the bivariate normal assumption. A theoretical curve, as a function of lag, can be developed based on various threshold values for the cumulative distribution function (see Deutsch and Journel, 1992, p. 139 and Goovaerts, 1998, p. 265). This theoretical curve can be compared to an empirical semivariogram based on indicators. More generally, if QQPlots show a marginal normal distribution, and the data appears to have bivariate normal distributions, it is reasonable to assume a full multivariate normal distribution for the data. Thus, the check for the bivariate normal distribution can be used for simple kriging, allowing a user to assure that quantile and probability maps are based on reasonable assumptions.

Kriging formulas

Credit for kriging can be spread among many authors. Kriging with covariance is equivalent to best linear unbiased prediction (BLUP), and simple, ordinary, and universal kriging contributions came from Wold (1938), Kolmogorov (1941), Wiener (1949), Gandin (1959), Goldberger (1962), and Henderson (1963). Spatial prediction using variograms is attributed to Gandin (1959, 1963) and Matheron (1962, 1969). See Journel (1983) for indicator kriging, Sullivan (1984) for probability kriging, and Matheron (1976) for disjunctive kriging. Cressie (1990) gives more details on the origins of kriging.

The Geostatistical Analyst uses predictors that can include measurement error. These models are discussed by Gandin (1959, 1960, 1963) and Cressie (1986, 1988, 1993, 127–135). These models include those commonly given in most geostatistics textbooks, which are often described as "exact" predictors. By exact, it is meant that if a prediction is made at a location where data has already been collected, then the predictor is the same value as the data that was collected there, and the prediction standard error is zero. This can cause strange-looking maps because there will be "jumps" in the predicted values wherever data has been collected. In the presence of measurement error, one may want to "filter" out the measurement and produce a smoother prediction map. Measurement error models are only possible for ordinary, simple, and universal kriging. All models were described here. Begin with notation. At times, it will be necessary to talk about multiple data locations, with multiple measurements per location (measurement error), for multiple types of variables (cokriging). We use $Z_j^k(\mathbf{s}_i)$ to denote the jth measurement of variable type k at the ith spatial location $\mathbf{s}_i$.

Estimating measurement error

If there are multiple observations per location, the Geostatistical Analyst can estimate the measurement error. The formula for computing measurement error is,

$$\hat{\sigma}_{ME}^2 = \frac{\displaystyle\sum_{\mathbf{s}_i \in D}\sum_{j=1}^{n_i}(Z_j(\mathbf{s}_i) - \overline{Z}(\mathbf{s}_i))^2}{N - n_D} \quad,$$

where D is the set of all data locations that have more than one measurement, $Z_j(\mathbf{s}_i)$ is the jth measurement at location $\mathbf{s}_i$, is the mean value at location $\mathbf{s}_i$, n_i is the number of observations at location $\mathbf{s}_i \in D$, $N = \Sigma_i n_i$ for all $\mathbf{s}_i$ in D, and n_D is the number of spatial locations in D. The slider is set at the position that corresponds with this value; that is, it is set at 100 ($\hat{\sigma}_{ME}^2$ / nugget) percent. Users can override $\hat{\sigma}_{ME}^2$ if they choose, and the nugget effect is constrained during estimation to be no smaller than $\hat{\sigma}_{ME}^2$; whenever the user overrides a nugget value or $\hat{\sigma}_{ME}^2$, then the inequality nugget $\geq \hat{\sigma}_{ME}^2$ is preserved.

Ordinary kriging

The interested reader should consult Cressie (1993, pgs. 127–135) for additional explanations of kriging with measurement error; here, a condensed version of the ordinary kriging implementation in Geostatistical Analyst is provided. As in Chapter 6, assume the data is a realization of a spatially autocorrelated process plus independent random errors:

$$Z_t(\mathbf{s}) = \mu(\mathbf{s}) + \varepsilon_t(\mathbf{s}),$$

but now decompose the random errors,

$$\varepsilon_t(\mathbf{s}) = Y(\mathbf{s}) + \eta(\mathbf{s}) + \delta_t(\mathbf{s}),$$

where $Z_t(\mathbf{s})$ denotes the tth realization at location $\mathbf{s}_i$, and let n_i be the number of measurements at location $\mathbf{s}_i$. Often $n_i = 1$, and if $n_i > 1$, it forms a measurement error model. The following assumptions are made:

- $m(\mathbf{s}) = m$ is an unknown, deterministic mean value.

- $Y(\mathbf{s})$ is a smooth second-order stationary process whose range of autocorrelation is detectable with an empirical semivariogram or covariance.

- $E(Y(\mathbf{s})) = 0$.

- $Cov(Y(\mathbf{s}), Y(\mathbf{s}+\mathbf{h})) = C_y(\mathbf{h})$, and there is no additional nugget effect in the process $Y(\mathbf{s})$.

- $h(\mathbf{s})$ is a smooth second-order stationary process whose variogram range is so close to 0 that it is smaller than all practical distances between data and prediction locations.

- $E(h(\mathbf{s})) = 0$.

- $Cov(h(\mathbf{s}), h(\mathbf{s}+\mathbf{h})) = C_h(\mathbf{h})$ with $C_h(¥) = 0$.

- $d_t(\mathbf{s})$ is a white-noise process composed of measurement errors.

- $E(d_t(\mathbf{s})) = 0$, for all $\mathbf{s}$ and t.

- $Cov(d_t(\mathbf{s}), d_u(\mathbf{s}+\mathbf{h})) = s^2$ if $\mathbf{h} = \mathbf{0}$ and $t = u$, otherwise it is 0.

- $Y(\bullet)$, $h(\bullet)$, and $d(\bullet)$ are independent of each other.

Assume here that the nugget effect, which is called v, is composed of two parts: microscale variation plus measurement error. That is, $v = C_\eta(\mathbf{0}) + \sigma^2$. From this model, you can deduce that,

$$Cov(Z_t(\mathbf{s}), Z_u(\mathbf{s}+\mathbf{h})) = \begin{cases} C_y(\mathbf{h}) + C_\eta(\mathbf{h}) & \text{if} \quad \mathbf{h} \neq \mathbf{0} \\ C_y(\mathbf{0}) + C_\eta(\mathbf{0}) & \text{if} \quad \mathbf{h} = \mathbf{0} \text{ and } t \neq u \\ C_y(\mathbf{0}) + C_\eta(\mathbf{0}) + \sigma^2 & \text{if} \quad \mathbf{h} = \mathbf{0} \text{ and } t = u \end{cases}$$

If there is measurement error, you will want to predict the filtered (noiseless) quantity $S(\mathbf{s}_0) \equiv \mu + Y(\mathbf{s}_0) + \eta(\mathbf{s}_0)$ at location $\mathbf{s}_0$; that is, remove the measurement error. If there is no measurement error, $S(\mathbf{s}_0) = Z(\mathbf{s}_0)$. Ordinary kriging with measurement error is obtained for the linear predictor,

$$\hat{S}(\mathbf{s}_0) = \lambda'\mathbf{z},$$

then minimize,

$$E(S(\mathbf{s}_0) - \lambda'\mathbf{z})^2,$$

where $\mathbf{z}$ is a vector of the observed data, and λ is a vector of the kriging weights. An unbiasedness condition,

$$E(S(\mathbf{s}_0) - \lambda'\mathbf{z}) = 0,$$

implies $\lambda'\mathbf{1} = 1$, which causes the need to use a Lagrange multiplier when minimizing. Thus, obtaining the kriging equations,

$$\begin{pmatrix} \Sigma_z & \mathbf{1} \\ \mathbf{1'} & 0 \end{pmatrix} \begin{pmatrix} \lambda \\ m \end{pmatrix} = \begin{pmatrix} \mathbf{c} \\ 1 \end{pmatrix}$$

where m is the Lagrange multiplier, Σ_z is the covariance matrix among the data, and $\mathbf{c}$ is $Cov(\mathbf{z}, S(\mathbf{s}_0)) = Cov(\mathbf{z}, Y(\mathbf{s}_0) + \eta(\mathbf{s}_0))$. Assuming that the range of $\eta(\bullet)$ is very close to 0, you can assume $Cov(\mathbf{z}, \eta(\mathbf{s}_0)) = \mathbf{0}$ for all practical distances, except when $\mathbf{s}_0 = \mathbf{s}_i$, where $\mathbf{s}_i$ is one of the spatial locations for observed data; then $Cov(Z(\mathbf{s}_i), \eta(\mathbf{s}_i)) = C_\eta(\mathbf{0})$, which needs to be estimated. The total nugget effect can be estimated, but recall that it is composed of two parts, $v = \sigma^2 + C_\eta(\mathbf{0})$. If there is a separate estimate of σ^2, then you can estimate $C_\eta(\mathbf{0}) = v - \sigma^2$. This is equivalent to specifying a proportion of the nugget effect that is measurement error and a proportion that is microscale variation; $0 \le \pi < 1$, and identify $\sigma^2 = \pi v$ and $C_\eta(\mathbf{0}) = (1 - \pi)v$ can be specified. If there are multiple observations per location, then measurement error can be estimated as shown earlier.

Once σ^2 and $C_\eta(\mathbf{0})$ are specified, proceed with solving the kriging equations. If all of the nugget effect is microscale variation due to $\eta(\bullet)$ (i.e., no measurement error), then the solution to the kriging equations yields exact kriging. Solving for λ you obtain,

$$\lambda = \Sigma_z^{-1}(\mathbf{c} - \mathbf{1}m) \text{ where } m = (\mathbf{1}'\Sigma_z^{-1}\mathbf{c} - 1)/\mathbf{1}'\Sigma_z^{-1}\mathbf{1},$$

for the ordinary kriging predictor. Substituting in this λ, you get the mean-square-prediction error,

$$E(S(\mathbf{s}_0) - \lambda'\mathbf{z})^2$$
$$= C_y(\mathbf{0}) + C_\eta(\mathbf{0}) - \lambda'\mathbf{c} - m,$$
$$= C_y(\mathbf{0}) + (1 - \pi)v - \lambda'\mathbf{c} - m,$$

so the prediction standard errors are

$$\hat{\sigma}_S(\mathbf{s}_0) = \sqrt{C_y(\mathbf{0}) + (1 - \pi)v - \lambda'\mathbf{c} - m}$$

Predicting a new value for cross-validation and validation

During cross-validation, you do not want to predict $S(\mathbf{s}_0)$, the noiseless version of data, but must predict $Z_u(\mathbf{s}_0)$, with measurement error, in order for the prediction standard errors to reflect the root-mean-square prediction error from cross-validation. Prediction of a "new value" is obtained for the linear predictor

$$\hat{Z}_u(\mathbf{s}_0) = \lambda'\mathbf{z},$$

then minimize,

$$E(Z_u(\mathbf{s}_0) - \lambda'\mathbf{z})^2.$$

Assume, in effect, that if $\mathbf{s}_0 = \mathbf{s}_i \in D$, then $u > n_i$. Proceeding as before, the kriging equations are obtained,

$$\begin{pmatrix} \Sigma_z & \mathbf{1} \\ \mathbf{1}' & 0 \end{pmatrix}\begin{pmatrix} \lambda \\ m \end{pmatrix} = \begin{pmatrix} \mathbf{c} \\ 1 \end{pmatrix},$$

where m is the Lagrange multiplier, Σ_z is the covariance matrix among the data and $\mathbf{c}$ is $Cov(\mathbf{z}, Z_u(\mathbf{s}_0)) = Cov(\mathbf{z}, Y(\mathbf{s}_0) + \eta(\mathbf{s}_0) + \delta_u(\mathbf{s}_0))$. Solving for λ, we obtain,

$$\lambda = \Sigma_z^{-1}(\mathbf{c} - \mathbf{1}m), \text{ where } m = (\mathbf{1}'\Sigma_z^{-1}\mathbf{c} - 1)/\mathbf{1}'\Sigma_z^{-1}\mathbf{1}.$$

Notice that when $\mathbf{s}_0 = \mathbf{s}_i \in D$, then the prediction $\hat{Z}_u(\mathbf{s}_i)$ is usually *not* equal to one of the observed values $z_t(\mathbf{s}_i)$; $t \le n$. However, substituting in λ to get the mean-square prediction error yields,

$$E(Z_u(\mathbf{s}_0) - \lambda'\mathbf{z})^2$$
$$= C_y(\mathbf{0}) + C_\eta(\mathbf{0}) + \sigma^2 - \lambda'\mathbf{c} - m,$$
$$= C_y(\mathbf{0}) + v - \lambda'\mathbf{c} - m,$$

so the prediction standard errors are

$$\hat{\sigma}_Z(\mathbf{s}_0) = \sqrt{C_y(\mathbf{0}) + v - \lambda'\mathbf{c} - m} \quad .$$

This should be compared to the prediction standard errors $\hat{\sigma}_S(\mathbf{s}_0)$ for the noiseless version. Notice that when $\mathbf{s}_0 = \mathbf{s}_i$ for one of the observed data locations $\mathbf{s}_i \in D$, then neither of the prediction standard errors will be 0.

Probability and quantile maps

If the random errors are normally distributed with stationarity (either second-order or intrinsic), then the prediction error $\hat{S}(\mathbf{s}_0) - S(\mathbf{s}_0)$ has a normal distribution with zero mean and variance $\hat{\sigma}_S^2(\mathbf{s}_0)$. Normality allows the computing of a probability map or, equivalently, a quantile map.

Simple kriging

Here a condensed version of the simple kriging implementation in the Geostatistical Analyst is given. Refer to the appendix on ordinary kriging for the model and assumptions. For simple kriging, one assumption is changed to:

$\mu(\mathbf{s})$ is a *known*, deterministic mean function.

As for ordinary kriging, it is necessary to predict the filtered (noiseless) quantity, $S(\mathbf{s}_0) \equiv \mu(\mathbf{s}_0) + Y(\mathbf{s}_0) + \eta(\mathbf{s}_0)$ at location $\mathbf{s}_0$.

Prediction with measurement error

Simple kriging with measurement error is obtained for the linear predictor,

$$(\mathbf{s}_0) = \lambda\text{'}\mathbf{z} + k$$

then minimize,

$$E\,(S(\mathbf{s}_0) - \lambda\text{'}\mathbf{z} - k)^2 = \mathrm{Var}[Y(\mathbf{s}_0) + \eta(\mathbf{s}_0) - \lambda\text{'}\mathbf{z}] + [\mu(\mathbf{s}_0) - \lambda\text{'}\mu - k]^2,$$

where μ is the vector of known means for all of the observed data. The minimization is obtained by setting $k = \mu(\mathbf{s}_0) - \lambda\text{'}\mu$ and $\lambda = \Sigma_z^{-1}\mathbf{c}$, where Σ_z is the covariance matrix among the data and $\mathbf{c}$ is $\mathrm{Cov}(\mathbf{z}, Y(\mathbf{s}_0) + \eta(\mathbf{s}_0))$. Then obtain the simple kriging predictor,

$$(\mathbf{s}_0) = \lambda\text{'}\mathbf{z} + k = \mathbf{c}\text{'}\Sigma_z^{-1}(\mathbf{z} - \mu) + \mu(\mathbf{s}_0).$$

Substituting to get the mean squared prediction errors,

$$E(S(\mathbf{s}_0) - \lambda\text{'}\mathbf{z} - k)^2$$
$$= C_y(\mathbf{0}) + C_\eta(\mathbf{0}) - \mathbf{c}\text{'}\Sigma_z^{-1}\mathbf{c}$$
$$= C_y(\mathbf{0}) + (1 - \pi)v - \mathbf{c}\text{'}\Sigma_z^{-1}\mathbf{c},$$

so the prediction standard errors are

$$\hat{\sigma}_S(\mathbf{s}_0) = \sqrt{C_y(\mathbf{0}) + (1 - \pi)v - \lambda\text{'}\mathbf{c}}$$

Predicting a new value for cross-validation

During cross-validation, it is not desirable to predict the noiseless version of the data—rather, to predict it with measurement error in order for the prediction standard errors to reflect the mean-square prediction error from cross-validation. Prediction of a "new value" is obtained for the linear predictor,

$$_u(\mathbf{s}_0) = \lambda\text{'}\mathbf{z} + k,$$

then minimize,

$$E(Z_u(\mathbf{s}_0) - \lambda\text{'}\mathbf{z} - k)^2.$$

Assume, in effect, that if $\mathbf{s}_0 = \mathbf{s}_i \in D$, then $u > n_i$. Proceeding as done earlier, the kriging predictor is obtained,

$$_u(\mathbf{s}_0) = \lambda\text{'}\mathbf{z} + k = \mathbf{c}\text{'}\Sigma_z^{-1}(\mathbf{z} - \mu) + \mu(\mathbf{s}_0),$$

with mean-square prediction errors,

$$E(Z_u(\mathbf{s}_0) - \lambda\text{'}\mathbf{z} - k)^2$$
$$= C_y(\mathbf{0}) + C_\eta(\mathbf{0}) + \sigma^2 - \mathbf{c}\text{'}\Sigma_z^{-1}\mathbf{c}$$
$$= C_y(\mathbf{0}) + v + \mathbf{c}\text{'}\Sigma_z^{-1}\mathbf{c},$$

so the prediction standard errors are

$$\hat{\sigma}_Z(\mathbf{s}_0) = \sqrt{C_y(\mathbf{0}) + v - \lambda\text{'}\mathbf{c}}.$$

This should be compared to the prediction standard errors for the noiseless version. Notice that when $\mathbf{s}_0 = \mathbf{s}_i$ for one of the observed data locations $\mathbf{s}_i \in D$, then neither of the prediction standard errors will be 0.

Probability and quantile maps

If the data comes from a joint multivariate normal distribution, where

$$\begin{bmatrix} S(\mathbf{s}_0) \\ \mathbf{z} \end{bmatrix} \sim N\left(\begin{bmatrix} \mu(\mathbf{s}_0) \\ \mu \end{bmatrix}, \begin{bmatrix} C_y(\mathbf{0}) + C_\eta(\mathbf{0}) & \mathbf{c} \\ \mathbf{c'} & \Sigma_z \end{bmatrix} \right)$$

then $\hat{S}(\mathbf{s}_0)$ is the conditional expectation, $E(S(\mathbf{s}_0)|\mathbf{z})$, and it is a well-known property of the multivariate normal distribution that the distribution of $\hat{S}(\mathbf{s}_0)$ is,

$$S(\mathbf{s}_0)|\mathbf{z} \sim N(\mathbf{c'}\Sigma_z^{-1}(\mathbf{z} - \mu) + \mu(\mathbf{s}_0), C_y(\mathbf{0}) + C_\eta(\mathbf{0}) - \mathbf{c'}\Sigma_z^{-1}\mathbf{c}).$$

Because the predictor also has a normal distribution, normality allows the computation of a probability map or, equivalently, a quantile map. Also notice that the conditional expectation $E(S(\mathbf{s}_0)|\mathbf{z})$ is the best predictor, in the sense of having the smallest mean-square prediction error, of all predictors, linear or not.

Universal kriging

Assume the following model,

$$Z_t(\mathbf{s}) = [\mathbf{x}(\mathbf{s})]'\beta + \varepsilon_t(\mathbf{s}),$$

but now decompose the random errors,

$$\varepsilon_t(\mathbf{s}) = Y(\mathbf{s}) + \eta(\mathbf{s}) + \delta_t(\mathbf{s}),$$

where $\mathbf{X}$ is a design matrix and β is a vector of parameters, and otherwise it is similar to the model for ordinary kriging, with the same assumptions except,

$$\mu(\mathbf{s}) = [\mathbf{x}(\mathbf{s})]'\beta \ , \text{ where } \mathbf{x}(\mathbf{s}) \text{ is a vector of observed covariates}$$
and β is a vector of *unknown* parameters.

Prediction with measurement error

As for ordinary kriging, predict the filtered (noiseless) quantity $S(\mathbf{s}_0) \equiv [\mathbf{x}(\mathbf{s}_0)]'\beta + Y(\mathbf{s}_0) + \eta(\mathbf{s}_0)$ at location $\mathbf{s}_0$. $\mathbf{X}$ has a column of ones, and other columns contain polynomial functions of the spatial coordinates at location $\mathbf{s}$. Universal kriging with measurement error is obtained for the linear predictor,

$$\hat{S}(\mathbf{s}_0) = \lambda'\mathbf{z},$$

then minimize,

$$E(S(\mathbf{s}_0) - \lambda'\mathbf{z})^2 \ ,$$

where $\mathbf{z}$ is a vector of the observed data, and λ is a vector of the kriging weights. An unbiasedness condition,

$$E(S(\mathbf{s}_0) - \lambda'\mathbf{z}) = 0 \ ,$$

implies $\mathbf{X}' \lambda = \mathbf{x}(\mathbf{s}_0)$. Proceeding as with ordinary kriging, the universal kriging equations are obtained,

$$\begin{pmatrix} \Sigma_z & \mathbf{X} \\ \mathbf{X}' & 0 \end{pmatrix} \begin{pmatrix} \lambda \\ \mathbf{m} \end{pmatrix} = \begin{pmatrix} \mathbf{c} \\ \mathbf{x}(\mathbf{s}_0) \end{pmatrix}$$

where $\mathbf{m}$ is a vector of Lagrange multipliers, Σ_z is the covariance matrix among the data, and $\mathbf{c}$ is $\mathrm{Cov}(\mathbf{z}, S(\mathbf{s}_0))$. Solving for λ, the universal kriging predictor is obtained,

$$\lambda = \Sigma_z^{-1}(\mathbf{c} - \mathbf{Xm}) \ , \text{ where } \mathbf{m} = (\mathbf{X}' \Sigma_z^{-1}\mathbf{X})^{-1}(\mathbf{X}' \Sigma_z^{-1} \mathbf{c} - \mathbf{x}(\mathbf{s}_0)).$$

Substituting to get the mean squared prediction errors,

$$E(S(\mathbf{s}_0) - \lambda'\mathbf{z})^2$$
$$= C_y(0) + C_\eta(0) - \lambda'(\mathbf{c}+\mathbf{Xm}),$$
$$= C_y(0) + (1 - \pi)\nu - \lambda'(\mathbf{c}+\mathbf{Xm}),$$

so the prediction standard errors are

$$\hat{\sigma}_S(\mathbf{s}_0) = \sqrt{C_y(0) + (1-\pi)\nu - \lambda'(\mathbf{c} - \mathbf{Xm})} \quad .$$

Predicting a new value for cross-validation

During cross-validation, do not predict $S(\mathbf{s}_0)$, the noiseless version of the data; rather, predict $Z_u(\mathbf{s}_0)$ with measurement error in order for the prediction standard errors to reflect the root-mean-square prediction error from cross-validation. Prediction of a "new value" is obtained for the linear predictor,

$$\hat{Z}_u(\mathbf{s}_0) = \lambda'\mathbf{z},$$

then minimize,

$$E(Z_u(\mathbf{s}_0) - \lambda'\mathbf{z})^2.$$

Assume, in effect, that if $\mathbf{s}_0 = \mathbf{s}_i \in D$, then $u > n_i$. Proceeding as before, the universal kriging equations are obtained,

$$\begin{pmatrix} \Sigma_z & \mathbf{X} \\ \mathbf{X}' & 0 \end{pmatrix} \begin{pmatrix} \lambda \\ \mathbf{m} \end{pmatrix} = \begin{pmatrix} \mathbf{c} \\ \mathbf{x}(\mathbf{s}_0) \end{pmatrix}.$$

Solving for λ, obtain the universal kriging predictor,

$$\lambda = \Sigma_z^{-1}(\mathbf{c} - \mathbf{Xm}) \text{ where } \mathbf{m} = (\mathbf{X}' \Sigma_z^{-1}\mathbf{X})^{-1}(\mathbf{X}' \Sigma_z^{-1} \mathbf{c} - \mathbf{x}(\mathbf{s}_0)).$$

Notice that when $\mathbf{s}_0 = \mathbf{s}_t \in D$, then the prediction $\hat{Z}_u(\mathbf{s}_0)$ is usually *not* equal to one of the observed values $z_t(\mathbf{s}_t)$; $t \leq n_t$. Substituting in λ to get the mean-square prediction error yields,

$$\mathrm{E}(Z_u(\mathbf{s}_0) - \lambda\text{'}\mathbf{z})^2 =$$
$$= C_y(\mathbf{0}) + C_\eta(\mathbf{0}) + \sigma^2 - \lambda\text{'}(\mathbf{c} + \mathbf{Xm}),$$
$$= C_y(\mathbf{0}) + v - \lambda\text{'}(\mathbf{c} + \mathbf{Xm}),$$

so the prediction standard errors are

$$\sqrt{C_y(\mathbf{0}) + v - \lambda\text{'}(\mathbf{c} - \mathbf{Xm})} \ ,$$

which should be compared to the prediction standard errors for the noiseless version. Notice that when $\mathbf{s}_0 = \mathbf{s}_t$ for one of the observed data locations $\mathbf{s}_t \in D$, then neither of the prediction standard errors will be 0.

Probability and quantile maps

If the random errors are normally distributed with stationarity (either second-order or intrinsic), then the prediction error $\hat{S}(\mathbf{s}_0) - S(\mathbf{s}_0)$ has a normal distribution with zero mean and variance $\hat{\sigma}_S(\mathbf{s}_0)$. Normality allows the computation of a probability map or, equivalently, a quantile map.

Lognormal linear kriging

If a log transformation is selected, lognormal kriging can be used for ordinary kriging, simple kriging, and universal kriging and is implemented as given in Cressie (1993). Following his notation, the prediction formulas are:

Ordinary Kriging—equation 3.2.40, p. 135 of Cressie (1993)

Simple Kriging—second equation on p. 136 of Cressie (1993)

Universal Kriging—Cressie (1993) equation 3.2.40 generalizes to,

$$\hat{p}_z(\mathbf{Z};\mathbf{s}_0) = \exp\{\hat{p}_Y(\mathbf{Z};\mathbf{s}_0) + \hat{\sigma}_Y^2(\mathbf{s}_0)/2 - \mathbf{m}_Y\,'[\mathbf{x}(\mathbf{s}_0)]\},$$

where $\mathbf{m}$ is the vector of Lagrange multipliers from the universal kriging equations and $\mathbf{x}(\mathbf{s}_0)$ is the vector of covariates at location $\mathbf{s}_0$, the prediction location. The prediction variance is given in Cressie (1993) equation 3.2.41, where:

Ordinary Kriging - μ_Y is replaced by,

$$\hat{\mu}_Y = \mathbf{1'}\boldsymbol{\Sigma}_Y^{-1}\mathbf{Y}/(\mathbf{1'}\boldsymbol{\Sigma}_Y^{-1}\mathbf{1})$$

Simple Kriging - μ_Y is known,

Universal Kriging - μ_Y is replaced by,

$$\hat{\mu}_Y(\mathbf{s}_0) = [\mathbf{x}(\mathbf{s}_0)]'(\mathbf{X'}\boldsymbol{\Sigma}_Y^{-1}\mathbf{X})^{-1}\mathbf{X'}\boldsymbol{\Sigma}_Y^{-1}\mathbf{Y}$$

where the vector $\mathbf{Y} = \log(\mathbf{Z})$ and each element of $\mathbf{Y}$ is assumed to have a normal distribution.

Transgaussian kriging

If a Box–Cox or arcsine transformation is selected, transgaussian kriging can be used for ordinary kriging and universal kriging, and is implemented as given in Cressie (1993, p. 137).

Indicator kriging

Indicator kriging is a nonlinear method, and only the exact form (i.e., measurement error is not filtered out) of ordinary kriging can be used on indicators. Assume the data is a realization of a spatially autocorrelated process,

$$Z(\mathbf{s}) = \mu + \varepsilon(\mathbf{s}),$$

and a binary (0 or 1) random variable is created by using a threshold,

$$Z^1(\mathbf{s}) = I(Z(\mathbf{s}) > c_1),$$

where $I(condition)$ is an indicator function that is 1 if $condition$ is true and 0, otherwise. Assume the binary data is also a realization of a spatially autocorrelated process (with a nugget effect possible),

$$Z^1(\mathbf{s}) = \mu_1 + \varepsilon^1(\mathbf{s}).$$

Indicator kriging is ordinary kriging (with 0 measurement error) of the binary variables $Z^1(\mathbf{s})$, and hence no filtering of any measurement error in $Z(\mathbf{s})$ is attempted. Another threshold can be used,

$$Z^2(\mathbf{s}) = I(Z(\mathbf{s}) > c_2),$$

with a model,

$$Z^2(\mathbf{s}) = \mu_2 + \varepsilon^2(\mathbf{s}).$$

Now use cokriging with both binary variables to predict $Z^1(\mathbf{s}_0)$. The theory and formulas are given by Journel (1983), Isaaks and Srivastava (1989), Cressie (1993, p. 281), Goovaerts (1997, p. 293), and Chiles and Delfiner (1999, p. 381).

Probability kriging

Like indicator kriging, probability kriging (Sullivan, 1984; Cressie, 1993, p. 283; Goovaerts, 1997, p. 301; Chiles and Delfiner, 1999, p. 385) is a nonlinear method, and it is not obvious how to filter out measurement error when using probability kriging. Assume the data is a realization of a spatially autocorrelated process plus independent random errors,

$$Z(\mathbf{s}) = \mu + \varepsilon(\mathbf{s}),$$

and a binary (0 or 1) random variable is created by using a threshold,

$$Z^1(\mathbf{s}) = I(Z(\mathbf{s}) > c),$$

where $I(condition)$ is an indicator function that is 1 if $condition$ is true and 0, otherwise. Assume the binary data is also a realization of a spatially autocorrelated process (with a nugget effect possible),

$$Z^1(\mathbf{s}) = \mu_1 + \varepsilon^1(\mathbf{s}).$$

Then, use cokriging to predict $Z^1(\mathbf{s}_0)$ using $\{Z^1(\mathbf{s})\}$ as the primary variable and the original data $\{Z(\mathbf{s})\}$ as the secondary variable in the cokriging equations. See the section on cokriging for further details.

Disjunctive kriging

In disjunctive kriging (Matheron, 1976), the predictor is of the form,

$$\hat{Z}(\mathbf{s}_0) = \sum_{s \in D} g_s(Z(\mathbf{s})),$$

where $g_s(Z(\mathbf{s}))$ is some function of the variable $Z(\mathbf{s})$. The Geostatistical Analyst uses the following predictor,

$$\hat{Z}(\mathbf{s}_0) = f_0 + \sum_{k>0} f_k \hat{H}_k(Y(\mathbf{s}_0)),$$

where

$$\hat{H}_k(Y(\mathbf{s}_0)) = \sum_{i=1}^{n} \lambda_{ki} H_k(Y(\mathbf{s}_i)),$$

f_i and λ_{ki} are coefficients, $H_k(Y(\mathbf{s}_i))$ are Hermite polynomials, and $Y(\mathbf{s}_i)$ and $Y(\mathbf{s}_j)$ have a bivariate normal distribution. The variable $Y(\mathbf{s})$ can be transformed (i.e., disjunctive kriging can be lognormal and transgaussian) and allows the user to examine the assumption of bivariate normality. The theory and practice of disjunctive kriging are complicated, and the Geostatistical Analyst follows the method as outlined in Rivoirard (1994).

Cokriging

Cokriging can be used when there are several variables. The exact formulas for cokriging are given by Journel and Huijbregts (1978, p. 324), Isaaks and Srivastava (1989, p. 400), Cressie (1991, p. 138), Goovaerts (1997, p. 224), and Chiles and Delfiner (1999, p. 298). Ordinary cokriging, simple cokriging, and universal cokriging allow measurement error models, just like their kriging counterparts. Similarly, indicator cokriging, probability cokriging, and disjunctive cokriging can only do exact prediction (i.e., measurement error is not filtered out).

Ordinary, simple, and universal cokriging

The universal kriging model is the most general, so assume,

$$Z_j^k(\mathbf{s}) = [\mathbf{x}_k(\mathbf{s})]'\beta_k + Y^k(\mathbf{s}) + \eta^k(\mathbf{s}) + \delta_j^k(\mathbf{s}),$$

where $\mathbf{X}_k$ is a design matrix and β_k is a vector of parameters for the kth variable type, with the following assumptions:

- $Y^k(\mathbf{s})$ is a smooth second-order stationary process whose variogram range is larger than the shortest distance between data points.

- $E(Y^k(\mathbf{s})) = 0$.

- $\mathrm{Cov}(Y^k(\mathbf{s}), Y^m(\mathbf{s}+\mathbf{h})) = C_y^{km}(\mathbf{h})$, with $C_y^{km}(\infty) = 0$ (i.e., there is no additional nugget effect in the process $Y^k(\mathbf{s})$).

- $\eta^k(\mathbf{s})$ is a smooth second-order stationary process whose variogram range is so close to 0 that it is shorter than all practical distances between data and prediction locations.

- $E(\eta^k(\mathbf{s})) = 0$.

- $\mathrm{Cov}(\eta^k(\mathbf{s}), \eta^m(\mathbf{s}+\mathbf{h})) = C_\eta^{km}(\mathbf{h})$ when k is equal to m, with $C_\eta^{km}(\infty) = 0$.

- $\mathrm{Cov}(\eta^k(\mathbf{s}), \eta^m(\mathbf{s}+\mathbf{h})) = 0$ when k is not equal to m.

- $\delta_j^k(\mathbf{s})$ is a white noise process composed of measurement errors.

- $E(\delta_j^k(\mathbf{s})) = 0$, for all k and j.

- $\mathrm{Cov}(\delta_j^k(\mathbf{s})\,\delta_j^k(\mathbf{s}+\mathbf{h})) = s_k^2$ if $\mathbf{h} = 0$; otherwise, it is 0.

- $\mathrm{Cov}(\delta_j^k(\mathbf{s}), d_t^k(\mathbf{s}+\mathbf{h})) = 0$ for i not equal to t.

$Y^k(\bullet)$, $\eta^l(\bullet)$, and $\delta^m(\bullet)$ are independent of each other for all k, l, and m. Assume here that the nugget effect v_i is composed of two parts: microscale variation plus measurement error; that is, $v_k = C_\eta^{kk}(0) + \sigma_k^2$. Also notice that there is no joint information at the scale of $\eta^k(\bullet)$ and $\eta^m(\bullet)$, so set their crosscovariance to 0. From this model, you can deduce that,

$$Cov(Z_j^k(\mathbf{s}), Z_t^m(\mathbf{s}+\mathbf{h})) =$$

$$\begin{cases} C_y^{km}(\mathbf{h}) & \text{if} & k \neq m \\ C_y^{kk}(\mathbf{h}) + C_\eta^{kk}(\mathbf{h}) & \text{if} & k = m \text{ and } \mathbf{h} \neq 0 \\ C_y^{kk}(0) + C_\eta^{kk}(0) & \text{if} & k = m \text{ and } \mathbf{h} = 0 \text{ and } j \neq t \\ C_y^{kk}(0) + C_\eta^{kk}(0) + \sigma_k^2 & \text{if} & k = m \text{ and } \mathbf{h} = 0 \text{ and } j = t \end{cases}$$

For simplicity, consider only two variable types; the ideas generalize easily for more types of variables. Predict the filtered (noiseless) quantity $S^1(\mathbf{s}_0) \equiv [\mathbf{x}_1(\mathbf{s}_0)]'\beta_1 + Y^1(\mathbf{s}_0) + \eta^1(\mathbf{s}_0)$ at location $\mathbf{s}_0$. Cokriging in the Geostatistical Analyst is obtained for the linear predictor,

$$\hat{S}^1(\mathbf{s}_0) = \lambda_1'\mathbf{z}_1 + \lambda_2'\mathbf{z}_2$$

then minimize,

$$E(Z(\mathbf{s}_0) - [\ \lambda_1'\mathbf{z}_1 + \lambda_2'\mathbf{z}_2])^2.$$

Proceeding, as with ordinary kriging, the following cokriging equations are obtained,

$$\begin{pmatrix} \Sigma_z & \mathbf{X} \\ \mathbf{X'} & 0 \end{pmatrix}\begin{pmatrix} \lambda \\ \mathbf{m} \end{pmatrix} = \begin{pmatrix} \mathbf{c} \\ \mathbf{x}_1(\mathbf{s}_0) \end{pmatrix},$$

where

$$\Sigma_z = \begin{pmatrix} \Sigma_{11} & \Sigma_{12} \\ \Sigma_{21} & \Sigma_{22} \end{pmatrix}, \ \mathbf{X} = \begin{pmatrix} \mathbf{X}_1 & \mathbf{0} \\ \mathbf{0} & \mathbf{X}_2 \end{pmatrix}, \ \mathbf{c} = \begin{pmatrix} \mathbf{c}_1 \\ \mathbf{c}_2 \end{pmatrix}, \ \lambda = \begin{pmatrix} \lambda_1 \\ \lambda_2 \end{pmatrix}, \ \mathbf{m} = \begin{pmatrix} \mathbf{m}_1 \\ \mathbf{m}_2 \end{pmatrix},$$

$\mathbf{m}_1$ and $\mathbf{m}_2$ are Lagrange multipliers, Σ_{km} is the covariance matrix among the data $\mathbf{z}_k$ and $\mathbf{z}_m$, and $\mathbf{c}_k$ is $\text{Cov}(\mathbf{z}_k, S_1(\mathbf{s}_0))$. Solving for λ, obtains,

$$\lambda = \Sigma_z^{-1}(\mathbf{c} - \mathbf{Xm}), \text{ where } \mathbf{m} = (\mathbf{X}' \, \Sigma_z^{-1} \mathbf{X})^{-1}(\mathbf{X}' \, \Sigma_z^{-1} \mathbf{c} - \mathbf{x}_1(\mathbf{s}_0)).$$

Substituting λ, get the mean-square prediction error,

$$E(S^1(\mathbf{s}_0) - \lambda'\mathbf{z})^2$$
$$= C_y^{11}(\mathbf{0}) + C_\eta^{11}(\mathbf{0}) - \lambda'(\mathbf{c} + \mathbf{Xm}),$$
$$= C_y^{11}(\mathbf{0}) + (1 - \pi_1)v_1 - \lambda'(\mathbf{c} + \mathbf{Xm}),$$

so the prediction standard errors are,

$$\hat{\sigma}_{S1}(\mathbf{s}_0) = \sqrt{C_y^{11}(\mathbf{0}) + (1 - \pi_1)v_1 - \lambda'(\mathbf{c} + \mathbf{Xm})}.$$

If

$$\mathbf{X} = \begin{pmatrix} 1 & 0 \\ 0 & 1 \end{pmatrix},$$

then ordinary cokriging is a special case of universal cokriging. For simple cokriging,

$$\hat{S}_1(\mathbf{s}_0) = \lambda'\mathbf{z} + k = \mathbf{c}'\Sigma_z^{-1}(\mathbf{z} - \mu) + \mu_1(\mathbf{s}_0),$$

with the prediction standard errors given by,

$$\hat{\sigma}_{S1}(\mathbf{s}_0) = \sqrt{C_y^{11}(\mathbf{0}) + (1 - \pi_1)v_1 - \mathbf{c}'\Sigma_z\mathbf{c}}.$$

Predicting new values for cross-validation can be developed just as with ordinary, simple, and universal kriging.

Indicator, probability, and disjunctive cokriging

Indicator, probability, and disjunctive cokriging are nonlinear methods, and only the exact form (i.e., measurement error is not filtered out) of ordinary cokriging can be used with these methods. Indicator cokriging is just cokriging of indicators; see Cressie (1993, p. 283), Goovaerts (1997, p. 297), and Chiles and Delfiner (1999, p. 386). Probability cokriging involves forming indicators on two variable types in addition to using the original data, and then using the ordinary cokriging equations. Disjunctive cokriging is a generalization of disjunctive kriging for bivariate Gaussian distributions (Muge and Cabecadas, 1989; Chiles and Delfiner, 1999, p. 419).

Cross Validation dialog box

Cross-validation

Cross-validation consists of removing data, one at a time, and then trying to predict it. Next, the predicted value can be compared to the actual (observed) value to assess how well the prediction is working. Notice that in geostatistics the semivariogram models are typically not reestimated each time data is removed. For more information on cross-validation, see Isaaks and Srivastava (1989, p. 351), Cressie (1993, p. 101), Goovaerts (1997, p. 105), Armstrong (1998, p. 115), Chiles and Delfiner (1999, p. 111), and Stein (1999, p. 215).

Cross-validation summaries

Summary statistics and graphs can be made by comparing the predicted value to the actual value from cross-validation. Let $\hat{Z}(\mathbf{s}_i)$ be the predicted value from cross-validation, let $z(\mathbf{s}_i)$ be the observed value, and let $\hat{\sigma}(\mathbf{s}_i)$ be the prediction standard error for location $\mathbf{s}_i$. Then some of the summary statistics given by the Geostatistical Analyst are:

1. Mean prediction errors,

$$\frac{\sum_{i=1}^{n}\left(\hat{Z}(\mathbf{s}_i) - z(\mathbf{s}_i)\right)}{n} .$$

2. Root-mean-square prediction errors,

$$\sqrt{\frac{\sum_{i=1}^{n}\left(\hat{Z}(\mathbf{s}_i) - z(\mathbf{s}_i)\right)^2}{n}} .$$

3. Average kriging standard error,

$$\sqrt{\frac{\sum_{i=1}^{n}\hat{\sigma}(\mathbf{s}_i)}{n}} .$$

4. Mean standardized prediction errors,

$$\frac{\sum_{i=1}^{n}\left(\hat{Z}(\mathbf{s}_i) - z(\mathbf{s}_i)\right)/\hat{\sigma}(\mathbf{s}_i)}{n} .$$

5. Root-mean-square standardized prediction errors,

$$\sqrt{\frac{\sum_{i=1}^{n}\left[\left(\hat{Z}(\mathbf{s}_i) - z(\mathbf{s}_i)\right)/\hat{\sigma}(\mathbf{s}_i)\right]^2}{n}} .$$

Appendix

B

IN THIS APPENDIX

- **A comparison of the Geostatistical Analyst methods**

This appendix provides an overview of the methods that are available with the Geostatistical Analyst. The following chart describes the characteristics of each method, summarizes its advandages and disadvantages, and shows the type of output it creates. By comparing the differences between these methods you can determine which ones you should use in your application.

A Comparison of the Geostatistical Analyst methods

Method	Deterministic/ Stochastic	Output Surface Types	Computing Time/ Modeling Time[1]	Exact Interpolator	Advantages	Disadvantages	Assumptions[2]
Inverse Distance Weighted	Deterministic	Prediction	Fast/Fast	Yes	Few parameter decisions	No assessment of prediction errors; produces "bulls eyes" around data locations	None
Global polynomial	Deterministic	Prediction	Fast/Fast	No	Few parameter decisions	No assessment of prediction errors; may be too smooth; edge points have large influence	None
Local polynomial	Deterministic	Prediction	Moderately Fast/Moderate	No	More parameter decisions	No assessment of prediction errors; may be too automatic	None
Radial basis functions	Deterministic	Prediction	Moderately Fast/Moderate	Yes	Flexible and automatic with some parameter decisions	No assessment of prediction errors; may be too automatic	None
Kriging	Stochastic	Prediction; Prediction Standard Errors; Probability; Quantile	Moderately Fast/Slower	Yes without measurement error; No with measurement error	Very flexible; allows assessment of spatial autocorrelation; can obtain prediction standard errors; many parameter decisions	Need to make many decisions on transformations, trends, models, parameters, and neighborhoods	Data comes from a stationary stochastic process, and some methods require that the data comes from a normal distribution
Cokriging	Stochastic	Prediction; Prediction Standard Errors; Probability; Quantile	Moderate/ Slowest	Yes without measurement error; No with measurement error	Very flexible; can use information in multiple datasets; allows assessment of spatial cross-correlation; many parameter decisions	Need to make many decisions on transformations, trends, models, parameters, and neighborhoods	Data comes from a stationary stochastic process, and some methods require that the data comes from a normal distribution

1. Computing time is computer-processing time to create a surface. Modeling time includes user-processing time to make decisions on model parameters and search neighborhoods.
2. We assume that all methods are predicting a smooth surface from noisy data.

Descriptions

IDW: IDW is a quick deterministic interpolator that is exact. There are very few decisions to make regarding model parameters. It can be a good way to take a first look at an interpolated surface. However, there is no assessment of prediction errors and IDW can produce "bulls eyes" around data locations. There are no assumptions required of the data.

Global polynomial: Global polynomial is a quick deterministic interpolator that is smooth (inexact). There are very few decisions to make regarding model parameters. It is best used for surfaces that change slowly and gradually. However, there is no assessment of prediction errors and it may be too smooth. Locations at the edge of the data can have a large effect on the surface. There are no assumptions required of the data.

Local polynomial: Local polynomial is a moderately quick deterministic interpolator that is smooth (inexact). It is more flexible than the global polynomial method, but there are more parameter decisions. There is no assessment of prediction errors. The method provides prediction surfaces that are comparable to kriging with measurement errors. Local polynomial methods do not allow you to investigate the autocorrelation of the data, making it less flexible and more automatic than kriging. There are no assumptions required of the data.

Radial basis functions: Radial basis functions are moderately quick deterministic interpolators that are exact. They are much more flexible than IDW, but there are more parameter decisions. There is no assessment of prediction errors. The method provides prediction surfaces that are comparable to the exact form of kriging. Radial basis functions do not allow you to investigate the autocorrelation of the data, making it less flexible and more automatic than kriging. Radial basis functions make no assumptions about the data.

Kriging: Kriging is a moderately quick interpolator that can be exact if the data has no measurement error, or smoothed if the data has measurement error. It is very flexible and allows you to investigate the spatial autocorrelation in the data. Because kriging uses statistical models, it allows a variety of map outputs, including predictions, prediction standard errors, probability, and quantile maps. The flexibility of kriging can require a lot of decision-making relative to other methods, or you can take the parameter defaults. Kriging assumes the data comes from a stationary stochastic process, and some methods require that the data comes from a normal distribution.

Cokriging: Cokriging is a moderately quick interpolator that can be exact if the data has no measurement error, or smoothed if the data has measurement error. It can use information in multiple datasets. Cokriging is very flexible and allows you to investigate the spatial autocorrelation and cross-correlation in the data. Because cokriging uses statistical models, it allows a variety of map outputs, including predictions, prediction standard errors, probability, and quantile maps. The flexibility of cokriging requires the most decision-making of all methods, or you can take the parameter defaults. Cokriging assumes the data comes from a stationary stochastic process, and some methods require that the data comes from a normal distribution.

Glossary

anisotropy

A property of a spatial process or data where spatial dependence (autocorrelation) changes with both the distance and the direction between two locations.

autocorrelation

Statistical correlation between spatial random variables of the same type, attribute, name, and so on, where the correlation depends on the distance and/or direction that separates the locations. Compare to crosscorrelation.

bandwidth

This term, when used for binning the empirical semivariogram/covariance, is some maximum width of a bin when using the sector method. The sector method forms bins between radial lines that diverge. The maximum divergence is called the bandwidth, beyond which the lines (no longer radial) become parallel.

bin

A classification of lags, where all lags that have similar distance and direction are put into the same bin. Bins are commonly formed by a grid or a sector method.

cokriging

A statistical interpolation method that uses data from multiple data types (multiple attributes) to predict (interpolate) values of the primary data type (primary attribute). Cokriging also provides standard errors of the predictions. See also kriging.

correlation

Covariance that is scaled so that values range from -1, when variables vary opposite of each other, to 1 when they vary together. See also covariance.

covariance

The statistical tendency of two variables of the same type, attribute, name, and so on, to vary in ways that are related to each other. Positive covariance occurs when both variables tend to be above their respective means together, and negative covariance occurs if one variable tends to be above its mean when the other variable is below its mean. See also correlation, and compare to crosscovariance.

crosscorrelation

Statistical correlation between spatial random variables of different types, attributes, names, and so on, where the correlation depends on the distance and/or direction that separates the locations. Compare to autocorrelation.

crosscovariance

The statistical tendency of variables of different types, attributes, names, and so on, to vary in ways that are related to each other. Positive crosscovariance occurs when both variables tend to be above their respective means together, and negative crosscovariance occurs if one variable tends to be above its mean when the other variable is below its mean. Compare to covariance.

cross-validation

The procedure where one data is removed and the rest of the data is used to predict the removed data. Full cross-validation is done by removing each data in the dataset and using the rest of the data to predict it.

crossvariogram

A function of the distance and direction separating two locations, used to quantify cross-correlation. The crossvariogram is defined as the variance of the difference between two variables of different types or attributes at two locations. The crossvariogram generally increases with distance, and is described by nugget, sill, and range parameters.

deterministic

A type or part of a model where the outcome is completely and exactly known based on known input; the fixed (nonrandom) components of a model. In the Geostatistical Analyst, all interpolation methods that do not have random components (IDW, global and local polynomial, and radial basis functions) are deterministic. The statistical methods (kriging, cokriging) may have deterministic (nonrandom) components, often called trend (as in universal kriging).

detrending

The process of removing the trend by subtracting the trend surface (usually polynomial functions of the spatial x- and y-coordinates) from the original data values. The resulting values, after having the trend removed, are called residuals.

directional influences

Natural or physical processes that affect the measured trait or attribute such that the magnitude of the effects on the attribute vary in different directions.

dissimilarity

Becoming less and less alike. The semivariogram is a dissimilarity function because it increases with distance, indicating that values are becoming less alike as they get farther apart. Thus, the higher the semivariogram value, the more dissimilar the values.

empirical

A term used to mean that the quantity depends on the data, observations, or experiment only; that is, it is not a model or part of a model. For example, empirical semivariograms are computed on data only, which is in contrast to theoretical semivariogram models.

estimation

The process of forming a statistic from observed data to estimate parameters in a model or distribution.

first-order polynomial

The order of a polynomial is the largest integer m in the power terms (e.g., x^m). For a first-order polynomial the largest m is 1. In the spatial context, where x and y are spatial coordinates, a polynomial will contain terms $x^m y^n$, and a first-order polynomial can contain all terms where $m + n = 1$ (e.g., $b_0 + b_1 x + b_2 y$). See also second-order polynomial.

geostatistics

General: Statistical methodologies that use spatial coordinates to help formulate models used in estimation and prediction. In the Geostatistical Analyst: Exploratory and interpolation methods that use information on the spatial coordinates of the data.

global polynomial interpolation

One of the deterministic interpolation methods used in the Geostatistical Analyst. The interpolated surface is not forced to go through the data, and the method does not have standard errors associated with it.

histogram

A bar graph where data is divided into groups. The width of the bars shows the range of values in each group, and the height of the bar indicates how many values are in each group.

interpolate

Predicting values at locations where data has not been observed, using data from locations where data has been collected. Usually, interpolation is for predictions within the area where data has been collected, rather then extending predictions to areas outside of the data-collection area.

intrinsic stationarity

An assumption that the data comes from a random process with a constant mean, and a semivariogram that only depends on the distance and direction separating any two locations.

inverse distance weighted interpolation

One of the deterministic interpolation methods used in the Geostatistical Analyst. The interpolated surface goes through the data, and the method does not have standard errors associated with it.

isotropy

A property of a natural process or data where spatial dependence (autocorrelation) changes only with the distance between two locations (direction is unimportant).

kriging

A statistical interpolation method that uses data from a single data type (single attribute) to predict (interpolate) values of that same data type at unsampled locations. Kriging also provides standard errors of the predictions. See also cokriging.

lag

The line (vector) that separates any two locations. A lag has length (distance) and direction (orientation).

least-squares fit

A model (line, surface, or smooth function) that is fit to data by finding the parameters of the model that minimize the squared differences between each data value and the model.

linear model of coregionalization

A model for semivariograms/covariances and crosscovariances formed by taking a linear combination of component semivariogram/covariance models. This model is used for cokriging methods.

local polynomial interpolation

One of the deterministic interpolation methods used in the Geostatistical Analyst. The interpolated surface is not forced to go through the data; the method does not have standard errors associated with it.

long-range variation

Variation can often be decomposed into components, each of which vary over different spatial resolutions or scales. Long-range variation refers to variation at the coarse scale, and is usually modeled with deterministic components such as polynomials, also known as trend.

mean stationarity

A property of a spatial process where all of the spatial random variables have the same mean value.

nugget

A parameter of a covariance or semivariogram model that represents independent error, measurement error and/or microscale variation at spatial scales that are too fine to detect. The nugget effect is seen as a discontinuity at the origin of either the covariance or semivariogram model.

ordinary kriging

Spatial prediction (interpolation) using semivariogram or covariance models that rely on spatial relationships among the data. Ordinary kriging makes certain assumptions about the model, such as intrinsic stationarity, and that the true mean of the data is constant but unknown.

partial sill

A parameter of a covariance or semivariogram model that represents the variance of a spatially autocorrelated process without any nugget effect. In the semivariogram model, the partial sill is the difference between the nugget and the sill.

polynomial

A function composed by summing powers of its variables. In the spatial context, where x-coordinates and y-coordinates are the variables, a polynomial has terms like 1, x, x^2, y, y^2, xy, x^2y, and so on, all of which are added together with coefficients, $b_0 + b_1x + b_2y + \ldots$ In general, terms of the form $b_i x^m y^n$ can be summed, where m and n are nonnegative integers.

prediction

The process of forming a statistic from observed data to predict random variables at locations where data has not been collected.

prediction standard error

The square-root of the prediction variance, which is the variation associated with the difference between the true and predicted value. The prediction standard error quantifies the uncertainty of the prediction. A rule of thumb is that 95 percent of the time the true value will be within the interval formed by taking the predicted value ± 2 times the prediction standard error if data are normally distributed.

probability map

A surface that gives the probability that the variable of interest is above (or below) some threshold value that the user specifies.

QQPlot

A scatter-plot, where the quantiles of two distributions are plotted against each other.

quantile

The p-th quantile, where p is between 0 and 1, is the value that has a proportion p of the data below the value. For theoretical distributions, the p-th quantile is the value that has p probability below the value.

radial basis functions

One of the deterministic interpolation methods used in the Geostatistical Analyst. The interpolated surface is forced to go through the data, and the method does not have standard errors associated with it.

regression

A statistical method where a variable, often called the response or dependent variable, is made up of a function (often linear) of one or more other variables which are called covariates, explanatory, or independent variables. The function can be fitted by least squares, among other methods.

residuals

Values formed by subtracting the trend surface (usually, polynomial functions of the spatial x- and y-coordinates) from the original data values.

range

A parameter of a covariance or semivariogram model that represents a distance beyond which there is little or no autocorrelation among variables.

searching neighborhood

A polygon that forms a subset of data around the prediction location. Only data within the searching neighborhood will be used for interpolation.

second-order polynomial

The order of a polynomial is the largest integer m in the power terms (e.g., x^m). A second-order polynomial has two as the largest m. In the spatial context, where x and y are spatial coordinates, a polynomial will contain terms $x^m y^n$, and a second-order polynomial can contain all terms where m + n = 2 (e.g., $b_0 + b_1 x + b_2 y + b_3 x^2 + b_4 y^2 + b_5 xy$). See also first-order polynomial.

second-order stationarity

An assumption that the data comes from a random process with a constant mean, and spatial covariance that only depends on the distance and direction separating any two locations.

semicrossvariogram

The crossvariogram divided by two.

semivariogram

The variogram divided by two.

semivariogram values

The value of the semivariogram function for some distance and direction.

short-range variation

Variation can often be decomposed into components, each of which vary over different spatial resolution or scales. Short-range variation refers to variation at the fine scale, and is usually modeled as spatially dependent random variation.

sill

A parameter of a variogram or semivariogram model that represents a value that the semivariogram tends to when distances get very large. At large distances, variables become uncorrelated, so the sill of the semivariogram is equal to the variance of the random variable. Some theoretical semivariograms do not have a sill. All semivariogram models used in the Geostatistical Analyst have a sill.

spatial dependence

The notion that things near to each other are more similar than things farther apart.

spherical model

A function of specific form with nugget, range, and sill parameters that can be used for a semivariogram or covariance model.

spline interpolation

One of the deterministic interpolation methods used in the Geostatistical Analyst; a special case of radial basis functions. The interpolated surface is forced to go through the data, and no standard errors are available.

stationarity

All statistical properties of an attribute depend only on the relative locations of attribute values. See mean stationarity, intrinsic stationarity, and second-order stationarity.

surface

A function of the spatial coordinates where the function represents some variable of interest, either what actually occurred in nature or a mathematical model of the variable.

trend

A surface composed of fixed parameters, often polynomials of the x- and y-coordinates. The nonrandom part of a spatial model describing an attribute. The trend usually models the long-range or coarse-scale variation, leaving random errors to model the fine-scale variation.

unimodal

A curve with a single global maximum value, without any local maximums.

univariate distribution

A function for a single variable that gives the probabilities that the variable will take a given value.

validation

The procedure where part of the data is removed and the rest of the data is used to predict the removed part of the data.

variogram

A function of the distance and direction separating two locations, used to quantify autocorrelation. The variogram is defined as the variance of the difference between two variables at two locations. The variogram generally increases with distance, and is described by nugget, sill, and range parameters.

variography

The process of estimating the theoretical semivariogram. It begins with exploratory data analysis, then computing the empirical semivariogram, binning, fitting a semivariogram model, and using diagnostics to assess the fitted model.

References

This section contains additional references and the literature cited in this book.

1. Abramowitz, M. and Stegun, I.A. 1965. Handbook of Mathematical Functions. Dover, New York.

2. Armstrong, M. 1998. *Basic Linear Geostatistics.* Springer, Berlin. 153 p.

3. Bishop, C.M. 1995. *Neural Networks for Pattern Recognition.* Oxford Press, Oxford, 482 p.

4. Chiles, J. and Delfiner, P. 1999. *Geostatistics. Modeling Spatial Uncertainty.* John Wiley and Sons, New York. 695.

5. Cook, D., Majure, J.J., Symanzik, J., and Cressie, N. 1996. Dynamic graphics in a GIS: Exploring and analyzing multvariate spatial data using linked software. Computational Statistics: Special Issue on Computer Aided Analyses of Spatial Data, 11(4): 467–480.

6. Cook, D., Symanzik, J., Majure, J. J., and Cressie, N. 1997. Dynamic graphics in a GIS: More examples using linked software. Computers and Geosciences: Special Issue of Exploratory Cartographic Visualization, 23(1):371–385.

7. Cressie, N. 1985. Fitting variogram models by weighted least squares. *Journal of the International Association for Mathematical Geology* **17**: 653–702.

8. Cressie, N. 1986. Kriging nonstationary data. *Journal of the American Statistical Association* **81**: 625–634.

9. Cressie, N. 1988. Spatial prediction and ordinary kriging. *Mathematical Geology* **20**: 405–421. (Erratum, *Mathematical Geology* **21**: 493–494).

10. Cressie, N. 1990. The origins of kriging. *Mathematical Geology* **22**: 239–252.

11. Cressie, N. 1993. *Statistics for Spatial Data, revised ed.* John Wiley and Sons, New York. 900 p.

12. Gandin L.S. 1959. The problem on optimal interpolation. *Trudy GGO* **99**: 67–75 (In Russian).

13. Gandin L.S. 1960. On optimal interpolation and extrapolation of meteorological fields. *Trudy GGO* **114**: 75–89 (In Russian).

14. Gandin, L.S. 1963. *Objective Analysis of Meteorological Fields.* Gidrometeorologicheskoe Izdatel'stvo (GIMIZ), Leningrad (translated by Israel Program for Scientific Translations, Jerusalem, 1965).

15. Goldberger, A.S. 1962. Best linear unbiased prediction in the generalized linear regression model. *Journal of the American Statistical Association* **57**: 369–375.

16. Goovaerts, P. 1997. *Geostatistics for Natural Resources Evaluation.* Oxford University Press, New York. 483 p.

17. Henderson, C.R. 1963. Selection index and expected genetic advance. In Statistical Genetics and Plant Breeding, W.D. Hanson and H.F. Robinson, eds., Publication 982, National Academy of Sciences, National Research Council, Washington, D.C. pp. 361–379.

18. Isaaks, E.H. and Srivastava, R.M. 1989. *An Introduction to Applied Geostatistics.* Oxford University Press, New York. 561 p.

19. Journel, A.G. 1983. Nonparametric estimation of spatial distributions. *Journal of the International Association for Mathematical Geology* **15**: 445–468.

20. Journel, A.G. and Huijbregts, C.J. 1978. *Mining Geostatistics.* Academic Press, London. 600 p.

21. Kolmogorov, A. N. 1941. Interpolation and extrapolation of stationary random sequences. *Isvestiia Akademii Nauk SSSR, Seriia Matematicheskiia 5*: 3–14. (Translation, 1926, Memo RM-3090-PR, Rand Corp., Santa Monica, CA).

22. Krivoruchko, K., Gribov, A., Ver Hoef, J.2000. *Predicting Exact, Filtered, and New Values using Kriging*. AAPG Hedberg Research Conference, "Applied Reservoir Characterization Using Geostatistics", December 3-6, 2000, The Woodlands, Texas.

23. Matheron, G. 1962. *Traité de Géostatistique Appliquée, Tome I. Mémoires du Bureau de Recherches Géologiques et Minières*, **No. 14**, Editions Technip, Paris.

24. Matheron, G. 1969. Le Krigeage Universel. *Cahiers du Centre de Morphologie Mathematique*, **No. 1**, Fontainebleau, France.

25. Matheron, G. 1965. *Les variables régionalisées et leur estmation. Une application de la théorie des fonctions aléatoires aux Sciences de la Nature*. Masson, Paris.

26. Matheron, G. 1976. A simple substitute for conditional expectation: The disjunctive kriging. In *Advanced Geostatistics in the Mining Industry*, M. Guarascio, M. David, and C. Huijbregts, eds., Reidel, Dordrecht, 237–251.

27. Morisita, M. 1959. Measuring of the dispersion and analysis of distribution patterns. *Memoires of the Faculty of Science, Kyushu University, Series E. Biology* **2**: 215–235.

28. Muge, F.H. and Cabecadas, G. 1989. A geostatistical approach to eutrophication modelling. In *Geostatistics,* **Vol. 1**, M. Armstrong ed., Kluwer, Dordrecht, The Netherlands, pgs 445–457.

29. Rivoirard, J. 1994. *Introduction to Disjunctive Kriging and Non-Linear Geostatistics*. Oxford University Press, Oxford. 180 p.

30. Snedecor, G.W. and Cochran, W.G. 1989. Statistical Methods (8th ed.). Iowa State University Press, Ames, IA.

31. Stein, M.L. 1999. *Interpolation of Spatial Data. Some Theory for Kriging*. Springer, New York. 247 p.

32. Sullivan, J. 1984. Conditional recovery estimation through probability kriging—theory and practice. In *Geostatistics for Natural Resources Characterization, Part I*. G. Verly, M. David, A. Journel, and A. Marechal, eds., Reidel, Dordrect, 365–384.

33. Tobler, Waldo, 1970. A computer movie simulating urban growth in the Detroit region. Economic Geography 46(2), 234-240.

34. Ver Hoef, J.M. and Cressie, N. 1993. Multivariable spatial prediction. *Mathematical Geology* **25**: 219–240.

35. Weiner, N. 1949. *Extrapolation, Interpolation, and Smoothing of Stationary Time Series*. MIT Press, Cambridge, MA.

36. Wold, H. 1938. *A Study in the Analysis of Stationary Time Series*. Almqvist and Wiksells, Uppsala.

Index

A

Angle of rotation 170
Angle tolerance 65
Anisotropical ellipse
  major axis 31
  minor axis 31
Anisotropy 30, 65, 69, 255
  altering the parameters 177
  angle of rotation 170
  concepts 65
  defined 279
  exploring for direction autocorrelation 176
  major range 170
  minor range 170
  modeling anisotropy 177
  neighborhood search 181
  principals 170
  spatial autocorrelation 106
  the formulas 255
ArcCatalog
  geostatistical layers 225
  metadata for a geostatistical layer 226
  previewing geostatistical data 225
  starting 225
ArcMap
  interaction with ESDA tools 82
  starting 14
Arcsine
  affecting distributions 95
  defined mathematically 200
  when to use 200
Artificial neural networks 126
Autocorrelation 28, 53, 59, 61, 133
  cokriging 165
  defined 279
  spatial. *See also* Spatial autocorrelation
Average empirical semivariance 56
Average standard error 35
  comparison 197
  cross-validation 190
  validation 190

Averaged semivariogram 61
Averaged semivariogram values 61

B

Back transformation
  normal score transformation 201
Bandwidth 65
  defined 279
Bin
  defined 279
Binary variables
  indicator kriging 155
  principles 154
  probability kriging 156
Binning 28, 62
  angle tolerance 65
  bandwidth 65
  directional binning 66
  directional influences 65
  grid method 66
  radial sector method 65
  semivariogram surface 64
  the mathematics 253
Bivariate distribution
  checking for 209
Bivariate Distribution dialog box
  identifying the controls 208
Bivariate normal distribution 207
  disjunctive kriging 206
  explained 206
  formulas 260
  p value 206
  principles 206
  probability map 206
  quantile map 206
Box–Cox
  defined mathematically 200
  effects on distributions 95
  when to use 200

Brushing. *See also* Selections
  in the Semivariogram/Covariance Cloud tool
    82
  making selections in ArcMap 82
  making selections with ESDA 82

C

Cell declustering
  formulas 251
Cell method
  declustering 212
Circular model
  formula 256
Classification 230
  of a geostatistical layer 230
  setting class ranges manually 230
  with a predefined method 233
  with equal interval 232
  with manual breaks 234
  with quantile 232
  with smart quantiles 232
Clipping 43
Cokriging
  as a prediction method 135
  constant mean 165
  creating a prediction map 166
  defined 279
  indicator, probability, and disjunctive
    cokriging 272
  mathematical formulas 271
  model explained 165
  models 134
  ordinary, simple, and universal cokriging
    mathematical formulas 271
  principles 165
Comparing models 38
Comparison 79
  average standard error 197
  concerns 197
  mean 197

Comparison (continued)
  performing 199
  principles 197
  root-mean-square prediction error 197
  standardized mean 197
  standardized root-mean-square prediction
    error 197
  validation 197
Comparison dialog box 198
  cross-validation statistics 197
  identifying the controls 198
Completely regularized spline 128
  principles 126
Constant mean
  cokriging 165
  disjunctive kriging 159
  in an ordinary kriging example 54
  indicator kriging 154
  ordinary kriging 138
  probability kriging 156
  simple kriging 143
  universal kriging 150
Continuous
  spatially 132
  values 132
Continuous surface 50
Contours
  and the geostatistical layer 220
  displaying the geostatistical layer as 228
Coregionalization models 258
Correlation
  defined 279
Covariance 59, 109, 175
  adding shifts 173
  altering the anisotropy parameters 177
  changing the lag size and number 179
  changing the partial sill and nugget 179
  cross-covariance function 172
  defined 279
  directional 170
  directional autocorrelation 176
  empirical cross-covariance 173

Covariance (continued)
  fitting models formulas 259
  formulas 168
  functions 169
  handling measurement error 180
  maximum cross-covariance 173
  minimum cross-covariance 173
  modeling anisotropy 177
  models 172
  partial sill principles 168
  range principles 168
  selecting a model 175
  Semivariogram/Covariance Cloud tool 91
  sill 168
  sill principles 168
Covariance functions 168
Covariance models
  formulas 255
Covariance surface
  Cross-Covariance Cloud tool 94
Covariation 109
  among multiple datasets 109
Cross-correlation
  cokriging 165
Cross-validation 263
  average standard errors 190
  defined 280
  error plot 190
  examining the predicted fit 193
  local polynomial 123
  mathematical formulas 263, 272
  mean prediction error 190
  objective of 35
  prediction standard errors 190
  principles 189
  QQPlot 190
  root-mean-square prediction error
    190, 191, 197
  saving statistics to a file 194
  scatter plot 189
  selecting a particular point 193

Cross-validation (continued)
   standard error plot 190
   standard normal distribution 190
   standard prediction errors 190
   summary statistics mathematical
      formulas 273
Cross-Validation dialog box 17
   identifying the controls 192
Crosscorrelation
   defined 280
Crosscovariance 93
   concepts 109
   defined 280
   exploring with the Crosscovariance Cloud
      tool 109
   exploring with the Histogram tool 109
   using the Crosscovariance Cloud tool 111
Crosscovariance cloud 93
Crosscovariance Cloud tool
   covariance surface 94
   cross-correlation between datasets 109
   general description 93
   Lag Size 94
   Number of Lags 94
   Search Direction 94
Crosscovariance models 172, 258
Crossvariogram
   defined 280
Cumulative distributions
   described 88

D

Data
   examining the distribution
      explained 95
      in an example 19
      using the histogram tool 96, 98
   global trends 21. *See also* Global trends
   understanding distributions
      with the QQPlot 97, 98

Data classification
   principles 230. *See also* Geostatistical
      layers
Data layers
   adding to ArcMap 14
Declustering 211
   cell method 212
      performing 214
   polygonal method 212
   preferential sampling 211
   principles 211
Declustering dialog box
   identifying the controls 213
Dependency rules 59
Deterministic
   defined 280
Deterministic component 69, 216
Deterministic interpolation 49, 53, 78
Deterministic interpolation techniques 113
   global 113
   local 113
Deterministic methods 50, 78
   global 103
   local 103
Detrending 69
   defined 280
Detrending dialog
   setting the window 218
Detrending dialog box
   identifying the controls 217
Diagnostics 35
   performing 79
Directional autocorrelation 74
   how to look for 176
Directional binning 66
Directional components
   anisotropy 69
   global trends 69
Directional differences
   Semivariogram/Covariance Cloud tool 107

Directional influences 30, 69, 74
   affecting the data 24
   defined 280
   exploring for directional autocorrelation 176
   exploring with the Semivariogram/Covariance
      Cloud 109
   searching neighborhoods 74
   using the Semivariogram/Covariance Cloud
      tool 108
Directional search 65
Directional semivariograms 30
Directional variation 106, 108
Disjunctive kriging
   bivariate normal 159
   constant mean 159
   creating a prediction map 160
      examining the bivariate distribution 164
      with declustering 163
   creating a probability map 161
   creating a standard error of indicators map
      162
   mathematical formulas 270
   model described 159
   principles 159
   trends 159
Dissimilarity
   defined 280
Distribution modeling
   direct 252
   Gaussian mixture 252
   linear 252
Distributions
   asymmetric 97
   bivariate normal 206
   checking for bivariate distribution 209
   examining with the Normal QQPlot 97
   general descriptions 95
   kurtosis 85
   leptokurtic 85
   modeling with normal score transformation
      205

Distributions (continued)
  normal 85
  platykurtic 85
  probability density 95
  skewed 96
  skewness 85
  stationarity 95
  symmetry 85
  tail 85
  transformations 95
  univariate normal 206
  using the Histogram tool 98
Drawing order
  in ArcMap 223

E

Elevation surface 50
Empirical
  defined 280
Empirical covariance functions 171
Empirical semivariogram
      29, 53, 56, 61, 63, 66
  concepts 61, 62
  fitting a model 67
  functions 171
  in an ordinary kriging example 56
  Semivariogram/Covariance Cloud tool 91
Empirical semivariogram surface 171
Entropy
  maximum entropy 87
  minimum entropy 87
  principles 87
  quartile 87
Equal interval 231
Error 35
Error plot
  cross-validation 190
  validation 190

ESDA tools
  Crosscovariance Cloud tool. See
      Crosscovariance Cloud tool
  General QQPlot
    explained 88
  Histogram tools. See Histogram
      tool; Histogram tools
  interacting with ArcMap 82
  Normal QQPlot
    construction of 88
    explained 88
  Semivariogram/Covariance cloud
    explained 91
  Trend analysis
    examining the global trend 103
    explained 90
    identifying global trends 105
  Voronoi map 86
    methods for assigning polygon values 86
Estimation
  defined 280
Exact interpolators 113
  explained 113
  Inverse Distance Weighted function 113
  measurement error 169
  radial basis functions (RBF) 113, 126
Exploratory Spatial Data Analysis (ESDA) 81
  ArcMap and ESDA 82
  associated properties of selected points 83
  brushing 82
  explained 82
  highlighting 82
  linking 82
  querying 82
  selecting 82
  selecting points 82
  tools
    Crosscovariance Cloud 84
    General QQPlot 84
    Histogram 84
    Normal QQPlot 84

Exploratory Spatial Data Analysis (ESDA)
      (continued)
  tools (continued)
    Semivariogram/Covariance Cloud 84
    Trend Analysis 84
    Voronoi Map 84
  transformations 82
  views
    Crosscovariance Cloud 82
    General QQPlot 82
    Histogram 82
    Normal QQPlot 82
    Semivariogram/Covariance Cloud 82
    Trend Analysis 82
    Voronoi Map 82
Exploring your data
  in an example 19
Exponential model
  concepts 71
  formula 257

F

Filled contours
  and the geostatistical layer 220
  displaying the geostatistical layer as 227
Filtered value
  measurement error 169
First and third quartiles 84
First-order polynomial 51, 123
  defined 280
Fitting a model
  in an ordinary kriging example 56
Fitting covariance models
  formulas 259
Fitting semivariogram models
  formulas 259
Fixed trend 103

G

G matrix 56, 57
G vector 57
  in an ordinary kriging example 57
Gamma matrix 55
  in an example 56
  in an ordinary kriging example 55
Gaussian mixture
  normal score transformation method 252
Gaussian model
  formula 257
General QQPlot
  explained 88
General QQPlot tool
  general description 88
Geostatistical Analyst toolbar
  adding to ArcMap 14
Geostatistical interpolation 49, 78
Geostatistical interpolation techniques 131
  creating surfaces 131
Geostatistical layer
  adding 222
  adding a group layer 222
  altering class breaks manually 234
  assigning data
    Equal interval 230, 231
    Quantile 230, 231
    Smart quantiles 230, 232
  changing color interactively 229
  changing color scheme 229
  changing drawing order 223
  changing the name 17, 224
  classifying with a predefined method 233
  classifying with equal interval 231
  classifying with quantiles 231
  classifying with smart quantiles 232
  contours 220
  copying 224
  data classification 230
  displaying as a grid 227

Geostatistical layer (continued)
  displaying as a hillshade 228
  displaying as contours 228
  displaying as filled contours 227
  exporting to a raster 238
  exporting to vector format 238
  extrapolating 236
  filled contours 220
  grid 220
  hillshade 220
  managing 224
  map extent 220
  method properties 240
  model parameters 220, 224
  predicting specific locations 242
  previewing data in ArcCatalog 225
  principles 220
  removing 224
  saving a map 237
  selecting points 241
  setting class ranges manually 230
  setting scale range 235
  starting ArcCatalog 225
  symbology 220
  transparency 220
  turning display on and off 223
  using map tips 241
  using method properties 240
  viewing in ArcCatalog 225
  viewing metadata 226
  zooming and panning 223
Geostatistical techniques
  autocorrelation 53
  certainty 53
  concepts 53
  creating the matrices 53
  empirical semivariogram 53
  fitting a model 53
  interpolation 132
  making a prediction 53
  prediction surface 53

Geostatistics 78
  defined 281
  principles 132
Global deterministic interpolation 103
Global outliers 101
  Histogram tool 101
  Semivariogram/Covariance Cloud tool 101
Global polynomial 248
  concepts 51
  cubic polynomial 120
  first-order polynomial 51
  formulas 248
  linear polynomial 120
  principles 120
  quadratic polynomial 120
  second-order polynomial 51
  third-order polynomial 51
Global polynomial interpolation
  creating a map 122
  creating a prediction map 122
  defined 281
  first-order 51
  formulas 248
  how it works 120
  second-order 51
  third-order polynomial 51
  when to use 120
Global trends. *See also* Trends
  concepts 69
  fixed 103
  looking for 103
Grid
  and the geostatistical layer 220
  displaying a geostatistical layer as 227
Grid spacing
  as an indicator of lag size 66
Group layer
  adding 222

H

Hillshade
  adding 47
  and the geostatistical layer 220
  displaying the geostatistical layer as 228
Histogram
  defined 281
  in an example 19
  normally distributed data 19, 20
  skewed data 19
  symmetric data 20
  unimodal data 20
Histogram tool
  examining distributions 96, 98
  exploring the crosscovariance 109
  frequency distribution
    1st and 3rd quartiles 84
    kurtosis 85
    mean 84
    median 84
    skewness 85
    standard deviation 85
    statistics summary 84
    variance 84
  general description 84
  identifying global outliers 101
  looking for outliers 99
Histogram tools 109
Hole effect model
  formula 257

I

IDW. *See* Inverse Distance Weighted (IDW)
  interpolation
Indicator kriging
  binary variable 154
  constant mean 134, 154
  creating a probability map 155
  indicator variable 154

Indicator kriging (continued)
  mathematical formulas 269
  model 154
  model described 154
  multiple thresholds 154
  primary variable 154
  principles 154
  secondary variable 154
Indicator kriging technique
  in an example 39
Indicator prediction value 40
Indicator variable
  indicator kriging 156
  probability kriging 156
Inexact interpolator 113
  global polynomial 113
  local polynomial 113
Interpolate
  defined 281
Interpolation techniques
  deterministic 49, 53, 113
  geostatistical 49, 53, 113
Intrinsic stationarity
  and ordinary kriging 54
  concepts 59
  defined 281
  semivariogram 61
Inverse Distance Weighted (IDW) 53
  concepts 50
  similarities to kriging 53, 74
Inverse Distance Weighted (IDW) interpolation
  114
  creating a map 118
  creating a prediction map 118
  creating a prediction map using Validation
    119
  cross-validation 114
  exact interpolator 117
  how surface is calculated 117
  optimal power 114
  power function 114

Inverse Distance Weighted (IDW) interpolation
  (continued)
  principles 114
  root-mean-square prediction error 114
  search neighborhood 115
    shape 116
  sectors 116
  shape of the neighborhood 116
Inverse Distance Weighted interpolation
  defined 281
Inverse Distance Weighting (IDW) 54, 74
Inverse multiquadric spline
  principles 126, 128
Isotropy
  defined 281
  general principles 106
  neighborhood search 181

J

J-Bessel model
  formula 258

K

K-Bessel model
  formula 257
Kriging 74
  as a prediction method 135
  autocorrelation 53, 133, 134
  certainty 53
  concepts 53
  creating the matrices 53
  defined 281
  deterministic trend 133
  empirical semivariogram 53
  error term 133
  fitting a model 53
  logarithmic transformations 137
  making a prediction 53
  mathematical formulas 261

Kriging (continued)
  output surface types 135
  prediction maps 135
  prediction surface 53
  predictors 172
  principles 132
  probability and predictions 133
  probability maps 135
  quantile map 135
  random error 134
  standard error of indicators map 135
  standard errors 172
  transformations 134
  trend 134
  unbiased predictor 137
Kriging equations 54, 55
Kriging family 131
  Disjunctive 131
  Indicator 131
  Ordinary 131
  Probability 131
  Simple 131
  Universal 131
Kriging map
  using default parameters 136
Kriging methods
  transformation methods 137
  trend options 137
Kriging models 133
  cokriging 134
  disjunctive cokriging 134
  indicator cokriging 134
  ordinary cokriging 134
  probability cokriging 134
  probability kriging 134
  simple cokriging 134
  universal cokriging 134
Kriging standard error
  in an ordinary kriging example 58

Kriging tasks
  producing a prediction 131
  quantifying the spatial structure 131. *See also* Variography
Kriging variance
  in an ordinary kriging example 58
Kriging weights 74
Kurtosis 85

L

Lag 31
  defined 281
  size 64
    choosing 66
Lag size 28, 171
Lag vector 73
Lagrange multiplier 77
Least-squares fit 53
  defined 281
Least-squares regression line 56
Leptokurtic 85
Linear
  normal score transformation method 252
Linear combination of models 255
Linear model of coregionalization
  defined 281
Linking. *See* Selections
Local outliers
  in a Voronoi map 102
Local polynomial 52
  cross-validation 124
  formulas 248
  order 123
  principles 123
  root-mean-square prediction error 124
  search neighborhood 123
Local polynomial interpolation 52, 123
  creating a map using 125
  creating a prediction map 125
  defined 282

Local polynomial interpolation (continued)
  formulas 248
  how it works 123
  when to use 124
Local variation 28, 51
Log transformation
  defined mathematically 200
  when to use 200
Logarithmic transformation
  effects on distributions 95
Lognormal kriging. *See also* Transformations
  mathematical formulas 269
Long-range variation
  defined 282

M

Major range
  anisotropy 170
Major/Minor axis 33
Map composition
  saving 237
Map elements
  adding 47
Map production
  in an example 42
Map tips
  for a geostatistical layer 241
Matrices 53
Mean
  comparison 197
  explained 86
Mean error 35
Mean prediction error
  cross-validation 190
  validation 190
Mean stationarity 59
  defined 282
Measurement error 32, 169
  concepts 68
  formulas 261

Measurement error (continued)
  microscale variation 168, 169
  principles 169
Measurement error model
  formulas 169
Measurement variation 169
Measures of location
  first and third quartiles 84
  mean 84
  median 84
Measures of shape
  kurtosis 85
  skewness 85
Measures of spread
  standard deviation 84
  variance 84
Median
  described 87
  Voronoi map 87
Method properties
  changing 240
  using 240
Microscale variation 32
Minimize the statistical expectation 54
Minor range
  anisotropy 170
Modeling process
  compare the models 18, 79
  explore the data 18, 79
  fit a model 18
  perform diagnostics 18, 79
  represent the data 18, 79
Models
  comparing
    principles. *See* Comparing models
  comparison concerns
    optimality 197
    validity 197
Multiquadric function
  principles 126

Multiquadric Spline
  principles 128
Multivariate normal distribution 132

N

Negative standard errors 56
Neighborhood search
  altering the map view 188
  altering the shape of the neighborhood 186
  anisotropy 181
  changing the number of points 185
  determining the prediction for a specific
    location 187
  directional autocorrelation 181
  isotropy 181
  major axis 181
  maximum number of points 183
  minimum number of points 182
  principals 181
  sectors 182
  semimajor axis 182
  semiminor axis 182
  shape 181
  viewing the neighborhood within a map 188
Normal distribution
  applying transformations 137
  bell-shaped curve 95
  described 95
  examining with the Histogram tool 96
Normal distributions
  examining with the Normal QQPlot 97
Normal QQPlot
  cumulative distributions 88
  described 97
  explained 88
Normal QQPlot tool
  using with distributions 96
Normal score transformation 137
  back transformation 201
  comparing to other transformations 203

Normal score transformation (continued)
  cumulative distribution principles 201
  direct approximation 201
  formulas 251
  Gaussian kernels 201
  linear approximation 201
  mathematics 251
  modeling distributions 205
  standard normal principles 201
Normal Score Transformation distribution
    dialog
  identifying controls 202
Nugget 28, 32
  concepts 68
  defined 282
  local variation 68
  measurement error 68
  spatial variation 68
Nugget effect
  formula 256
Nugget Error Modeling check box 32
Number of lags 171

O

Omnidirectional semivariogram 66
Ordered
  values 132
Ordinary kriging 53, 54, 57, 138
  binning 55
  constant mean 54
  creating a map 139
  creating a prediction map 139
    applying transformation 141
    using detrending 142
  creating a prediction map using validation
    140
  creating a prediction standard error map 140
  cross-validation mathematical formulas 263
  defined 282
  empirical semivariogram 56

Ordinary kriging (continued)
  fitting a model 56
  fitting a model in an example 72
  fitting the spherical model in an example 73
  g vector 57, 76
  gamma matrix 76
  in an example 26
  kriging equations in an example 54
  kriging standard error 58
  kriging variance in an example 58
  making a prediction 57
  mathematical formulas 262
  model 134
  model described 138
  principles 138
  probability maps mathematical formulas 264
  quantile maps mathematical formulas 264
  random error 54
  specifying the search neighborhood 75
  trends 138
  use of measurement error models 169
  validation mathematical formulas 263
  weight vector in an example 57
Outliers
  general description 99
  identifying global and local 101
  looking for
    with the Histogram tool 99
    with the Semivariogram/Covariance Cloud
      tool 99
    with Voronoi Mapping 100
  looking for global and local
    explained 99
  using the Histogram tool 101
  using the Semivariogram/Covariance Cloud
    tool 101
  using the Voronoi map 102
Output Layer Information dialog box 17

P

Partial sill 28, 68
  defined 282
Pentaspherical model
  formula 256
Platykurtic 85
Polygonal method
  declustering 212
Polynomial
  defined 282
Polynomials 22, 51
Power function
  inverse distance weighted 114
Predicted kriging variance 58
Prediction 74
  defined 282
  making in an ordinary kriging example 57
Prediction error 35
Prediction map
  as an output surface type 135
  local polynomial interpolation 122
  ordinary kriging 139
  with cokriging 166
  with disjunctive kriging 160
  with global polynomial 122
  with IDW 118
  with inverse distance weighted 118
  with local polynomial 125
  with ordinary kriging
    using detrending 142
    while applying a transformation 141
  with radial basis functions 129
  with simple kriging 144
    while applying a transformation 147, 148
    while examining bivariate distribution 149
  with the defaults 136
  with universal kriging 151
Prediction map using validation
  created with IDW 119
Prediction map with declustering
  creating with disjunctive kriging 163

Prediction maps
  types of 135
    probability map 135
    quantile map 135
    standard error maps 135
Prediction methods
  cokriging 135
  kriging 135
Prediction of error map
  creating wtih disjunctive kriging 161
Prediction of standard error of indicators map
  creating with disjunctive kriging 162
Prediction standard error
  defined 282
Prediction standard error map
  creating with ordinary kriging 140
  creating with simple kriging 146
  creating with universal kriging 152
Prediction standard errors 37
  cross-validation 190
  validation 190
Prediction surface 53
  creating 75
Prediction unbiased 54
Preferential sampling
  declustering 211
  weight data 212
Probability kriging
  binary variable 156
  constant mean 156
  creating a probability map 157
  indicator variable 156
  mathematical formulas 270
  model described 156
Probability map
  as an output surface type 135
  creating with indicator kriging 155
  creating with probability kriging 157
  creating with simple kriging 145
  defined 282
Probability mapping 39

Probability maps
    creating with disjunctive kriging 161
    ordinary kriging mathematical formulas 264
    simple kriging mathematical formulas 266
    universal kriging mathematical formulas 268

Q

QQPlot 35
    cross-validation 190
    defined 282
    General 21
    normal
        in an example 20
    principles 88
    validation 190
Quantile 231
    defined 282
Quantile maps
    as an output surface type 135
    creating with simple kriging 145
    ordinary kriging mathematical formulas 264
    simple kriging mathematical formulas 266
    universal kriging mathematical formulas 268
Quartiles
    first and third 84

R

Radial basis functions
    defined 283
Radial basis functions (RBF) 52, 126
    artificial neural networks 126
    completely regularized spline 126
    concepts 127
    creating a map 129
    creating a prediction map 129
    formulas 248, 250
    how it works 126
    inverse multiquadric spline 126
    multiquadric function 126

Radial basis functions (RBF) (continued)
    principles 126
    spline with tension 52, 126
    thin-plate spline 52, 126
    weights 128
    when to use 127
Radial sectors 65
Random errors 54, 69
    cokriging 165
    in an ordinary kriging example 54
    principles 133
    second-order stationarity 137
Random process 54
    and ordinary kriging 54
Random processes
    making predictions 59
    with dependence 59
Random short-range variation 103
Range 28, 31, 68
    defined 283
    principles 168
Range of the model 73
Raster
    exporting a geostatistical layer to 238
Rational quadratic model
    formula 257
RBF. See Radial basis functions (RBF)
Regression
    defined 283
Replication 60
Residuals 26
    defined 283
    modeling 21
    simple kriging 143
    trends 216
RMSPE. See Root-mean-square prediction
        error
Root-mean-square error 35
Root-mean-square prediction error
    comparison 38, 197
    cross-validation 190, 191

Root-mean-square prediction error (continued)
    inverse distance weighted 114
    validation 190, 191
Root-mean-square standardized prediction error
    comparison 38

S

Scale
    and the geostatistical layer 235
Scatter plots
    cross-validation 189
    validation 189
Scatterplots 35
Search Direction tool 30
    in an example 24
Search neighborhood 115. See also
        Neighborhood search
    accounting for directional influences 74
    influences on shape 116
    inverse distance weighted 117
    local polynomial 123
    sectors 74
Searching neighborhood
    defined 283
Searching Neighborhood dialog
    altering the map view 188
    altering the shape of the neighborhood 186
    changing the number of points 185
    determining the prediction for a specific
        location 187
Searching Neighborhood dialog box 33
    identifying the controls 184
Second-order polynomial 21, 22, 51
    defined 283
Second-order stationarity 59, 137
    defined 283
    kriging assumption 137
Sectors 33, 116
    inverse distance weighted 116

Selections
 brushing 82
 linking 82
Semicrossvariogram
 defined 283
Semimajor axes 182
Semiminor axes 182
Semivariance 28
 in an ordinary kriging example 56
Semivariance/Covariance
 goal of 28
Semivariogram 28
 altering the anisotropy parameters 177
 binning 62
 binning concepts 62
 changing the lag size and number 179
 changing the partial sill and nugget 179
 circular model formula 256
 combining models 71
 creating the cloud 61
 defined 283
 directional 170
 empirical semivariogram 91
 exploring for directional autocorrelation 176
 exponential formula 257
 exponential model 67
 fitting a model 67, 72
 functions 171
 Gaussian model formula 257
 handling measurement error 180
 hole effect model formula 257
 J-Bessel model formula 258
 K-Bessel model formula 257
 modeling anisotropy 177
 nugget 168
 nugget effect formula 256
 partial sill 68, 168
 pentaspherical model formula 256
 principles 168
 quantifying spatial autocorrelation 65
 radial sector method 65

Semivariogram (continued)
 range 68, 168
 rational quadratic model formula 257
 selecting a model 175
 sill 68, 168
 spherical model 67
 spherical model formula 256
 stable model formula 258
 tetraspherical model formula 256
Semivariogram graph 29
Semivariogram model
 circular formula 256
 exponential formula 257
 formulas 255
 Gaussian formula 257
 hole effect formula 257
 J-Bessel formula 258
 K-Bessel formula 257
 nugget effect formula 256
 pentaspherical formula 256
 Rational quadratic formula 257
 spherical formula 256
 stable formula 258
 tetraspherical formula 256
 types of 67
  Circular 67
  Exponential 67
  Gaussian 67
  Hole Effect 67
  J-Bessel 67
  K-Bessel 67
  Pentaspherical 67
  Rational Quadratic 67
  Spherical 67
  Stable 67
  Tetraspherical 67
Semivariogram surface 29
 concepts 64
 Semivariogram/Covariance Cloud tool 92
Semivariogram values
 defined 283

Semivariogram/Covariance
 general description 91
 handling measurement error 180
Semivariogram/Covariance Cloud 91
Semivariogram/Covariance Cloud tool 91
 bins 92
 empirical semivariogram 91
 exploring spatial structure 106
 identifying outliers 99, 101
 Lag Size 92
 looking for directional influences 107
 looking for outliers 99
 Number of Lags 92
 outliers 91
 Search Direction 92
 Semivariogram Surface 92
 spatial autocorrelation 91
 using for global and local outliers 99
 using to explore directional influences 108
 using to explore spatial structure 108
Semivariogram/Covariance dialog
 changing the lag size and number 179
 changing the partial sill and nugget 179
Semivariogram/Covariance dialog box
 identifying the controls 174
Semivariogram/Covariance Modeling dialog box
  16, 28
 identifying the controls 174
Semivariograms
 functions 168
 selecting a model 175
Shifts 173
Short-range variation 26, 103
 defined 283
Sill 31, 68
 defined 283
 nugget effect 168
  measurement error 168
  microscale variation 168
 partial sill 168
 value 73

Simple kriging 143
  constant mean 143
  creating a prediction map 144
    applying a transformation 147
    applying a transformation with declusing
      148
    examine bivariate distribution 149
  creating a prediction standard error map 146
  creating a probability map 145
  creating a quantile map 145
  mathematical formulas 265
  model described 143
  predicting a new value for cross-validation
    mathematical formula 265
  prediction with measurement error
    mathematical formula 265
  probability maps
    mathematical formulas 266
  quantile maps
    mathematical formula 266
  residuals 143
  trends 143
  use of measurement error models 169
Skewness 85
Spatial autocorrelation 23, 53, 59, 62, 106
  anisotropy 106
  concepts 113
  explained 106
  isotropy 106
  stationarity 106
Spatial covariation
  using the Crosscovariance Cloud tool 111
Spatial dependence 54, 62
  defined 283
Spatial modeling 61
Spatial structure 106, 108
  exploring
    with the Semivariogram/Covariance Cloud
      tool 106
  understanding through variography 108
  using the Semivariogram/Covariance Cloud
    tool 108

Spherical model 28, 73
  defined 284
  formula 256
Spline interpolation
  defined 284
Spline with tension 52
  principles 126
Square root transformation. *See*
    Transformations
Squared difference 53
Stable model
  formula 258
Standard deviation
  explained 85
  Voronoi map 87
Standard error plot
  cross-validation 190
  validation 190
Standard errors 172
Standard errors map 135
Standard errors of indicators map 135
Standard normal distribution
  cross-validation 190
  validation 190
Standard prediction error
  cross-validation 190
  validation 190
Standardized error 35
Standardized root-mean-square prediction error
  comparison 197
Stationarity 106
  concepts 59
  defined 284
  intrinsic stationarity 59
  replication 59
  second-order stationarity 59
  spatial autocorrelation 106
  trends 103
Statistical values 132
  continuous 132
  Ordered Categorical 132
  Unordered Categorical 132

Subsets
  creating 79, 243
  performing validation 244
Sum of the weighting 54
Summary statistics 84
Surface
  defined 284
Surface types
  overview 135
  prediction map 135
  probability map 135
  quantile map 135
  standard error of indicators map 135
  standard errors map 135
Surface-fitting methodology 18
Surfaces
  create using default settings 15
  creating using ESDA tools 81
Symbology
  and the geostatistical layer 220
  changing the color interactively 229
  changing the color scheme 229

T

Tetraspherical model
  formula 256
Thin plate
  principles 126
Thin plate sline 52
Third-order polynomial 51
Threshold 39, 153
Transformation
  normal distributions 137
  with histogram 82
  with Normal QQPlot 82
Transformations 137
  approximation methods
    direct 201
    Gaussian Kernels 201
    linear 201

Transformations (continued)
  arcsine 200
  arcsine transformations 137
  back transformations 82
  Box–Cox 200
  Box–Cox transformation
    log transformation 137, 200
  checking for the bivariate normal distribution
    206
  comparing NST to other tra 203
  constant variance 200
  distributions and arcsine 95
  distributions and Box–Cox 95
  distributions and logarithmic 95
  effects on predictions 82
  logarithmic 200
  modeling distributions 205
  modeling distributions with NST 205
  normally distributed 82
  NST 201
    comparing to arcsine 203
    comparing to Box–Cox 203
    comparing to log transformation 203
    comparing to other transformations 203
    cumulative distribution 201
    direct approximation 201
    Gaussian Kernels approximation 201
    linear approximation 201
    standard normal 201
  primary variable 137
  principles 137, 200
  secondary variable 137
  skewed data 82
  standard normal distribution
    cumulative distribution 201
  trends 137
  using 204
Transgaussian kriging 137, 200
Transparency
  adding 47
  and the geostatistical layer 220

Trend
  defined 284
Trend analysis 90
Trend Analysis tool
  directional trends 90
  general description 90
  identifying global trends 105
  in an example 21, 103. *See also* ESDA
    tools: Trend analysis: explained
  looking for global trends 105
  polynomials 90
Trends 51, 69, 90
  cokriging 165
  deterministic method 103
  fixed 216
  geostatistical method 103
  global. *See also* Global trends
  nugget effect 103
  ordinary kriging 138
  principles 216
  random errors 103, 216
  random short-range variation 103
  removal 26, 27, 28, 103, 137, 216
  residuals 103, 216
  setting the window size 218
  simple kriging 143
  spatial autocorrelation 103
  stationarity 103
  universal kriging 150

U

Unbiased predictions 54
Unbiased predictor 137
Unbiasedness 55
Unbiasedness constraint 55
Unimodal
  defined 284
Univariate distribution
  defined 284
Univariate normal 206

Univariate normal distribution
  checking for with QQPlots 206
Universal kriging
  constant mean 150
  creating a prediction map 151
  creating a prediction standard error map 152
  mathematical formulas 267
  model described 150
  predicting a new value for cross-validation
    mathematical formula 267
  prediction with measurement error
    mathematical formula 267
  principles 150
  probability maps
    mathematical formulas 268
  quantile maps
    mathematical formulas 268
  trends 150
  use of measurement error models 169
Unordered
  values 132

V

Validation
  average standard errors 190
  creating a prediction map using validation
    using IDW 119
  creating subsets 195, 243
  defined 284
  error plot 190
  examining the predicted fit 193
  mathematical formulas 263
  mean prediction error 190
  performing using subsets 244
  performing validation 196
  prediction standard error 190
  principles 189
  QQPlot 190
  root-mean-square prediction error 190, 191
  saving statistics to a file 194

Validation (continued)
scatter plot 189
selecting a particular point 193
standard error plot 190
standard normal distribution 190
standard prediction errors 190
Values. *See* Statistical values
Variance 84
Variogram
defined 284
Variogram models 16
combining of 71
Variography 16, 131, 168
defined 284
goal of 62
Variography dialog box 174
identifying the controls 174
Vector format
exporting a geostatistical layer to 238
Vector g 55
Visualization
3D 50
Voronoi
general concepts 86
local influence 87
local outliers 87
local smoothing 87
local variation 87
maximum entropy 87
minimum entropy 87
quartile 87
Voronoi map
general concepts 86
local influence 87
local outliers 87
local smoothing 87
local variation 87
Voronoi Map tool
general description 86
identifying global and local outliers 101
looking for outliers 100

Voronoi methods
cluster 87
entropy 87
finding outliers 102
interquartile range 87
mean 86
median 87
mode 86
simple 86
standard deviation 87

W

Weight 54
Weight vector
in an ordinary kriging example 57
Weighted sum 54
Weights
in an ordinary kriging example 57

Z

Zooming and panning a layer 223